GOOD ITALY, BAD ITALY

GOOD
ITALY
BAD
ITALY

*Why Italy Must Conquer Its
Demons to Face the Future*

BILL EMMOTT

YALE UNIVERSITY PRESS
NEW HAVEN AND LONDON

For information about this and other Yale University Press publications, please contact:

U.S. Office: sales.press@yale.edu   yalebooks.com
Europe Office: sales@yaleup.co.uk   www.yalebooks.co.uk

Set in Janson MT by IDSUK (DataConnection) Ltd

Cartoons by Peter Schrank; charts by Adam Meara

Printed in Great Britain by TJ International Ltd, Padstow, Cornwall

Library of Congress Cataloging-in-Publication Data

Emmott, Bill.
   Good Italy, bad Italy : why Italy must conquer its demons to face the future/Bill Emmott.
      p. cm.
   ISBN 978-0-300-18630-7 (cl : alk. paper)
   1. Italy—Politics and government—1994- 2. Italy--Economic conditions—1994- 3. Italy—Social conditions—1994- 4. Italy—Economic policy. 5. Political corruption—Italy. 6. Global Financial Crisis, 2008–2009. 7. Berlusconi, Silvio, 1936- I. Title.
   DG583.5.E66 2012
   945.093—dc23

                                                                          2012007652

A catalogue record for this book is available from the British Library.

10 9 8 7 6 5 4 3 2 1
2016 2015 2014 2013 2012

For Carol

Contents

Acknowledgements		viii
1	Italy's second chance	1
2	*L'inferno politico*	29
3	*Il purgatorio economico*	72
4	Inspirations from Turin	108
5	Hope in the South	139
6	Enterprise obstructed	184
7	Potential displayed	211
8	Good Italy, Bad Italy	254
	Notes	281
	Further reading	289
	Index	291

Acknowledgements

This must begin with a confession. For all Italy's undoubted attractions, it is plain that one man has been chiefly responsible for making this old Asia hand become so engaged with and fascinated by his country. His name is Silvio Berlusconi.

A more positive influence has been my dear friend Annalisa Piras, who as London correspondent for La7 television and then L'Espresso came to interview me after *The Economist*'s 'unfit' cover, and ever thereafter urged me to stay interested and even to write a book. On reading an early, clumsy draft of the first chapter of the Italian predecessor to this book, she observed that what I was really saying was that Italy was divided between 'la Buona Italia' and 'la Mala Italia'. She is now the director and producer of our documentary film on Italy which will shortly be released. Her husband Michael Trow and children Cordelia and Flavia also deserve thanks for tolerating her long absences while we were shooting that film together, a venture which assisted some of the research for this book.

My former colleagues at *The Economist* are next in line for gratitude, for giving me such a wonderful place to work for 26 years until 2006, but even more for doing the investigation into Silvio Berlusconi that prompted our 'unfit' cover in 2001. Those most directly associated with that investigation were Tim Laxton and David Lane, who wrote the main article together, Xan Smiley, then Europe editor, who wrote the leader, and Clive Crook, my deputy editor, who oversaw the issue that week. In addition, Oscar Grut, the company's legal counsel, and Marisa Pappalardo, our Italian lawyer, gave us essential support as well as fighting the libel cases brought against us by Mr Berlusconi.

For the expansion and updating of this book, which was originally published in Italian as *Forza, Italia: Come Ripartire dopo Berlusconi* in 2010, I received invaluable research help from five Italians then completing Masters degrees at the London School of Economics: Filippo Costa-Buranelli, Eleonora Pauletta d'Anna, Giulia Paravicini-Crespi, Giovanni Cina and Tommaso Giarrizzo.

I would like to give thanks to the Rete per l'Eccellenza Nazionale, the 'Network for National Excellence', for all the members' help, enthusiasm and suggestions, but especially to Alessandro Fusacchia, the founding president, to Francesco Luccisano, his successor and my main contact there, and to Sara Callegari, Vincenzo D'Innella Capano, Davide Canavesio, Elena Fenili, Marco Ferrara, Francesca Galli, Marinella Giannelli, Alex Giordano, Eva Giovannini, Serenella Mattera, Morena Ragone, Emilio Roca, Davide Rubini, Daria Santucci, Jacopo Silva and Lorenzo Tortora de Falco for helping with my travels, arrangements and research.

Francesco Grillo and his colleagues at his Vision & Value consultancy in Rome were a great inspiration in the hunt for what Francesco calls 'positive viruses'. Gianni Riotta provided dozens of ideas, as well as generous hospitality, first in Rome and then in Milan. Stefania Giannini, rector of the University for Foreigners in Perugia was wonderfully hospitable and helpful during my stumbling efforts to learn Italian, as was my teacher, Sabrina Cittadini. In addition to all the people who kindly gave up their time to be interviewed by me, I am particularly grateful to the following for their ideas, criticism and assistance: Roger Abravanel, Giuliano Amato, Marco Annunziata, Giancarlo Aragona, Matteo Arpe, Natalia Augias, Paola Bianchi, Luca De Biase, Tito Boeri, Emma Bonino, Ferruccio de Bortoli, Giovanni Brauzzi, Mario Calabresi, Edward Chaplin, Arianna Ciccone, Vittorio Colao, Giulia Crivelli, Mario Draghi, John Elkann, Alessio Falorni, Paolo Fulci, Paolo Gubitta, Daniela Hamaui, James Hansen, Richard Holloway, John Hooper, Paola Lanzarini, Enrico Letta, Riccardo Luna, Bruno Manfellotto, Claudia Millo, Mario Monti, Guido Nassimbeni, Pierleone Ottolenghi, Francesca Paci, Nando Pagnoncelli, Fabio Petroni, Chris Potter, Alessandro Profumo, Yakuta Rajabali, Ignazio Rocca di Torrepadula, Cristina and Enrico Sassoon, Beppe Severgnini, Rachel Shelmerdine, Alessandro Spaventa, Paola Subacchi, Maurizio Viroli and Ignazio Visco. Peter Schrank's farewell drawing when I resigned from *The Economist* in 2006 inspired me to ask him to draw the cartoons for this book. Adam Meara drew the charts, using data kindly supplied by Christopher Wilson.

At Yale University Press, Phoebe Clapham has been an admirable, enthusiastic and effective editor. My literary agent, Arthur Goodhart, provided as always tireless support and persistence in helping me see this project through to fruition.

My wife, Carol, as always, deserves the greatest and sincerest gratitude of all, especially for tolerating with such equanimity my frequent and sometimes lengthy disappearances into deepest Italy, both for this book and for the documentary film.

Bill Emmott
Somerset

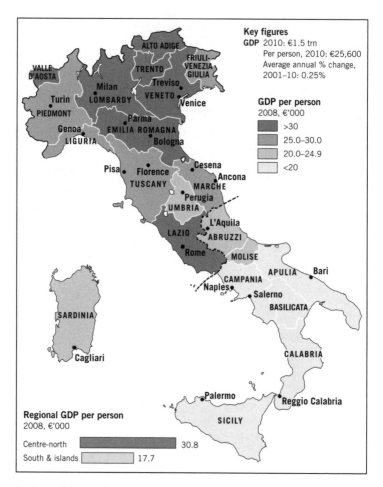

Italy and its regions
Source: *The Economist*

CHAPTER 1

Italy's Second Chance

For most of the big, rich countries of the West, the financial crisis of 2008–10 and its worrying aftermath came as a genuine shock, the worst such economic shock since the Second World War. It was made even more humbling by the sense that their control over world affairs is ebbing away, thanks to the rise of China, India and other previously poor countries, and thanks to the ageing of their populations. It was far from being the first big post-war crisis – the oil-price hike and runaway inflation of the 1970s had long ago jolted Europe and North America out of any post-1945 complacency – but it was the first time that the West really felt as if it might be teetering on the edge of an abyss of long-term decline and even of a serious crisis in its democracies, over inequality, over the need for austerity, over immigration, over the apparently excessive power of some big corporate groups, especially banks.

For one country, however, a country that had been a founder member of the European Union (EU) in 1957, whose capital city gave the EU's founding treaty its name, and which, deep in its history, could claim to have invented or at least developed many of the foundations of western capitalism and civilization, the sense of crisis was and is not really new. That country is Italy. The crisis it found itself in during 2011–12, both in its economy and its democracy, was the second such crisis it had faced in the past twenty years. In one sense, at least, it can therefore count itself lucky: having failed on the first occasion, in the early 1990s, to truly rebuild and reform either its politics or its economy after a nasty shock, it now has a second chance to do so. And that second chance can, at least in principle, be informed by experience, by knowledge of why reforms or renewal failed to take hold the first time round.

The comparison between the 1992–94 Italian crisis and today's is quite spooky. Twenty years ago, a discredited, paralysed government collapsed, and alongside that collapse there occurred a financial crisis, brought about by the fact that Italy's government debts had risen to the then-colossal level of 120 per cent of the country's annual economic output, its gross domestic product (GDP), and the fact that international investors had lost faith in the Italian government's ability both to maintain its currency and to service its debts. The response was to throw out, albeit temporarily, the politicians from government and instead to install a technocrat, a non-politician, as prime minister. Twenty years ago the chosen man was Carlo Azeglio Ciampi, former governor of the Bank of Italy, the country's central bank.

In 2011, as the government of Silvio Berlusconi became more and more paralysed and discredited at home and abroad, and as faith in Italy's ability to service its debts started to wobble alongside faith in the still-young European single currency, the euro, with which Italy had replaced its lira, the central bank governor was not available: Mario Draghi had just been appointed president of the European Central Bank. But another 'super-Mario' was available: Mario Monti, a distinguished economist who had served as European Commissioner for the single market and for competition between 1995 and 2004. Once again, normal politics was suspended, and, with the support of the main political parties, a 'technical government' was installed in November 2011 in the hope of launching a reform programme, mainly for the economy but also again for political institutions, including the electoral system, the various layers of local government and the justice system.

It was *déjà vu* all over again, in the famous phrase coined by Yogi Berra, the American baseball player and coach. And so it is, albeit with two curious complications, and a third complication that raises the stakes considerably.

The first complication is that having had a humdinger of a political crisis in the early 1990s, when most of the political establishment went on trial for corruption and the main parties all collapsed, Italy then sleepwalked into a new dark political alley, even if one with thoroughly modern characteristics, one from which it is far from clear that it is yet emerging. The new alley was represented, or one could say built, by the former property developer turned media mogul Silvio Berlusconi. It consisted of the merging of vast wealth and media power, arising from a quasi-monopoly in commercial television and a dominant position in advertising sales, with the very institutions of government that would normally be expected to regulate such power.

The modern character of Italy's new democratic crisis is its mediatic nature, the fact that Mr Berlusconi became, when he entered politics in 1994, the first Italian post-war political leader to harness television to his cause. But it has had a very traditional character, too, in the way he turned government towards his own interests, issuing (and passing) a whole series of *ad personam* laws that benefited him and his companies, and in the way in which, beneath him, he built a whole superstructure, a spider's web[1] of favours and patronage to his supporters and those who collaborated with him, partly using his own money, partly the country's money.

The Italian story of the past twenty wasted years is thus a story of what happens when a billionaire businessman and his associates turn government to their own interests – and thus of how an economic and political crisis in a western democracy can be exploited by distinctly non-reformist forces. It is also a story of what happens when media power is concentrated in too few hands, and when the rest of the media and the cultural elite fail to take a stand or tell the truth in response. It is a story of what happens when the moral arbiters in a society – in this case, the Catholic Church – fall silent and become collaborators, and when other political parties become complicit. The fall, in November 2011, of the Berlusconi government and its replacement by Mario Monti's government of tech-

4

nicians reflected the weakening of that concentration of power and a new willingness – at last – among the cultural and religious elite to stand up and be counted. But that new sentiment remains weak, Mr Berlusconi's media power and wealth remain intact, and it is abundantly clear that the man himself does not consider his resignation as prime minister to be an end to his political career or power. Indeed, the need of the Monti government for parliamentary support from Mr Berlusconi's own political party means that he has retained some leverage with which to protect that power and to keep open the chance of a return to government itself.

The second complication is linked to that complicity, and to a widespread failure, during both the 1990s and in the first decade of the twenty-first century, to tell, or face up to, the truth about Italy's economic situation and prospects. Perhaps, after the initial recovery from the financial crisis of 1992–94, and especially after Italy's successful effort to join the euro in the first wave of members when the European single currency was launched in 1999, some complacency was understandable – or at least a desire to hope for the best. After all, one of the benefits of joining the euro was that the country's borrowing costs fell towards those of the continent's best credit-risk, Germany, thus making the burden of a large debt more bearable. But when the global financial crisis erupted in 2008, after a year during which contracting interbank credit markets caused increasing pain and difficulties for European and North American banks, a process that culminated in the bankruptcy of the Lehman Brothers investment bank in September, the Italian response was one not just of complacency but of self-congratulation. That response was led by the Berlusconi government that had taken office in May 2008, but it was echoed and reinforced by wide swathes of Italian business and the media.

The self-congratulation arose from the idea that the 2008 financial crisis had exposed the fragility and even recklessness of economic models which Italians considered anathema, and which thus made Italy's economy look better by comparison: ones that had given a big role to service industries, especially financial services, ones in which household debts had risen rapidly, driving up consumption artificially, and ones that had substantially liberalized their economies and removed regulatory barriers to risk-taking. Principally, of course, that meant the United States and the United Kingdom, but also a neighbouring Mediterranean rival, Spain, whose property boom turned into a painful bust. To have a stable, non-reckless banking system like Italy's suddenly looked like a virtue, as did having low household debts and a still relatively large manufacturing sector, even though this latter virtue was, in truth, at least temporarily a vice, since, after Lehman's demise, the biggest immediate impact was on worldwide demand for manufactures.

Some *Schadenfreude*, or pleasure at the misfortune of others, can perhaps be forgiven. But the real trouble with this line of thinking was that it distracted attention from Italy's own weaknesses and vulnerabilities. It mistook for a benefit the fact that others were now joining Italy in a debt-ridden economic mess. Italy was no longer unusual in having an unsustainably large government debt burden: the public debt burdens of Britain, France, America and even Germany were, after 2008, rising rapidly towards Italian levels. But other people's sicknesses do not make you any healthier. Italy's long-term sickness remained: its economy had barely grown from the mid 1990s until 2008, thanks to slow or non-existent growth in productivity and to declining household incomes; and so its government debts were still dangerously high in relation to its annual output and thus to its ability to raise tax revenues. The post-2008 recession increased the ratio between the country's public debt and GDP to the same level it had attained in 1994, namely 120 per cent.

In his annual year-end press conference in 2010, Silvio Berlusconi boasted that Italy's economy was strong, its households rich, its exports recovering, its savings abundant, and said that there would be no need for any new budgetary stringency from the government during 2011. By the time he resigned from office on 12 November of that year, his government had introduced five different budgetary measures (though not all were implemented). Days before resigning, he still proclaimed that there was no crisis in Italy, for 'the restaurants are all full'. The bond markets, source of the Italian government's borrowing, thought differently, driving up Italy's borrowing costs as investors grew more worried about the country's future ability to service or repay its debts. The eruption in the summer and autumn of 2011 of a financial crisis that had, in reality, been developing for years seemed to come as a genuine surprise.

The third complication, the one that raises the stakes considerably, is the background to that supposedly surprising crisis. It is the fact that while in 1992–94 Italy's financial crisis was a problem chiefly for the country itself, in the new crisis twenty years later Italy's problems are intimately connected to those of the whole seventeen-country eurozone, the nations that all share Europe's single currency. Some Italians who are surprised to find themselves in a tight financial corner may blame the euro for their problems, believing this to be an imported crisis. Yet, while there is a small amount of truth to this, in terms of the timing, the larger risk is that Italy's crisis could be exported to the rest of the eurozone, which, given the importance of Europe and given the close integration of the global financial system, really means that it could be exported to the rest of the world, too.

The eurozone is weighed down by debts and by doubts, and certainly they are not just Italian ones. At their core, the problems of the European single currency arise from the fact that the countries that joined it in 1999 and thereafter disagree about whether inside the currency there should be collective responsibility for public debts, with corresponding rules and duties attached to them, as in the United States of America, or whether each country should simply stand on its own, dealing with its own debts according to agreed guidelines about how large those debts are supposed to be.

That latter form is the way in which the currency was set up by the 1992 Maastricht Treaty and then launched in 1999, with no collective responsibility, a formal ban on the bail-out of any member country, and with rules for acceptable levels of budget deficits and public debt as a ratio to GDP. Unfortunately, in order to get the euro launched on time and with a pleasing fanfare it was decided to waive the rules, 'temporarily', for several countries that did not then meet them. The biggest of those non-conformists was Italy. Then, shortly thereafter, even Germany and France decided to flout the rules about budget deficits. So the euro entered the storm of the global financial crisis with no collective responsibility for government debts but also no credible rules.

By 2011, Italy was not the eurozone's largest debtor, measured by the ratio of public debts to GDP: that honour was held by Greece, whose debts were rising well past 150 per cent of GDP. That country was forced into drastic austerity measures, slashing public sector wages and pensions, and yet still could not afford the borrowing costs being imposed on it by a worried international financial market. Hence talk spread of a potential Greek default on its debt, or of its more euphemistic equivalent, a 'debt restructuring', under which lenders would agree to cut the country's borrowing costs and give it longer to repay.

Once that talk became accepted and repeated even by the leading eurozone governments, France and Germany, markets inevitably began to wonder whether, if Greece were to be given such a benefit, other eurozone debtors might eventually want, or need, the same. So the markets started to price in the possibility of such future default-cum-restructurings, and even, more tentatively, the chances of the euro being abandoned altogether by a few countries or of it collapsing altogether. All countries' borrowing costs thus rose, except those of Germany, but borrowing costs for the biggest debtors rose the most. Greece accounts for about 2 per cent of eurozone GDP, and so neither its economy nor its debts are crucial. Italy, however, accounts for more than 13 per cent of eurozone GDP, and its public debts are, in absolute terms, the third largest in the world, after those of the United States and Japan.

So Greek doubts, and the timing of Greece's bail-out negotiations, did help determine Italy's financial fate in 2011. But as long as the Italian government showed no interest in either cutting government debt materially over the long term nor in bringing in reforms to promote faster economic growth, a debt crisis was inevitable at some stage or other. The euro crisis nevertheless makes Italy's financial troubles far more important and worrying for the rest of the world than they would otherwise have been. And both the original 2008–10 financial crisis and now the euro crisis mean that, unlike twenty years ago, Italy's efforts to solve its financial troubles will take place in distinctly difficult and unfavourable global circumstances. But that does not alter the underlying fact: that it is twenty years of neglect and complacency that have put Italy in the situation in which it now finds itself, twenty wasted years that could have been used to make the country stronger, more dynamic and less vulnerable.

With hindsight, it is clear that during those two decades, during which Mr Berlusconi was in power for nine years but governments of other stripes ruled for the other eleven years, steady, gradual measures to cut government spending, raise more tax revenue and liberalize the economy to achieve more growth could have enabled the country to avoid the current crisis. As Italy is the world's eighth largest economy and the eurozone's third largest economy (after Germany and France), this failure matters to the whole world. But also, the failure matters because it shows what happens when a country fails to acknowledge and face up to reality: it is like the band on the supposedly unsinkable *Titanic*, which played on even after the ship had hit an iceberg and started to sink. The iceberg should have been avoidable and the passengers saveable, if only the ship's designers had acknowledged the dangers and equipped the vessel with a sufficient number of lifeboats.

Why were those years wasted and the threats not recognized? Why was there not more reform, following the 1992–94 crisis? And what are the prospects that this time Italy will actually take its second chance, and make the changes necessary not just to survive but to restore its own dynamism? These are the questions this book sets out to answer, because they are questions that puzzled its author and that sent him off, journeying around Italy, in the first place. He was, admittedly, initially provoked by the return to office in 2001 of Silvio Berlusconi, and thus of the merging of corporate and governmental power involved in that return, for this merging challenged basic principles of the separation and balancing of powers in a democracy. But also, Italy offered and continues to offer a further challenge, a further source of interest: it is a country that has never fully embraced liberal economic or political ideas, a country that had at one time prospered despite not being liberal but was now foundering. So could liberal ideas stand a chance of being accepted, at last, as a solution to the country's current problems? That is what your author hoped to find out.

* * *

First, however, it was necessary to put into proportion a surprising psychological discovery – surprising at least to someone relatively new to Italy. This was Italians' declared pessimism and defeatism. To illustrate, wherever I went in Italy, a basic introductory conversation seemed to go something like this:

'Why on earth are you writing a book about Italy?'

'Well, why not? Don't you think your country is interesting?'

'Not really. Italy doesn't matter to anyone. And anyway it's all hopeless. The politicians are all corrupt. Nothing can be done. Nobody cares. You know the story: we are all individuals who can't work as a team. Our industry is being wiped out by China and India. Our universities are useless. Our justice system is sick. We're all getting older, and no one is having children any more. I wouldn't bother if I were you. Have another grappa.'

'But you have been celebrating your 150th anniversary as a nation. What would Cavour, Mazzini and Garibaldi think if they heard you talking like that? Aren't you proud to be an Italian?'

'Yes, yes, but although we have been a country for 150 years, we've never been a nation. It is only soccer that unites us, and generally not even that. Anyway, as I told you, nothing can be done and nobody wants to try.'

'But what about ... [and then I would list examples of things I'd come across in Italy that had been changed, towns that had transformed themselves, companies that had conquered world markets, etc.]? Of course Italy can be changed. And I rather believe that you might really be more patriotic and even hopeful than you appear to be. Or am I just a naïve foreigner, seduced by Italy's charms, unable to see the truth?'

Usually, my Italian companions were too polite to answer. But they did look secretly more than a little pleased. Cynical as they might seem, most Italians I met actually wanted to be more positive, more optimistic. And, despite the apparently negative question, most seemed strangely interested in what a foreigner might have to say about their country.

It is funny though. I have written lots of books about Japan, and no Japanese has ever asked me why I was doing so. I doubt if a Frenchman would ask why a foreigner was bothering to write about France, though he would surely make clear that he had no intention of reading the drivel the foreigner was bound to produce. And an Englishman? Well, he would probably smile benignly, offer his full assistance, profess to be slightly embarrassed by the foreigner's attention to his humble country, and then walk swiftly away in case the foreigner might actually ask for something. But all would take it for granted that others would and should be interested in them. Just not in Italy. At least not on the surface.

My Italian interrogators, admittedly, did add a further wrinkle to this question. Many went on to say that writing about Italy was all very well but they hoped that I had noticed that there was not one Italy but two, the North and the South. These were essentially different countries. If I was interested in data, which no doubt as a boring economist I would be, I had better understand that in Italy averages mean nothing: to use them is like saying that a person with his head in an oven and his feet in the fridge is comfortable, on average. The two halves are so different that general statistics are grossly misleading.

There is plainly truth in this, even if it is often exaggerated. People have been praising northern Italy as 'southern Bavaria' and dismissing southern Italy as 'northern Arabia' for centuries. But does it really tell us anything? People may be richer in the North, but there are problems there too. Corrupt politicians aren't only in the South, and nor are mafiosi, alas, and if we look at other popular worries such as third-rate universities, tensions over immigration or falling competitiveness, they are plainly national issues, not regional ones.

Instead, the question that I began to ask myself, as I travelled around Italy, was whether this sort of geographical distinction was really the most important one to make if we were trying to understand how the country had gone wrong and what might be done about it. Yes, yes, the South and the North are very different, as for that matter are Piedmont and the Marche, Liguria and Friuli. Every analyst or historian of Italy notes, within barely the first few hours of study, that local loyalties, known to Italians as '*campanilismo*' or 'bell-towerism', remain much more powerful than national ones. Even inter-regional marriages are less common than you might expect. But standing further back, looking from afar, I wondered whether it might actually be more useful to think of Italy's divide in a different way.

What I started to ponder, at the suggestion of an Italian friend and collaborator in London, Annalisa Piras,[2] was whether Italy's most important division, in fact its most important division through centuries of history, might not be geographical but moral or philosophical. What we mean is a divide between what could be called the Bad Italy and the Good Italy, *la Mala Italia* and *la Buona Italia*. This is, you might say, just a matter of opinion, of values, but we would respond by saying that the divide is more than just that: it is a divide between selfish, closed, unmeritocratic and often criminal ways of doing things, and more open, community-minded and progressive ways. It is a divide that is just as powerful and sometimes destructive within regions as it is between them.

This, after all, is a very Italian sort of divide. For it was this that Italy's greatest poet, Dante Alighieri, was writing about in *La Divina Commedia* (Divine Comedy) in the early fourteenth century. His extraordinary poem follows his journey, guided by Virgil, through *l'Inferno* (Hell) and *il Purgatorio* (Purgatory) before arriving in *il Paradiso* (Heaven). Dante's religious allegory of contemporary political sin, conflict, morals and love is concerned chiefly with the city state from which he had been exiled, Florence. But today it can be applied to the whole country. Just as in Dante's time, Italy's ills today reflect the country's loss of its moral compass, as well as the failure of enough people to show moral courage, to take a stand. President John F. Kennedy paraphrased Dante well when he misquoted him as having said that 'the hottest place in Hell should be for those that in times of great crisis maintain their neutrality'.

The Bad Italy is not Italy at all, but it is certainly Italian. It is not Italy because it is all about individual and clannish selfishness and so does not deserve to be ascribed to the whole nation. It starts of course with corruption and criminality, but is better described more broadly as the urge to seek power in order to use it for self-interested purposes, to amass power to reward friends, family, bag-carriers and sexual partners regardless of merit or ability, and by doing so to build clans and other networks that are beholden to you, and that live by enriching themselves at the expense of others, by closing doors rather than opening them, by excluding rather than including. This is the tendency that, in its milder form, has populated Italian university faculties with huge numbers of relatives of staff, rather than with meritocratically selected professors, but in its most virulent form builds secret networks of business-people and politicians, Church organizations and mafia groups.

We are all selfish, and biologists take great pleasure in explaining to us that even our acts of love or generosity can be explained by selfish motives. And I know all about the ambivalence deep in every Italian, the belief that laws should be enforced and obeyed, taxes paid, just not by him. Yet today there is something extra about the Bad Italy. This sort of selfishness involves a special and even wilfully destructive disregard for any wider community or, especially, national interests, institutions, laws and values.

This Bad Italy can best be compared to a parasite or, worse, a cancer. It is not a cancer that spreads and kills quickly, but one that grows bit by bit, gradually weakening its host. Certainly, that cancer has been spreading in recent years, flouting the hopes of many, both outside and inside Italy, that after the huge corruption scandal of the early 1990s known as 'Tangentopoli' or 'Bribesville', which brought down the old political establishment, it would recede. It did recede for a while as the big Christian Democrat and Socialist Party power-brokers such as Bettino Craxi[3] were exiled, pushed out of office or even jailed, as a new electoral law and direct elections for city mayors created new political incentives, and as a contemporaneous financial crisis forced a wave of privatization, liberalization and, most notably, banking reform (most notably because, as budding robbers point out, banks are where the money is, which makes them prime targets for corrupt networks and political interference).

Yet since then, facilitated and inspired by those at the very top of government, especially though not only by Mr Berlusconi, the cancer has spread again. After that small spate of fairly liberal economic reforms in the 1990s, little more has been done and the economy has stagnated, gradually slipping behind those of its European neighbours and leaving Italy with some of the highest rates of unemployment for the under-30s in the EU and, as previously stated, the second highest ratio (after Greece) of public debt to GDP. Battling over corruption, over scandals, and over the spoils of office has been the favoured political activity, far more favoured than actually governing, still less reforming, the country.

No Italian with their eyes open can honestly claim otherwise. At best you can say that both sides in politics are guilty of it, and argue that things might have been worse. You can also, with justice, say that ordinary Italians share the blame too, for every time each group's particular rights or privileges have been threatened they have kicked up a fuss and tried (usually successfully) to block change. There is a reason why the phrase '*cosi fan tutte*' is not just the title of a Mozart opera but also something of a national slogan: everybody is doing it, so why shouldn't I? But to accept that the cancer has spread is not to say that everything is hopeless. However many grappas I drink (and I have drunk quite a few), I cannot accept the idea that this Bad Italy has triumphed or will inevitably always do so. There is just too much evidence on the other side.

If the Bad Italy is supreme, how is it that an Italian[*] became the world's youngest ever three-Michelin-star chef at the age of 27, or that the country is so rich in entrepreneurs despite the known difficulties in starting a business? How can Italy still have been the world's fifth-largest manufacturer in 2009 (after the US, China, Japan and Germany, in that order, according to a study by IHS Global Insight, an economic consultancy),[4] if it is being destroyed by Chinese competition? How can the 'Eurostar' and 'Frecciarossa' (Red Arrow) high-speed trains on which I have been travelling round the country be so much more comfortable and punctual than English ones (even if they are not really any faster)?

If it is all hopeless, how can I have encountered Italian companies leading the world in selling fitness equipment, sunglasses, cashmere clothing, light aircraft, chocolate, children's cartoons and much else besides, or new anti-mafia movements, or towns that have found new post-industrial life or have pushed out the criminals, or Venice's extraordinary flood-control scheme? How come, if Italians don't care and think it is all hopeless, Italy still leads Europe in

---

[*] Massimiliano Alajmo of Le Calandre in Padua, owned with his brother Raffaele.

the proportion of its people, young and old, who volunteer to do unpaid community or charity work? In some way at least, virtually every foreigner who goes to live in Italy, or buys a holiday home there, starts to notice it: there is so much skill, entrepreneurial energy, creativity and even enthusiasm for taking part in collective activities, to place against the obvious weaknesses and political horror stories. Not everybody is doing it. There is dynamism there, but it is waiting to be released, to be encouraged.

It is plainly not an easy struggle, nor always a winning one. But the Good Italy is there, fighting away. I do not believe that I am just seeing a few rays of light in a dark cave, as if I was pointing out that Saddam Hussein was really a good family man or that there is some spark of creativity in North Korea. The Good Italy is more than that, much more.

Some characteristics of the Good Italy and the Bad Italy overlap, to be sure: the personal networks, the importance of mutual obligations, for example. But the difference is one of motivation and an essential openness. For this Good Italy is not simply about selfishness, even though with those biologists and with our great Scottish economist Adam Smith I recognize that self-interest plays an unavoidable and positive part, the invisible hand that guides us to prosperity, as he said in his seminal book *The Wealth of Nations* (1776). With him, however, I believe also in the importance of 'moral sentiments', of fellow-feeling, of cooperative instincts, of creativity for common purposes, of a sense of collective interest and collective endeavour, as essential ingredients in a successful capitalism and a successful society.

Even Wen Jiabao, the Chinese prime minister, teased westerners during the global financial crisis by telling them he likes to carry Smith's less well-known book, *The Theory of Moral Sentiments* (1759), to imply that he knew more than they did about supposed western morality and how essential it is in capitalist societies. In some ways, however, this talk is actually reminiscent of the words of David Cameron, Britain's Conservative prime minister since May 2010, in his frequent calls for a 'Big Society' to take over responsibilities and provide public services much better than the state does. He describes this as the core idea of his premiership; if it contains any substance at all (which cynics of course doubt, as cynics always do), then it represents a desire that Britain should in this respect be more like Italy.

For that is where the Good Italy resides, in moral sentiments, fellow-feeling, and cooperative instincts, in its 'Big Society', but also in a spirit of openness, a desire for progress and modernity, a desire with Smith for 'the wealth of nations' not just the wealth of individuals and groups. Over the centuries, it seems to me, this Good Italy has battled regularly against the Bad Italy, trying to beat back the cancerous efforts of the latter to eat away at excellence, at quality, at merit, at justice, at fairness, at truth itself. If it had failed, Italy really would not exist.

The Bad Italy is, in truth, where my contact with the country began, as previously noted, when in 2001 my colleagues and I at *The Economist* decided to publish a big investigation of the financial scandals and conflicts of interest surrounding Mr Berlusconi, who was then campaigning to become prime minister for a second time.

The headline on our cover said 'Why Silvio Berlusconi is unfit to lead Italy'[5], and we carried on the campaign against him with further articles and covers during the next few years, earning two libel suits[6] from him as our reward. So I became fully versed in the Bad Italy, becoming treated in my then role as *The Economist*'s editor-in-chief as a sort of public enemy of the prime minister. His brother's[7] newspaper, *Il Giornale*, honoured me in that role by repeating Mr Berlusconi's dismissal of us as '*The E-Communist*', and reinforced the point by printing my photograph and pointing out that I look like Lenin. When I stood down as editor in 2006, the same newspaper described me less amusingly in its story about my departure as 'the anti-Italian'.

Yet that is certainly not true. And, much more important, I had steadily become convinced, through my increasing contact with the country, that Italy is not simply defined by the scandals, corruption and criminality about which the foreign press understandably writes so much. So I decided to look for the Good Italy, the positive side to the nation, to try to see what it might amount to and to think about what could be done to make it stronger. What might someone who was actually 'fit to lead' that country do to liberate the Good Italy?

The confidence to do this grew and grew as I began to find and talk to more and more young people who turned out to be open-minded, positive in attitude, connected to the world and dedicated to changing things for the better. A number of these inspiring individuals and groups will be featured in the book, including the splendid anti-mafia organizations Addiopizzo ('Goodbye, protection money') and E Adesso Ammazzateci Tutti ('Now kill us all'), founded by young people in Palermo and Reggio Calabria respectively, entrepreneurs' groups, think-tanks and several groups formed by young parliamentarians. But pre-eminent among those that I met, and who gave me my contrarian confidence, were the young organizers and members of RENA, the immodestly or at least ambitiously named Rete per l'Eccellenza Nazionale, or Network for National Excellence, in Rome, Turin, Bari, Padua – in fact, all over the country.

RENA is a thoroughly modern sort of network, a network of people linked in practical terms by the internet and by conferences, but in conceptual terms by a shared objective and a shared set of values. The network, which is quite new, consists chiefly of more than 100 young professionals. By 'young', by the way, I mean people aged broadly between 25 and 45, bright and energetic types who can make this 55-year-old feel ancient and a little staid. They are working in companies, universities, government, think-tanks, the media or for themselves, mostly in Italy but a few abroad. Their shared objective is simple: to make Italy better, by spreading 'best practices' in various fields and teaching people what they consider to be a sense of civic duty. Their shared values are of meritocracy, opportunity and democracy. But their most important shared value, from my point of view, is enthusiasm, of an infectious sort and, for the purposes of this book, their willingness to make arrangements for me all over the country. If Dante had his Virgil and Beatrice to guide him through Hell, Purgatory and Heaven, I had the young members of RENA, along with some other generous enthusiasts.

The point of looking for the Good Italy is not just to make Italians feel better about themselves, nor indeed to give this author a good time as he toured the country: it also has implications for economic and social policy-makers. People have often remarked that Italy is an economic and political creature that should not in principle be capable of flying but does, one that breaks all the normal rules of economic aerodynamics, rather like a bumble bee. They then devote their time to working out how it does so. I think that analogy is wrong. It reflects a mistaken view that there is some standard model for success as an economy and society, some formula that everyone must follow. Yet a mere glance at the world shows that this is not really true or at least meaningful, for there are vast differences between France and America, Japan and Britain, Italy and China, all of which have succeeded in achieving great progress, despite their diversities.

Japan, in fact, is the country that persuaded me to think in this way, to think about economies and societies as a struggle between the good and the bad. When Japan was booming in the 1980s, attracting the sort of adulatory attention that China does today, it was widely assumed that since things were going so well for the country, everything that it did must be good, even if it defied explanation. To defy explanation was said to be just part of the eternal mystery of the East, the inscrutable nature of Japan. Then when the 1990s brought a financial crash and stagnation for Japan, the reasoning flip-flopped, transforming itself into a widely held view that everything in Japan must now be bad, must be negative.

Yet the country had not been transformed overnight. What had really happened, surely, was that the balance between the good and the bad, the positive and the negative, had shifted. The power of vested interests, the weight of corruption, the burden of politics, the importance of protected and uncompetitive industries had grown, tipping the balance against the good forces that had previously been victorious. The task for policy-makers is to tip the balance back again, not to change the country from top to bottom.

It is the same in Italy. This country has become one of the richest in the world, one of the greatest in the world, thanks to the success of the Good Italy in overcoming the dead-weight, the burden of the Bad, especially in the 1950s, 60s and 70s. The reason why Italy does fly, why it doesn't tumble tragically to the ground, is that the Good Italy stops it from crashing, by fighting back against the Bad, by pushing back the line between the two. There has been enough Good, in other words, to counteract the Bad.

The trouble now, in the second decade of the twenty-first century, is that the Bad is well on top and the country is heading towards decline and even disaster if the balance is not changed. Slow growth and political paralysis have made Italy the biggest threat to Europe's single currency, the euro, for the Bad has such a tight grip that neither investors nor other governments can muster sufficient confidence that Italy can turn itself round. In that, however, it is not alone: it is, as was said earlier, a symbol of what could happen in other western democracies.

No doubt, it is not a simple matter, not just a battle as in old western films between the goodies and the baddies, the white hats and the black hats. Often, the strengths of Italy, the good things, bring with them some strange, hard-to-understand contradictions.

For example, Italy is famously a country that hates state control, in which residents do everything they can not just to avoid paying taxes but also to avoid their lives being interfered with. Yet it is also a country in which any attempts to cut back the state, whether by reducing public spending or by reforming regulations, are fought against bitterly. The state is an enemy but it is also apparently a friend. It is as if America's anti-government 'Tea Party' movement, made famous in 2010 by Sarah Palin, had merged with the Communist Party.

Next, look out of the train or car window, especially in north-eastern Italy but also all over the South. This is a country in which, as was mentioned earlier, *campanilismo* or local loyalties are strong, in which community activism can also be impressive, and so where you might expect local control and 'nimbyism' (not in my backyard) would be supreme. Yet it is also a country in which local environmental controls are poor, in which urban sprawl has disfigured the outskirts of many towns and cities, in which local governing bodies have often failed to protect their apparent local interests. This is well known in the South, where during the 1960s and 1970s big industrial projects – oil refineries, steelworks, car factories – were introduced in Sicily, Calabria and Puglia in the vain hope that this might trigger self-sustaining growth. But it is also true in the richer North, especially the north-eastern region of the Veneto, around Venice, and right across the Po river valley to Turin in the north-west.

Now, here is a social conundrum. We all know, and rather admire, the fact that to Italians the most important value of all is family. Cold-hearted analysts look at this as the sign of a low-trust society, in which only those whose genes you share can really be trusted. Novelists and film-makers see it as the cuddly side of Cosa Nostra, of the mafia, whether in Sicily in *The Godfather* or New Jersey in *The Sopranos*. Others take the warmer view that Italians know from birth the things that Anglo-Saxons learn only as they get older, that people matter more than material things or money, and that your mother matters most of all. But if all that is so, why are Italians no longer having children, why is the birth rate now one of the lowest in Europe? Soon, it would seem, there will be no one left to trust. Perhaps that is why Italians are also among Europe's keenest users of the Facebook social networking service, despite relatively poor internet service?

And finally a cultural and economic puzzle. Italy is famous for its art and for its history: Italians, especially in government bodies, can be heard to boast that the country holds 70 per cent of the world's artistic patrimony (a rather western-centric estimate, by the way, which neither Indians nor Chinese would be very happy with), and more UNESCO 'world heritage sites' (forty-five) than any other country. It also has the longest Mediterranean coastline of any developed country. So naturally tourism, art and culture must be one of Italy's great strengths and economic assets, especially now that cheap travel and rising affluence is making international tourism available to more and more people?

Well, not really, or at least not as much as you might expect: Italy's receipts from international tourism are lower than in either France or Spain. Moreover, in one of the most shocking events of 2010, part of the historic city of Pompeii collapsed, thanks to bad management and neglect, and some more collapsed the following year, as if to show that Italians don't care enough about their own heritage, their own tourist assets – or at least the Italian state doesn't. Just outside Rome, a few hundred metres from Hadrian's Villa, one of the great tourist sites of the world, a huge new landfill site for waste is being dug, under emergency powers assumed by the Lazio regional government, ignoring archaeological damage and the likelihood of off-putting smells wafting across Hadrian's ruins. It is as if Italy has given up on tourism and culture, or just doesn't care. You might interject the notion that Spain has simply cornered the market in cheap mass tourism, and there is some truth to that, but Italy's tourism receipts were ahead of Spain's as recently as 1995. There must be a bit more to this than meets the eye.

There is a bit more than meets the eye to almost everything in Italy. Straightforward explanations are rarely sufficient, the full truth is rarely revealed and stories rarely seem to come to an end. What can be said, however, is that a country that was highly dynamic during the 1950s, 60s and 70s, with new industries being created, new fortunes being made, and new leaders coming to the fore in every walk of life, has become strikingly sclerotic. The same basic characteristics of Italy prevailed then as now: localism, family fealties, the importance of networks of mutual obligation, households' high propensity to save, the power of the Catholic Church and so on. By comparison to France, Britain or Germany, indeed, in many ways

Italy has long been rather feudal in its nature. But in its post-war heyday, its feudalism managed also to be dynamic, to accommodate and even welcome change. The Good Italy, the new elements of Italy, were able to elbow their way past the obstacles erected by the bad Italy.

Now, feudal Italy has lost that dynamism, but the Good Italy is still there, even if it fumbled its chance to restore the dynamism twenty years ago. The question is how to restore it now, amid Italy's new financial and political crisis. The journey of this book, a more humdrum, secular and certainly more humble modern version of Dante's, amid a different modern sort of comedy, is a journey to try to understand why the dynamism faded and to see what could be done about it. Like Dante, one might as well begin in *l'Inferno*. At least after we have looked at politics, things can only get better.

CHAPTER 2

L'Inferno Politico

If you have been following Italian political events, you could be forgiven for wondering whether the political scene there in recent years should best be categorized, whether by Dante or by a modern observer, as a type of hell or as some sort of paradise. It depends on whose point of view you are taking.

After all, the countless nights of partying with scantily clad young women that the 75-year-old prime minister, Silvio Berlusconi, held at his villas between 2008 and his fall from office in 2011 could place politics in either category. The life of the government leader and his closest male associates appeared roughly to resemble the reward supposedly promised to Islamist suicide bombers when they ascend to heaven, except that the dozens and dozens of girls at Mr Berlusconi's parties are fairly unlikely, shall we say, to have been virgins.

This is the man whose most enduring political legacy from his total of nearly nine years in power (1994, 2001–06; 2008–11) could prove merely to be that he replaced *la dolce vita*[1] as the great global cliché about Italy with a phrase he is said to have learned from his friend the late Colonel Muammar Qaddafi of Libya: bunga-bunga. Those involved – that is, those whose telephone conversations about it were tapped and then publicized – seemed unable to agree upon exactly what a bunga-bunga party, or in some versions dance, consists of, but it sounds exotically salacious and is certainly memorable. And the numbers of people involved are quite extraordinary: in one court case alone it has been claimed that 131 prostitutes were supplied by one businessman for parties and other events.

No one, certainly, could be more different to Mr Berlusconi and his way of doing things than his successor in the prime minister's office at Palazzo Chigi, Mario Monti, a 69-year-old whose immediately previous role was as president of Bocconi, a private business and economics university in Milan. Monogamous, hard-working, with an instinct for seriousness leavened by a sharp sense of humour, Mr Monti has a deep interest in economic policy which his predecessor utterly lacked. One of Mr Berlusconi's finance ministers during his 2001–06 government told me, off the record, that whenever there had been a need to discuss economic policy Mr Berlusconi would leave the table, saying it was up to the ministers to decide, and would go off and watch a football game on the television. Mr Monti would be likelier to desert a football game in order to discuss economics.

The temptation now is to treat Mr Berlusconi as being essentially a historical figure, a strange but interesting phenomenon of the 1990s and the first decade of the twenty-first century, a true one-off. But that would be a mistake, for two important reasons. The first is that Mr Berlusconi personally does not consider himself to be history: he saw his departure from office on 12 November 2011 as strictly temporary. At the next general elections, which are due at the latest in the spring of 2013, despite his many denials he is very likely to run again, to lead his political party, in whatever form it takes at that time, and to attempt again to form a government. The second is that the effect of Mr Berlusconi anyway goes well beyond the man himself, both in terms of explaining what did and did not happen between the crisis of the early 1990s and today, and of explaining how other political parties, forces and institutions see themselves and the practice of politics now. *'Berlusconismo'*, as populist, media-obsessed, power-accumulating politics is known to many Italian commentators, is an integral part of Italian political life, and will be for years to come.

Bunga-bunga may now be especially memorable and even familiar around the world, but probably the best and more revealing slogan dreamt up by Mr Berlusconi was actually *'Forza Italia'*, the name of the new political party he formed in 1994 and with which he made his triumphal entry into parliament and – albeit on that first occasion for less than eight months – to Palazzo Chigi. Translatable as 'Come on Italy' or, better, as 'Courage Italy', the name was borrowed from the football terraces, venues with which he was already familiar as the owner since 1986 of the AC Milan football club. It was the original expression of his essential approach to achieving electoral success: to seek to monopolize optimism, to promote and promise pleasure, and to convey a positive view of Italy and Italians.

At that time, in the early 1990s, it was not at all clear to many Italians that Mr Berlusconi was a representative of what this author is calling '*la Mala Italia*'. It was a moment of great scandal in politics, a moment essentially of the fall of the old political regime. Mr Berlusconi represented change, novelty, even a popular touch. As a self-made man, a hugely successful businessman who had risen from a modest upbringing in Milan as the son of a bank employee, he could even be said to represent an Italian version of 'the American dream', an idea he and his supporters later fostered in a pamphlet about his life that was prepared for the 2001 elections called 'Una Storia Italiana' (An Italian Story). Not many people recognized that his name had long before been associated with the old political establishment, as a member of a Masonic Lodge, 'P2' or 'Propaganda Due', that was accused of plotting all sorts of misdeeds.

When he entered politics in the wake of a crisis both of political corruption and of the public finances, many observers thus concluded that this successful businessman might prove to be good at governing, or at least at making things happen, but he would probably lack skills in the political arts. Nearly two decades later, years during which he proved to be the single most influential person in Italian politics, the general conclusion is the exact opposite: that he has been pretty cack-handed at governing but is a genius at the political arts.

It is a testament to that genius that neither Italian voters nor the country's supposed moral guide, the Catholic

Church, took an especially moralistic view of Mr Berlusconi's personal behaviour; even after his trial opened on 6 April 2011 on charges of employing an illegally[2] under-age prostitute, Karima El-Mahroug,[3] and of abusing his power to get her released from police custody, the opinion-poll ratings for his party, the Popolo della Libertà ('People of Liberty', the current name for the former Forza Italia) remained at about 25–27 per cent, which, while not spectacularly strong, were also not the ratings of a party considered to be led by a pariah. Some say that through the brazenness of his behaviour, and the constant round of scandals (the Karima/Ruby affair was already the third major sex scandal since he returned to office in May 2008), he has anaesthetized Italians to each successive outrage; others that his control when in office of the news broad-casts both of the public broadcasting channels of RAI and of his own commercial channels at Mediaset mean that he suppresses the news; others that his Italian supporters[4] simply do not care.

The Catholic Church in Italy, and indeed the Vatican establishment itself, have tut-tutted about Mr Berlusconi's scandals from time to time, but until 2010–11 essentially turned a blind eye both to the fact that he has now twice divorced and to this old man's antics with young girls, presumably on the view that the benefits that the Church obtained from having Mr Berlusconi's coalitions in govern-ment exceeded any moral damage done. One of those benefits consisted of the blocking of social and legal reforms that are anathema to the Vatican: gay marriage, *in vitro* fertilization and other 'bio-ethical' measures that have advanced more rapidly in other western European countries than in Italy. Another was the restoration in 2005 of a valuable exemption for the Church from tax on its vast holdings of property that are used for commercial activities, a saving estimated by a journalist from *l'Espresso* magazine, Stefano Livadiotti, as being worth 700 million euros annually.[5] This restoration, by Mr Berlusconi's then governing majority, reversed a decision by the Court of Cassation the previous year, which had upheld efforts by municipal governments to levy the tax on the Church. In February 2012, the Monti government announced that it planned to restore this tax.

There can be little doubt where Dante would have placed both Mr Berlusconi personally, much of the rest of the political establishment, and even the leaders of the Catholic Church, as a punishment for what they have done or, in the Church's case, not done: firmly in Hell. His purpose was moral, and since among Dante's circles of sin were included those for the lustful, the gluttonous, the fraudulent, the self-indulgent and, worst of all, the *ignavi*, or those who fail to take a moral stand, all terms perfectly apt for the governing class, it is hard to imagine him looking leniently either on the current Italian political scene or on the Church establishment who, in his view, ought to speak out strongly against immorality of all kinds. What is the Church for, after all, if it fails to offer moral guidance, as is laid down in the scriptures?

Some of these political sins that would have drawn Dante's condemnation, especially lust, can be ascribed directly and principally to Mr Berlusconi personally, though part of his innovation in that regard is in reality his openness about sex and his brazen social life, rather than the fact of it. Previous prime ministers have not, it is safe to say, all been puritans.

Throughout his commercial and political career, he has made self-indulgence and pleasure-seeking a central part of his public image, an image that is more like that of a star from 'reality' television, or one in a racy version of a Broadway musical, than of a conventional policy-maker or political wheeler-dealer. He has always sought to act the playboy in a very public way, though admittedly it is only since he turned 70 years old and divorced for the second time that he appears to have turned to younger and younger girls, and eventually to bunga-bunga, sealing his Dantean fate. Hypocrisy is one of the few sins that is hard to associate with Silvio Berlusconi. One of his more truthful statements, made in 2009 when a rather older call girl, Patrizia D'Addario, had released recordings of her nights with him, was 'I am not a saint.'

It would be wrong, however, to attribute all the sins of politics to him. As noted earlier, his rise to political power occurred just when sinfulness by others in the form of corruption caused the collapse of the post-war Italian party system, in 1992–93, in the scandal known as 'Tangentopoli' (roughly, 'Bribesville') if you are referring to the culprits, who were initially centred in Milan, or as 'Mani Pulite' ('Clean Hands'), if you are referring to the investigation. This scandal coincided with the worst financial crisis Italy had experienced since 1945.

In the scandal, prosecuting magistrates led by Antonio Di Pietro, now a politician himself,[6] for a while successfully pursued leading politicians from the previously dominant Christian Democratic Party and the Socialist

Party on charges of lining their pockets and party funds with the proceeds from bribes given to secure public works contracts. Mr Berlusconi's political mentor, Bettino Craxi, was pelted with coins in the street by demonstrators, was forced into exile in Tunisia by attempts to prosecute him, and died there in 2000.

The scale of this assault on the incumbent political parties can be seen from the fact that requests for the lifting of parliamentary immunity were lodged by magistrates for more than 200 of the 630 members of the Chamber of Deputies. The discredited dominant parties both crumbled. And yet, lest we become too excited by this exposure of corruption, we should note that although more than 3,000 people were put on trial during the Mani Pulite campaign, more than 2,000 escaped conviction simply because their cases eventually expired thanks to the statute of limitations. The campaign exposed corruption, but it did not really punish it in a comprehensive way. Moreover, the political establishment took its revenge on Mr Di Pietro through a successful smear campaign, which led him to resign from the judiciary and later, once he had cleared his name, to enter politics.

Nevertheless, Mani Pulite marked the beginning of a new era in Italian politics, one that fittingly coincided with the end of the Cold War and a new era in global politics too. This was fitting because the party system, and the complexion of Italian governments from 1948 onwards, had been shaped by the Cold War. Italy's second biggest party from 1948 until 1992 was the Communist Party (PCI by its Italian initials). Coalition governments during that long period were all formed around the biggest party, the Christian Democrats (DC by its Italian initials), implicitly in order to keep the PCI out of power as well as to exclude the smaller extreme-right-wing neo-fascist party, the Italian Social Movement (MSI). With the fall of the Soviet Union, the PCI fell too, discredited by the demise of its Russian allies.[7] Suddenly, politics lost its old core and stability, while also becoming much more inclusive.

What hasn't changed

Yet was the post-1992 era really new? It looked new, if you took Silvio Berlusconi as its symbol and at face value, since he formed a new party almost out of nothing, used a new, highly personal and televisual style of campaigning, and came from a business background rather than a political one. Yet from a Dantean, sin-spotting point of view, or even just as a student of politics, you might well question how new this era really was.

For Mr Berlusconi had during the 1980s been a close ally of the very old-style Mr Craxi, and had obtained his national commercial TV licences, and eventual near monopoly, courtesy of the same Mr Craxi, in other words through political contacts, which may or may not have been corrupt but were certainly a case of private profit from state power. Furthermore, as previously noted, Mr Berlusconi had been among the list of members of a secret network, organized by a Masonic Lodge known as 'P2',[8] that was exposed during a previous corruption (and indeed anti-mafia) investigation in 1981. Mr Berlusconi was no newcomer.

Mr Berlusconi has long been fond of claiming that since he entered politics in 1994 he has been persecuted by left-wing magistrates. Yet in fact his encounters with the judiciary began much, much earlier, in 1979, encounters which led to successive criminal cases during the 1980s for alleged corruption, false accounting and other crimes. It is at least as plausible to say that Mr Berlusconi entered politics in order to protect himself against further prosecution. There is no doubt that some prosecutors are politically motivated against him, but that explanation is insufficient to explain away all or even most of the charges.[9]

Although he has not stemmed the flow of trials, while in office he has been extremely successful at using new laws to reduce the risks posed to him by trials, such as by decriminalizing the offence of false accounting (of which he has often been accused), shortening the statute of limitations for other crimes, and using laws that have temporarily permitted him to refuse to appear in court (before later being struck down by the Constitutional Court) in order to delay trials by several years. So if entering politics was a gambit to avoid jail, it worked.

From a broadly liberal point of view, the sad, missed opportunity represented by Mr Berlusconi also began long before 1994. As this book will confirm, Italians can often be heard saying that what their country needs is innovators, willing to disrupt the old ways of doing things. Mr Berlusconi was just such a disruptive innovator when he entered the advertising and television businesses in the 1970s and early 1980s, confronting a complacent and conservative establishment in those industries who thought this upstart would inevitably fail.

An important part of his method for proving them wrong was the very traditional tactic of building and then exploiting political contacts, as outlined earlier in connection with Mr Craxi. Since such tactics are also standard in his original industry, property development, this was not surprising. Nevertheless he did also innovate in the selling of advertising and in commercial TV. The missed liberal opportunity is that once he had succeeded, this disruptive innovator set about ensuring (through his political ties and then by entering politics himself) that no one else could follow him and disrupt his own success. It is a classic story: first break in, and then rebuild a stronger wall behind you to keep everyone else out.

In politics, Mr Berlusconi's rallying call in 1994, by means of which he struck a governing alliance with the MSI and, even more crucially, the new quasi-separatist Northern League and the rump of the old DC, now the Union of Democrats of the Centre (UDC), was a very traditional one: he said he wanted to 'save Italy from communism'. The fall of the old system that led eventually to his rise to power had also coincided with the killings in Palermo, in May and July 1992 respectively, of Giovanni Falcone and Piero Borsellino, the two magistrates who were leading a major investigative campaign against that oldest and most traditional of sources of political power, the mafia. Several of Mr Berlusconi's closest and longest-serving associates – most notably Marcello Dell'Utri, a Sicilian senator for Forza Italia who worked for many of Mr Berlusconi's companies during the 1970s and 1980s – have been convicted of crimes that include conspiracy with the mafia.[10] So for all his many claims to be a liberal and a modernizer, Mr Berlusconi was in reality a protector of the status quo.

That first Berlusconi government, as previously noted, lasted only eight months before a dispute with the Northern League brought it down. It was followed by a confusing period of changing party names and initials, in which independent, centrist and left-wing parties formed five different governments within six years, amid the creation of strangely named political assemblages on the centre and left called 'the Ulivo' (Olive Tree, led by Romano Prodi) and 'Margherita' (often translated as Daisy, led by Francesco Rutelli), before Mr Berlusconi won power again in 2001 for the centre-right and held office for the unusually long (for Italy) period of five years. Yet, for all the name changes and political fragmentation, the continuity in Italian politics is at least as striking as the change.

There were changes, for sure, especially at local level following the direct election of town mayors from 1993 onwards (a reform that had been fiercely opposed by the old Christian Democrat establishment). The electoral law was changed twice, in 1993 and in 2005, first to reduce and then to increase the amount of proportional representation in the system, and on both occasions to provide an extra incentive – a 'majority prize' of extra seats – to parties to form large coalitions before elections rather than after them, with prime ministerial candidates named in advance, in a general hope of making Italian politics more bi-polar, with two main parties or coalitions confronting each other and alternating in government, rather like the much-admired (in Italy) situation in Britain. The idea was to avoid the pre-1992 situation of frequent changes in multi-party government coalitions, all of which contained and were largely steered by just one party, the Christian Democrats.

On the face of it, this partially succeeded, for by 2008 the country did indeed have two large parties confronting each other on the right and the left: respectively Silvio Berlusconi's People of Liberty (PdL) and the Democratic Party (PD), which was formed in 2007 out of the former socialists, former communists and leftist inclined members of the former Christian Democrats. Yet both of these parties are in reality rather artificial.

It cannot be known for sure until and unless Mr Berlusconi actually leaves the political scene, but the PdL looks and feels very much like a personal political support group rather than an enduring party. It benefited hugely from a merger in 2009 with the National Alliance (AN) party led by Gianfranco Fini, the new name for the old neo-fascist MSI, but that then splintered away again the following year when Mr Fini (a former foreign minister during the 2001–06 government, and by then speaker of the Chamber of Deputies) decided to plan for a post-Berlusconi future by forming his own new party, Future and Liberty (FeL). Moreover, the coalitions formed around Forza Italia and then the PdL have looked even more artificial, consisting as they have of governments containing both the Northern League, whose very essence is that of opposing fiscal support for the South, and the AN, whose base is in the South and so depends on protecting that very fiscal support.

Meanwhile the Democratic Party had two leaders (Walter Veltroni and Pier Luigi Bersani) during its first four years of life, and at all times has had at least half a dozen others jockeying to be the party's prime ministerial candidate, thanks to the open primary votes the party adopted for that purpose. One of those who had been instrumental in bringing about its creation, Francesco Rutelli, a senator, a former mayor of Rome and the only-just unsuccessful[11] prime ministerial candidate for the 'Margherita' coalition against Mr Berlusconi in 2001, deserted the new party after just ten months to form his own tiny group, Alliance for Italy. The Democratic Party has not yet forged a solid agreement as to what its proposed programme for the country is, nor has it put down roots as a party organization. Its main problem is that the faction of the party that has the deepest roots and the strongest local organization is the very entity whose heritage it was formed to try to escape, namely the former Communist Party. And that part of the party in particular retains close ties to another well-organized interest group, the main trade union federations.

It may well be that the Democratic Party will not really find its voice, nor decide whether its future is as one party or several, until Mr Berlusconi leaves the political scene, for opposition to him is for the time being the main glue that holds it together. Its weakness is shown by the fact that on the left several small parties or movements have outdone the PD in terms of dynamism and even, at times, have been more successful in setting the political agenda: Antonio Di Pietro's Italia dei Valori (IdV), mentioned earlier; the Left Ecology Freedom (SEL) party formed in 2009 by Nichi Vendola, the charismatic, gay, ex-communist, devout Catholic president of the southern region of Puglia; the leaderless 'Purple People' movement; and the Five Star Movement formed and led by Beppe Grillo, a satirist.

Even when Mr Berlusconi left office in November 2011, the most dynamic, eye-catching element in the Democratic Party was not its leadership, who you might have expected to look triumphant, but the fast-rising young mayor of Florence, Matteo Renzi, who is just 37 years old, has been mayor only since 2009, is an active user of social networks for communication, and is a keen student of the success in Britain of Tony Blair and his 'new Labour' in 1997. One of the main proposals of this *rottamatore* or 'scrapper' is that all Italian politicians who have been in charge for the past twenty years should retire – including those on the left. His actual policy positions are rather vaguer, it must be said. Meanwhile the Democratic Party's old leadership publicly expressed strong support for the technical government led by Mario Monti while plainly, if mainly privately, squirming at the prospect of many of the Monti government's reforms – especially to pensions and the labour laws – which were opposed vehemently by the trade unions.

So an apparently transformed political scene is less different than it looks: its dominant figure after 1994 rested much of his appeal on anti-communism, and kept himself in power less through pure popularity than through old-fashioned coalition-building; the centrist and leftist parties are in reality factions formed around interest groups or individual leaders. Just as important, however, is the fact that the two general sins of Italian politics – corruption and excessive cost – remain as widespread as ever.

A costly *casta*

Corruption is, by definition, hard to measure. The incredibly slow and problematic nature of the Italian justice system makes it difficult to guage it by the number of successful prosecutions, either. It would be hard, however, to find a magistrate, political journalist or political scholar who thinks that it has diminished significantly since 1992, either at national or at local level.

Just two years after the Berlusconi government had won a huge majority in the 2008 elections, it was hit by the forced resignation of its minister for economic development, Claudio Scajola, amid a scandal involving a property developer, Diego Anemone, who had allegedly provided Mr Scajola with an ultra-cheap apartment in an expensive area of Rome, with a view of the Colosseum. Prosecutors released the information that Mr Anemone had a list of 400 names of politicians and officials with whom he dealt, which made this look like quite a traditional sort of political corruption scandal. Guido Bertolaso, head of the Civil Protection Agency, the body responsible for disaster relief and reconstruction, was also on the list, and had already been hit by allegations (well illustrated by leaked transcripts of telephone wiretaps) that he had taken favours in the form of prostitutes (whom Mr Bertolaso, who remained in his post for several months afterwards, said were not prostitutes but rather masseuses, necessary to help relieve the stress of his job).

Moreover, as is traditional in Italian politics, Mr Scajola remained a member of the Chamber of Deputies following his resignation, and even, as the Berlusconi government wobbled its way towards collapse during the autumn of 2011, began to look for a political comeback, either as a future leader of the centre-right himself, or, likelier, as a king-maker.

Telephone wiretaps provide some indication of the magnitude of the problem of corruption. This investigative practice is also heavily used in pursuit of organized crime, yet corruption and organized crime form strongly overlapping circles. According to government figures, in 2009 alone there were 119,000 phone interceptions and 11,000 cases of the bugging of premises. Barely a day seems to go by without hundreds of pages of wiretap transcripts landing on journalists' desks. Much of the evidence against Mr Berlusconi himself in the under-age prostitution case consists of wiretap transcripts, both of his own phone calls and those of the women involved.

That is one of the extraordinary aspects of Italian politics: that whatever use Mr Berlusconi was making of wiretaps by the country's intelligence services while he was prime minister, he must have known that others were also listening in to his phones too. Which in turn makes his personal behaviour, including his call to a Milan police office to ask them to release Karima El-Mahroug on the grounds that she was 'the niece of the Egyptian president', even more extraordinary in its recklessness or perhaps insouciance.

Despite the difficulties, Alberto Vannucci of the University of Pisa made a brave attempt to compare the level of corruption today with that of the early 1990s in an article[12] in the *Bulletin of Italian Politics* in 2009. He showed that the number of corruption-related crimes reported, the number of people involved in those reported crimes, and the number of convictions, were all considerably lower in 2004–06 than in 1992–95, at the height of Mani Pulite. But as he says, that does not tell you that there is less corruption now. For a start, on those measures you would also have to conclude that there had been less corruption in the 1980s too, as all those figures were then even lower, but if Mani Pulite proved anything it was that corruption had certainly been rife – it had just not been reported or exposed.

Moreover, indicators of perceptions of the level of corruption, which are available through direct opinion polls of Italians and through the transnational surveys conducted by the Transparency International anti-corruption non-governmental organization (NGO), based in Berlin, suggest the opposite: the perception is that corruption is more extensive now even than in the early 1990s. The 2010 poll of corruption perceptions by Transparency International placed Italy in an ignominious 67th place, just behind Rwanda. Even so, as Professor Vannucci also shows, the number of cases of alleged corruption reported annually in a newspaper normally considered to be vigilant and anti-establishment, *la Repubblica*, were also substantially lower by 2008 than in the first half of the 1990s.

On the twentieth anniversary of Mani Pulite, in February 2012, the president of the Corte di Conti, the Court of Accounts that has responsibility for dealing with official corruption, hit the headlines by stating that in the court's view corruption and misuse of public funds were costing the country 60 billion euros per year.

Broader measures of the overall illegal economy –
variously known as 'black', 'shadow', 'informal' or
'submersed' – which includes corruption, tax evasion of all
kinds, illegal labour and organized crime, also show no
substantial diminution: a paper[13] by ISTAT, the national
statistics agency, using official figures reckoned it was
somewhere between 16.3 per cent and 17.5 per cent of
GDP in 2008, a little lower than the 18.2–19.1 per cent in
2000 thanks possibly to increased efforts to reduce tax
evasion. Private economists' estimates often place it at
somewhere between 20 per cent and 25 per cent of GDP.
Those figures make Italy's illegal economy similar in size
to estimates of the black economy in Spain and Greece,
and roughly double the estimated size of such illegal
activities in Britain, Germany and America.

As Professor Vannucci outlines in his article, given the
way in which personal networks and relationships work in
Italy, and given the relative weakness there of regulatory
institutions, of civil society and of respect for legality, the
likeliest explanation for these divergent indicators of
declining numbers of corruption cases, rising public perceptions of corruption and diminishing media attention lies in
the fact that the line between 'normal' and 'abnormal' uses
and abuses of power or relationships is blurred, to say the
least. In a society such as Italy, where covert networks are
the norm, there arises a widespread acceptance of what
needs to be paid, to whom and for what, almost as if a
catalogue or guidebook had been drawn up.

It is when people appear to go beyond the accepted (if
informal) rules that anger, retaliation and exposure become
likelier. In the aforementioned cases of Mr Scajola (the

economic development minister) and Mr Bertolaso (head of the civil protection agency) in 2010, it was speculated that two things had happened: that they had gone beyond the norms; and that their patron, Mr Berlusconi, had lost the power or ability either to control or protect them. This speculation may not be accurate, but it illustrates a general way of thinking about corruption and power networks.

Furthermore, following the vast amount of exposure that occurred during and after Mani Pulite, the implicit catalogues and accepted practices will have adjusted themselves, with bribers and recipients of bribes aware that new channels and new forms of favour had become necessary to avoid prosecution. During the 1990s, when power appeared to become diffuse and rapidly changing as parties fragmented, the perception that strong, corrupt networks existed may have dimmed. But Mr Berlusconi's political success in surviving in government for five years in 2001–06, and then in being re-elected in 2008 with a seemingly stronger majority, will have had two effects: by concentrating power in the hands of those around him and in the coalition parties, the incentives and rewards for corruption will have increased again; and the perception will have grown among those not in those circles that rewards were now overwhelmingly accruing to insiders – regardless of whether it was true.

Corruption is part of the excessive cost of politics, a part of *la Mala Italia*, but only part. For entry into politics in Italy also brings an excellent, entirely legal income for men and women alike, and use of the country's quite staggeringly huge fleet of 72,000 official cars (known as 'Auto Blu'). The biggest non-fiction, current affairs bestseller in recent years was *La Casta* (The Caste), by two journalists from the *Corriere della Sera* newspaper,[14] which sold a million copies.[15] The authors regaled Italians with news that their members of parliament are paid salaries and allowances three times those of their French counterparts, that they grant themselves an extraordinary array of perks, including subsidized air travel and all those official cars, and that they become qualified for a parliamentary pension after only 30 months of service.[16]

Most of all, though, what *La Casta* highlighted was how politics has become a way to use public money for political patronage, and that this has not changed at all over the past twenty years. It is facilitated by the sheer number of political posts in the country, whether at national, regional, provincial, municipal or indeed European levels: roughly 150,000 in all, according to Cesare Salvi and Massimo Villone,[17] authors of another book, plus more than 275,000 others whose income is connected to political activities, through consulting projects, events, political foundations and so on. The authors of *La Casta* put the total number of people whose income derives from politics even higher, at 600,000, but the truth is that no one really knows. And this does not even include the hundreds of thousands, perhaps millions, of people given public sector jobs to secure their votes, a practice of clientelism that is especially widespread in the South.

What is clear is that on every measure – party financing, the cost of parliament, the number of posts, the size of allowances – the expense and reach of Italian politics holds world championship status. In the summer and autumn of 2011, the seemingly impossible began to happen:

serious talk broke out of cutting the cost of politics, as part of the fiscal austerity measures being forced upon Italy by the sovereign-debt crisis surrounding the euro (and within which Italy's government is by far the biggest debtor, owing nearly 1.9 trillion euros). But there was no need for *la Buona Italia* to get excited about this: Mr Berlusconi's coalition soon dropped the idea of cutting parliamentary benefits, pension rights or, heaven forbid, even the number of parliamentary seats, and then the Monti government also shied away from cutting political costs either.

The aforementioned Patrizia D'Addario, who was at the centre of the Berlusconi scandal circus in 2009, symbolized several of the political sins all in one. This (then) 42-year-old, glamorous single mother and prostitute had been recruited to attend the prime minister's parties by a businessman from Bari called Giampaolo Tarantini, who was himself looking for favours by building a network of highly placed contacts, according to magistrates.

Thanks to her release of tape recordings made in Mr Berlusconi's bedroom (in a bed said to have been given to him by Vladimir Putin of Russia), and to the resulting furore, Ms D'Addario attained the dizzy-but-serious heights of an interview with the *Financial Times*,[18] in which she claimed that as a result of her partying with the prime minister she had been promised by him a post as a Member of the European Parliament. This promise fell through, she said, when Mr Berlusconi's wife, Veronica Lario, filed for divorce, making prominent accusations about (among many other things) his granting of political posts to his girlfriends. Ms D'Addario told the *Financial*

Times interviewer: 'The system is like that. All of Italy functions like this.' Moreover, as is often the case with Italian scandals, within a year Ms D'Addario, her case and her accusations had been virtually forgotten, superseded by others.

Some things, in Italy, never seem to change. Scandals blow in, like storm-clouds, and the rain they release feels torrential for a while. But then they pass, and are virtually forgotten.

The politics of the plasma screen

Political scientists have, since the fall in 1992–93 of what is known in the Italian media as 'the first republic',[19] described Italy as being a 'democracy in transition', but they have had no idea what it is actually in a transition to, and no obvious 'second republic' has emerged. You can't be in transition without a destination, unless you are the character played by Tom Hanks in the 2004 movie *The Terminal*, which was loosely based on the true story of a stateless Iranian who lived in Paris Charles de Gaulle airport for nearly twenty years – roughly the duration so far of Italy's 'transition'. The Iranian finally left the terminal when he was taken to hospital – which is not a bad parallel for Italian politics. Few would deny that it is sick.

Yet there are two big ways in which Italian politics clearly has changed since the early 1990s. That change is represented, first, by the style and methods of Mr Berlusconi, in which television plays an essential part. The second big change is the rise of the Northern League (Lega Nord, in its Italian name) to its often pivotal role in coalition politics, which has altered the dynamics especially of the right-wing of politics, but also of the country as a whole.

Mr Berlusconi's general use of power is of a very traditional Italian sort: for self-protection, self-enrichment, and for the benefit of his friends and supporters. This makes it the epitome of *la Mala Italia*, as outlined in Chapter One. Despite what he says about protecting the country from communism, Mr Berlusconi has in fact not pursued much of an ideological agenda during his nearly nine years in office. He says he is a liberal, though more classically liberal reforms have been introduced by centre-left governments during the past fifteen years than by his own. It was the very lack of liberal reforms, in the view both of the bond markets and of the European Central Bank, that brought his government down in November 2011 amid the eurozone's financial crisis.

Yet the way he has sought, won and retained power has been extremely new – including the resulting fact that he succeeded in remaining in office for a full five-year term in 2001–06, which none of his post-war predecessors managed to do. The person who came closest to that achievement was his mentor, Bettino Craxi, who was in power for almost four years in 1983–87. Giulio Andreotti, unwilling star of Paolo Sorrentino's 2008 film about Italian politics and the mafia in the early 1990s, *Il Divo*, managed to be prime minister seven times, sometimes consecutively, but he never managed to remain in Palazzo Chigi for more than three years in a row.

Mr Berlusconi managed to survive in office and in power for so long by combining new techniques with old ones. The old ones concern money and coalition bargaining, for he has never been able to form a government on his own. In 2001 his Forza Italia party was the largest single party with 29.5 per cent of the vote, but still needed the Alleanza Nazionale and the Northern League in order to form a government. In 2008, his greatest electoral triumph was achieved by forming a common list with the AN, which gained an impressive combined 37.4 per cent of the votes, a success that led to a formal merger of the two parties a year later, but, as previously noted, that merger fell apart after just one further year. The Northern League's 8.3 per cent of the votes was still needed to form a government.

The new techniques, however, are just as important. They boil down, first, to the domination of television. And, second, to the use of television as the medium for conducting a permanent, personal electoral campaign, with some assistance, especially in the murkier aspects of campaigning, from print publications owned by the Berlusconi family, including two daily papers, *il Giornale* and *il Foglio*, plus a third, *Libero*, which collaborates closely with Mr Berlusconi and his party.

Through television, Mr Berlusconi has campaigned as a pure populist, but with two distinctions from the way in which populism is understood in other developed countries: first, his populism is permanent or constant, rather than being limited to election campaigns; second, it is not closely tied to policy-making – in other words, when in office he has not introduced much legislation or other policies, according to the opinion polls, as classic populists would – but rather has simply used it for the maintenance of personal support and domination of the political agenda, by means of declarations and interventions that are only rarely followed up by actual policy. On television, he is at least as much a performer as he is a politician.[20]

Television is far and away the most important communications medium in Italy, and, as already noted, Mr Berlusconi owns the three dominant commercial TV channels through his company Mediaset (Canale 5, Italia 1 and Rete 4). A poll[21] in 2008 found that more than 80 per cent of respondents said they got their news about the election campaign that year from television, and only 60 per cent said that they also got it from newspapers.

During the 1970s and 1980s, control of the three terrestrial channels of the public broadcaster, RAI, were shared between the country's three main political parties, the Christian Democrats, the Socialists and the Communist Party, and some vestiges of that system still remain, especially in the political talk shows of RAI2 and RAI3. But what Mr Berlusconi succeeded in doing during his periods in government, most strongly in 2008–11, was in taking full control of the news broadcasts of RAI, known in Italian as *telegiornale*, and using them to control the flow of information to the public as well as to maintain his own perpetual campaign. This left just two mainstream news broadcasts outside his control when in government: the ones on La7, the small commercial terrestrial channel owned by Telecom Italia, and on Sky Italia, Rupert Murdoch's satellite broadcaster.

In many developed countries, print newspapers set the news agenda for television, having the resources, space and independence to make investigations, reveal stories and offer opinions. This is not really true in Italy, where newspaper circulations are lower than in other European countries: a daily sale in 2004 of 115 copies[22] per 1,000 adults, which compares with 313 per 1,000 in Germany, 332 per 1,000 in Britain or, rather closer, 160 per 1,000 in France. Even more important, the broadcast and print media act in a more politicized way than elsewhere. The long tradition of party political sharing of power inside RAI is echoed by a quite overt tendency of daily newspapers to affiliate themselves with political parties, sometimes even being financed by them (or receiving public subsidies[23] as party organs).

The three *grandes dames* of the daily press, *il Corriere della Sera, la Repubblica* and *La Stampa*, are not party papers, but each has suffered from limitations as truly independent watchdogs at different moments in their histories. The *Corriere*'s parent company, RCS Mediagroup, is owned by fifteen main shareholders, who at times themselves form blocs to steer the paper's political position or style and frequently intervene to try to prevent critical coverage of themselves and their own businesses. In recent years, this has typically made editors of *il Corriere* very risk-averse, preferring an apparent political balance to taking any strong stances. *La Repubblica* is independent, but, being owned by Carlo De Benedetti's Gruppo Editoriale L'Espresso, it is fiercely anti-Berlusconi following long corporate battles from the 1980s onwards between Mr De Benedetti and Mr Berlusconi. The result is that *La Repubblica* and its associated weekly news magazine, *l'Espresso*, might as well be a political party in their own right. They also preach chiefly to the converted, to those who already agree with them, rather than changing anybody's minds.

Finally *La Stampa*[24] is owned by the Fiat car company and so its political position has frequently echoed the political interests of its owner, making it establishment-oriented during much of its history, and reluctant to take on the political powers that be. Currently, however, Fiat is fairly disconnected from Italian politics, having expanded production in Brazil, Poland and Serbia, having cut back in Italy, and being on the way to merging with the Chrysler car company in Detroit. Exor, the Agnelli family holding company that stands behind *La Stampa* and Fiat, is also more active abroad than at home. John Elkann, the 36-year-old chairman of Fiat and president of *La Stampa* who is the Agnelli family heir, is a thoroughly international person who seems to have no real interest in getting politically involved in Italy, and in 2009 he appointed as the new editor-in-chief of the paper Mario Calabresi, who at 39 was then by a long way the youngest editor of a mainstream daily. As a result of all this, *La Stampa* has become the most independent large-circulation daily paper in the country – albeit one whose circulation is heavily concentrated in north-west Italy.

The overall outcome, however, is that the media do not, as a rule, act in the Anglo-Saxon sense as a 'fourth estate', as a separate source of accountability for government and for the authoritative provision of facts and comment for readers. It is too politicized for that, which means that its views and revelations can readily be pigeonholed as being merely political tactics. This has been especially true of the various relatively left-wing talk shows on the RAI public TV channels in recent years, such as *Annozero* or *Parla Con Me*, as the hosts (respectively Michele Santoro and Serena Dandini) were clearly associated with left-wing positions. Arguably the only truly independent investigative star broadcaster is Milena Gabanelli, whose show *Report* uses freelance video journalists to build stories, rather like *Panorama* in Britain or *Sixty Minutes* in America, on issues of public policy and sometimes private abuse. As a result, Ms Gabanelli spends 60 per cent of her time, she says, fighting libel cases (so far, always successfully).

However Mr Berlusconi's newspapers have also been past masters at aggressive political tactics: *il Giornale* has frequently been used to spread scandalous stories about his political opponents, notably (after his split with the ruling party in 2010) Gianfranco Fini, in a process that a young anti-mafia (and now anti-Berlusconi) writer, Roberto Saviano,[25] has aptly called the '*macchina del fango*' or 'mud machine'. The same happened in the summer of 2011 to Mr Berlusconi's long-standing economy minister, Giulio Tremonti, who was attacked by *Il Giornale* at a moment when its owner seemed to believe that Mr Tremonti was plotting to unseat him, but also a moment when international investors responded by fleeing Italian government bonds and helping to precipitate a crisis for the euro. These two newspapers, it is widely believed, keep files on the private lives of politicians and other public figures, for use when politically convenient for their boss.

Il Foglio, the Berlusconi family's second daily paper, is not used as aggressively as the other two, but its editor, Giuliano Ferrara, was a minister in Mr Berlusconi's 1994 government, is a long-standing friend of his, writes many of his speeches and in 2011 launched a television programme on RAI, which he called *Radio Londra*, seemingly with the principal purpose of defending his by then beleaguered friend and attacking his enemies, especially magistrates. The name of the programme was especially brazen, intended as it was to imply an association with wartime broadcasts by exiled resistance groups, telling the truth in an era of falsehoods spread by occupying powers – which, sadly, is the opposite of what it actually does.

The conflict between Mr Berlusconi's business interests and his public role is extreme, even simply in business terms: it more or less guarantees that whenever he is in power or holds a blocking position in parliament, the barriers to new competition and innovation in commercial television will not be lowered. But his business power gives him political leverage too, through the influence his media ownership and his advertising company, Publitalia, give him over the activities and reputations of corporate Italy. By that means, he has managed to mute the criticism of him by other businessmen, even if he cannot snuff it out altogether.

Given that during his almost two decades in politics Mr Berlusconi was out of office for six years from 1995 to 2001 and then two further years in 2006–08, an important question to ask is why the left-wing governments in those periods did not simply pass a law covering the conflict of interest between media domination and the prime ministership, in order to remove his political advantage. In principle, it should have been simple to do so. Such a conflict of interest would not be legal in Germany, France or Britain. Accordingly, attempts were made to draw up and pass such legislation. But they failed. They failed partly because Mr Berlusconi's businesses lobbied hard against them and he was able to draw upon plenty of powerful allies in other businesses. They failed partly because of hubris or complacency on the left. Yet they also failed because, in the divided, fragmented coalition governments of the left, it proved possible for Mr Berlusconi and his allies to secure – yes, essentially buy – sufficient support on the left to block the legislation.

Thus the left, and its leadership, has been complicit in preserving the media power and conflict of interest about which they also complain and from which, in overall competitive terms, they have suffered. Politics in modern Italy is not always or even mostly about winning elections for the party or of implementing any policy agenda; it is a matter of personal gain and the personal accretion of power. If politics has found itself paralyzed and mistrusted, the cause of that has in large part been the willingness of many leaders of the left and indeed the centre of politics to compromise with Mr Berlusconi and his political methods. Dante would surely consign all such compromisers to *l'Inferno* for their failure to show moral courage; or perhaps it should be said that the *Mala Italia* inside them won out over whatever *Buona Italia* was there.

This, unfortunately, is a common theme: the opposition to Mr Berlusconi often has not opposed him strongly or effectively because they too would like to operate in the same way as him when they get the chance. A prime example is his attacks on the judiciary, which you might expect the left always to have opposed vehemently: they have criticized him when he has attacked particular magistrates or has complained about his own trials directly, but when he has attacked the magistracy by proposing reforms such as measures to make the judiciary more accountable to parliament, their criticism has been more muted, if it can be heard at all. They too would quite like to control the magistrates.

Media domination is a necessary explanation of Mr Berlusconi's enduring success, in the face of his many and evident weaknesses, but it is not a sufficient one. To that domination must be added the use he has made of it, and the way in which he has succeeded in striking a popular chord with a large enough group of Italians to be able to stay in power – and, just as crucially, to make his coalition allies believe they should keep on sticking with him. His populism, in other words, has been both important and sophisticated.

In this regard, Mr Berlusconi has been genuinely innovative, by comparison with previous generations of Italian political leaders. Beppe Severgnini, a columnist for *il Corriere della Sera* and bestselling author, sought in his book *La pancia degli Italiani: Berlusconi spiegato ai posteri*[26] ('Italians' Stomach: Berlusconi Explained to Posterity') to analyse how and why. He comes up with ten 'factors' that he argues have made Mr Berlusconi so special and acceptable. Four of them are pertinent for the present purpose: the 'human' factor, namely that he has the common touch, so that Italians feel he is 'one of us' rather than a remote, austere figure like normal politicians; the 'Hoover' factor, namely that he is a super salesman, rather like the door-to-door agents for vacuum cleaners in the past, able to seduce people into supporting him; the 'Zelig' factor, named after the character in Woody Allen's 1983 film, by which is meant that he has the ability to be completely different, sometimes opposite, things to different people; and finally the TINA factor, named after Margaret Thatcher's slogan 'there is no alternative', the idea that he has helped to create, through his constant campaigning, that all other possible prime ministers are weak, communist or unattractive in some other way. In the end, there was an alternative: the non-politician Mario Monti. But in a way this just proved Mr Berlusconi's point. No politician could displace him.

Northern 'separatism'

The second great innovation, or genuine change, in Italian politics has been very different, although populist campaigning has played a part there too. It is the rise of the Northern League, the nominally separatist party from the north of Italy, especially Lombardy, the region around Milan, and the Veneto and Friuli–Venezia Giulia regions near Venice. Technically, one strange fact about the Northern League is that it is the oldest political party currently represented in parliament – but that is because all the others have changed their names and forms so often since Mani Pulite. It was formed in 1991 by a merger of various regional parties including the Lombard League and the Veneto League. Its full name, in Italian, indicates its apparent purpose: Lega Nord per l'Indipendenza di Padania (Northern League for Padanian Independence). It has a newspaper called *La Padania* and a radio station called Radio Padania too.

The only thing missing, however, is a genuine region called Padania that could demand secession on some plausible historical or ethnic grounds. Such a country has never yet existed. Vaguely, the word Padania is derived from and associated with the valley of Italy's longest river, the Po, which starts west of Turin and flows all the way to Venice on the Adriatic coast. Yet no one in the party wants to be too precise about this, as politically they are more than happy to pick up votes further south, in Tuscany and Umbria, and further north in Trentino–Alto Adige near Austria.

Italy has, to be sure, been rife with regional divisions and resentment of the central government ever since Count Camillo Benso di Cavour created the unified country in 1861 along with his Savoy king, Vittorio Emmanuele II, with more than a little help from the swashbuckling Giuseppe Garibaldi. The region around Nice, Garibaldi's hometown, was handed to France shortly before unification, while extra bits were added to Italy from the defeated and collapsed Austro-Hungarian empire in 1919, notably Trentino–Alto Adige, the region known to the English as South Tyrol and which is partly German-speaking. Yet the pressure for actual secession, certainly since 1945, has been weak. Despite that, the Northern League staged a spectacular arrival in national Italian politics in the general elections of 1992–96, when the party came seemingly from nowhere to grab 8.4 per cent of the vote in 1994, with an extraordinary 173 seats in the two houses of parliament.

This was a time when outsiders were especially welcome in politics: the discrediting of the Christian Democrats and the Socialist Party, the fall of the Soviet Union, and a major national financial crisis all combined to lay the path for newcomers such as the Northern League (which supposedly stood for financial probity and 'clean government')[27] and of course Silvio Berlusconi (who didn't, but was new to formal politics). Not uncoincidentally, the League joined forces with Mr Berlusconi's Forza Italia to form a government, and found itself with its first ministers, even if the coalition collapsed after only eight months.

In those triumphant elections of 1992–96, the League's support was strongest in the North, with shares of the vote in the Chamber of Deputies elections in Lombardy (the region of Milan) of 24.8 per cent in 1996, in the Veneto (around Venice) of 29.8 per cent, and in Piedmont (around Turin) of 18.4 per cent. But the party's support was not confined to those regions: in that year, it also took 10.2 per cent of the vote in Liguria, the coastal strip around Genoa, 7.2 per cent in Emilia Romagna (the region of Bologna, traditionally leftist) and nearly 2 per cent even in Tuscany.

Since then, in electoral terms, two big things have happened to the League. In national elections, the party's fortunes have slumped and then soared again, falling back to less than 4 per cent in the 2001 Chamber elections and 4.58 per cent in 2006 before reviving to reach 8.3 per cent in 2008. The second, however, is that the League has steadily dug itself in in local government right across the north of Italy but has also been creeping into the Centre. By 2010 the party held 373 mayoralties (against 97 in 1998), 13 provincial presidencies and 2 regional presidencies (Piedmont and the Veneto). Among the mayoralties in

2010, seven were in Emilia Romagna, five in Liguria and one as far south as the Marche. The party is even expanding its presence in Abruzzo (east of Rome) and Sardinia.

That progress at local level is highly reminiscent of Britain's small party, the Liberal Democrats, in recent decades, for both parties have sought to build a reputation for good local administration. This fits also with the Northern League's flagship policy, of promoting fiscal federalism – which means, essentially, passing more control over the use of tax revenues to the regions and municipalities where they are raised. Chiefly, this is directed at stopping what is seen as the wasteful transfer of taxpayers' money to the south of Italy, but it is also presented as a policy aimed at increasing local accountability and control. At national level, however, the Northern League also stands for a policy that is anathema to the Lib Dems: tight control of immigration, with distinct flavours, in some regions, of outright xenophobia.

The phenomenon that has proceeded alongside this rise of the Northern League during the 1990s and 2000s is the growth of immigration. The 1982 manifesto of the party's main predecessor, the Lombard League, did not feature immigration: it favoured giving precedence to people from that region for jobs, housing and other things, but over all other Italians, not just foreigners. By 1991, the new Northern League did favour controls on immigration, along with tough penalties for illegal immigration and crimes by foreigners, in a country in which foreign-born residents by then made up only 1 per cent of the population. By 2010 that proportion had become more than 7 per cent, or 4 million people, many more of whom live in northern Italy than in the South, for that is where the jobs are easier to find. Not surprisingly, immigration came to occupy a more and more prominent place in Northern League manifestos.

Compared with other western European countries, to have 7 per cent of your population foreign-born is not outlandish: the figures[28] for France, Britain and Germany are 8.5 per cent, 10.2 per cent and 12.5 per cent respectively. But those countries, like Britain, have become accustomed to immigration over a much longer period – such a long period in fact that there many of those some would call 'immigrants' are actually citizens born in the country but with immigrant parents or even grandparents. Not in Italy. There the striking thing is that immigration has gone from virtually zero to 4 million in only twenty years, and there is every likelihood that the proportion of foreign-born citizens will rise further, for both normal reasons and abnormal ones: more immigrants will come from current and soon-to-be members of the European Union in the Balkans and eastern Europe; and the political instability now seen in North Africa and the Middle East is sure to bring more refugees, both economic and political, trying to cross the Mediterranean to Italy, Spain, France and Greece.

When the Berlusconi government fell in late 2011, the Northern League chose to be the only major political party to withhold its parliamentary support from the new technical government of Mario Monti. This in part reflected its desperation: by having been part of government for so long, the League had lost its character as an outsider and was losing support, even in local elections in its home regions. It also reflected a tactical bet by Mr Bossi that when disenchantment set in with the Monti government, that disenchantment would also involve anger against foreigners and the euro itself: foreigners because Germany was seen as being instrumental in forcing a change in government and in policy in Italy, the euro because its instability and the fact that it is controlled from Berlin (Germany again) and Frankfurt (home of the European Central Bank) could be cast as an outrage against Italian, and indeed Padanian, sovereignty. This is the first time a major Italian political party has come out clearly against European integration. It is a high-stakes bet, one that has the potential to become quite explosive in Italian politics. At least for Umberto Bossi personally it was a bet that failed, for he was forced in April 2012 to resign the party leadership in a most traditional sort of political scandal: a corruption investigation, concerning the alleged misuse of public funds for personal expenses, both for him and his son, amid accusations of links to the Calabrian mafia, the 'Ndrangheta.

Paralysis and conflict

Whatever happens to that anti-euro bet, the rise of the Northern League – whether you agree with the party or not – has been a pretty typical event in western democracies: populism, regionalism, xenophobia and resentment about taxes being wasted on other people are all themes that can be found in many other countries. A decline in trust for government and for political parties of all kinds is another common element. What is not so common, however, is the context in which Italian politics finds itself trying to deal with these themes: one of weak national political institutions that are in frequent conflict with one another, and an associated near-paralysis in policy-making and legislation.

During the long Berlusconi era, the most evident conflict has been that between the judiciary and the executive, which has mostly manifested itself as a personal conflict between the magistrates and the prime minister himself. But the conflict has been wider than just that personal one: the Tangentopoli/Mani Pulite scandals of the early 1990s arose because of an attempt by the judiciary to expose and punish abuses of political power, and nearly two decades later that attempt remains unresolved and incomplete, with new abuses by politicians of all parties being exposed regularly, often by the essentially illegitimate or at least unjust means of releasing transcripts of intercepted telephone conversations to the media. Apparent crimes are punished by public exposure but not by the due process of the courts, a situation that is itself ripe for abuse, on the part of magistrates, and ripe to be discredited or waved aside, on the side of politicians.

Everyone knows that the judicial system needs reform. It is a system that is designed to be just to the accused but ends up being unjust to virtually everybody. No one who paid attention to the trial of Amanda Knox and Raffaele Sollecito in Perugia in 2009–11 for the murder of an English student, Meredith Kercher, could doubt that, whatever they thought of the ultimate verdict in that case. The initial conviction of the American Knox and her former Italian boyfriend in 2009 was overturned on appeal in October 2011 amid vitriolic and hyperbolic accusations on all sides. The fact that this trial involved an English victim and an American defendant guaranteed the case much more publicity than other murder trials (who now remembers that a man remains convicted of the Kercher killing, Rudy Guede, who was born in Ivory Coast but raised in Perugia?). But that publicity also drew attention not just to the frailties of police procedure in Perugia, but also to the nature of criminal justice in Italy.

The fact that there are three levels of trial both in criminal and civil cases, thus with two opportunities for appeal, was supposed to make trials fair, especially by comparison with the manifestly unfair trials held during the Mussolini period. Instead, this makes them not just long but interminable, with returns to court every few years, and makes it very likely that statutes of limitations will intervene even in criminal trials.

This occurred in the case of Giulio Andreotti, the aforementioned 'il Divo', who dominated Italian politics in the late 1970s and 80s. He was found guilty of association with the mafia by the Court of Appeal of Palermo in 2003, but was discharged thanks to the statute of limitations and continues to sit in parliament as a Life Senator. Silvio Berlusconi too has been convicted twice (for perjury and for illegal political financing) but both times was discharged by the statute. Not surprisingly, one of his governments' main legislative initiatives has been to reduce the period of the statute of limitations for crimes of which their prime minister has been accused; this means that whatever happens in the trials, he will be likely to avoid conviction.

Long trials make convictions less likely in criminal cases and resolution either unlikely or extraordinarily slow in civil ones. This certainly imposes a burden on business, for the inability to enforce contracts, resolve disputes or deal with labour issues greatly increases the cost and risk of investing in Italy. The World Bank's 'Doing Business'[29] rankings for 2011 placed Italy 157th out of 183 countries in terms of enforcing contracts. To do so, on average, required 41 procedures, took 1,210 days and cost 29.9 per cent of the value of the claim. France, by contrast, ranked 7th, with 29 procedures, taking 331 days and costing 17.4 per cent of the value of the claim. As always in Italy, those averages will also disguise a huge difference in the performance of courts in, say, Trento in the North and Reggio Calabria in the South. It was to try to ease this burden on business that the Monti government proposed in early 2012 to set up a special business court to hear cases more swiftly.

The system is, also, however, unjust for individual claimants and defendants. In 2008 the average backlog of criminal proceedings just in the courts of First Instance ranged from 153 days in Trento to 554 days in Lecce, in Puglia. If you add the backlog of pre-trial investigations, a further 104–568 days, depending on the city, and then the backlogs in the Court of Appeal (253 days in Potenza, 1,500 days in Venice), you get a picture of vastly long-drawn-out trials, even before the final level, the Court of Cassation, rules on whether or not the lower courts have interpreted the law correctly.

Efforts to reform the justice system have been equally long-drawn-out. The one major revision of the Criminal

Procedure Code since 1948 was first launched by a bill in parliament in 1963, followed by a further law in 1965 delegating powers to the government to write a new code, a law which expired before the code was finished. The process began again in 1974 with a further law, setting up a ministerial committee that was chaired by a famous jurist, Gian Domenico Pisapia.[30] The fruits of the Pisapia Committee worked their way through parliamentary committees and finally entered law in 1988.

The main point of the 1988 Criminal Code was to introduce a more British-style adversarial approach to criminal trials, reducing the scope of the traditional and more French-style inquisitorial system. While it was designed to help ensure that the defence had a fair hearing, the result of this change was to make trials last even longer.

New reforms have often been proposed, especially by Mr Berlusconi's governments, but have so far got nowhere. With such an adversarial relationship between politicians, especially the prime minister himself, and the main institutions of the judiciary – the Superior Council of the Judiciary (CSM by its Italian initials), which recruits, transfers, promotes and regulates all judges and prosecutors, and the National Association of Magistrates, which represents them in public rather in the manner of a trade union – there is little chance of achieving any consensus. The 1948 Constitution protects judges and prosecutors from political interference, and no change to that can or will be countenanced. Much of the inefficiency of the judicial system arises from procedures and lack of resources – there is no computerized record of cases pending – but avoiding reforms to procedures and withholding resources are ready weapons for either side in this conflict.

Progress on judicial reform is glacial and, as the chapter on Turin (Chapter Four) will illustrate, chiefly a matter of local initiative. Not that progress on other reforms, when led by central government, is exactly spectacular. Since the mid 1990s, the number of laws, decrees and reforms that have made a big difference can be counted on the fingers of one hand. Pensions is one; labour reform, though largely for ill, is another; and there has been unsuccessful tinkering with public administration. So much talk, so much argument, so little action. That, more even than the corruption and illegality, is the true sickness of Italian politics.

CHAPTER 3

Il Purgatorio Economico

These days, we all have a view about southern Europe, and it is generally bad – at least if it is the economy we are talking about. In search of a nice headline and memorable phrase, during the 1990s research analysts in financial markets came up with the acronym 'PIGS' to group together the slow-growing, highly indebted countries of the European Union's south, namely Portugal, Italy, Greece and Spain. They were unified in the analysts' minds by thoughts of a monopolistic capitalism, of bloated public sectors, of a lack of dynamism, and of a clientelistic politics that uses public money to buy votes and give jobs to cronies. Useless, parasitic, hopeless economies, with dysfunctional, corrupt politics – in the common, northern European view, at least.

The good news for Italy during the global financial crisis of 2008–10 was that its place in this acronym was taken by Ireland, whose economy was neither monopolistic nor parasitic, but which had a huge, poorly regulated property boom that went bust and turned it into a troubled debtor. By contrast, Italy was said to have 'good fundamentals', by which was meant that it had not had a property boom but rather had high levels of household savings, apparently stable banks and, as noted in Chapter One, something much-envied during the 2008–10 crisis, namely a manufacturing sector that was larger than in most developed countries.

Good news rarely lasts, especially when it is founded on short-term concerns rather than longer-term realities. The bad news by 2011 was that bond markets began to look askance at Italy once again, and the acronym was simply lengthened to become PIIGS. What unified these five countries in analysts' minds was now the prospect of national insolvency: economic growth too slow (if it existed at all) to produce the revenue to service and reduce the PIIGS' vast public (i.e. sovereign) debts.

Greece was the most troubled and weakest of this ignoble group, with public debts equalling 150 per cent of GDP or more, widespread tax evasion among its citizens, and an economy that was heading backwards worryingly fast. But once that country moved towards a de facto default on its debts and therefore towards forcing the banks that had lent to it to write off a large part of those debts, attention switched to the eurozone's second-largest debtor, in terms of the ratio between its public debts and its GDP. If Greece might need a discount on its debts (technically known as a 'restructuring'), what was the risk that Italy might need, or want, one too?

Note was taken of the fact that, despite those suppos-edly good 'fundamentals', Italy had in fact failed to grow not just since the financial crisis began but also for more than a decade beforehand. Fundamentally, that did not look good at all. Indeed, its growth record in the period 2000–10 was worse than that of Greece. Moreover, Italian household savings are not actually as high as many people thought. Despite following quite a prudent budgetary policy since 2008, markets noted that it would not take much of a rise in Italy's borrowing costs to tip it over the edge and towards Greek-style insolvency: so banks sold their Italian government debt in order to avoid the danger of future write-offs, and the country's borrowing costs duly rose towards unaffordable levels. Unaffordable, that is, if the country looks like having virtually no economic growth in the next decade, either.

Sclerotic, even lazy, preferring *la dolce vita* or, for the lucky few, bunga-bunga: that became the northern European caricature of Italy. Yet it was not always like this. During the 1950s and 1960s, Italy was Europe's closest equivalent to what today is known as an 'emerging economy', showing fast, dynamic growth year after year. In fact, if you take its best period, 1950–70, Italy was behind only Japan and South Korea in terms of growth, and well ahead of other Organisation for Economic Co-operation and Development (OECD) member countries.

During those twenty years, Italy grew at an annual average growth rate in real GDP by 5.8 per cent per year compared with 8.9 per cent for Japan and 4.1 per cent for the rest of the OECD area.[1] Both Italy and Japan slowed after 1970, thanks chiefly to the oil-price shock of 1973 and to the currency revaluation and volatility that followed the end of the 'Bretton Woods' system of fixed exchange rates, but like Japan Italy still outperformed its rich counterparts: in 1970–90 its average annual growth rate was still 2.9 per cent compared with 4.0 per cent in Japan and 2.6 per cent in the rest of the OECD area.

This member of the PIIGS was actually a tiger. For had that epithet been invented by then for high-growth economies, Italy would surely have been known as the 'Mediterranean tiger', just as Ireland was later known as the 'Celtic tiger', following the example of the 'Asian tigers' of South Korea, Hong Kong, Singapore and Taiwan during the 1980s. It would be a stretch to use that phrase to describe Italy's economic achievement ever since the country was unified in 1861, but nevertheless it did represent an impressive catch-up[2] from a poor beginning: income per head in 1861 was only half that of Britain, a country it had caught up with on that measure by 1990, and for a few years surpassed.

The most dramatic period of that catch-up came after 1945. Italy's rapid post-war growth was facilitated both by increasingly liberalized world trade and by urbanization – which is also what helped Japan in that same period and China in later decades. The country was transformed from having a predominantly rural population – in 1939 more than 40 per cent of the Italian labour force was employed in agriculture and only 30 per cent in industry[3] – to an urban one, with all the productivity gains that such a move can bring, especially when using imported technology and management techniques to catch up with the world's leaders, notably America.

That urbanization brought with it a virtuous cycle of rising wages, especially as workers migrated in their millions from the poor South to the richer, more industrial North, which boosted consumer demand for the products emanating from those northern factories.[4] It wasn't a smooth process – there was, for example, a crisis of inflation, wage claims and loss of export competitiveness in 1963[5] – but then neither was that of Japan, whose post-war 'miracle' was peppered with violent strikes in the 1950s and a post-Olympics financial crisis in 1964.

Where Japan's industrial expansion in the 1950s, 60s, 70s and 80s came from heavy industry and then increasingly high-technology industries, Italy's depended far more on consumer goods and consumer durables made by small entrepreneurial firms, though with increasing emphasis on design and marketing.

Heavier industries (defence, steel, chemicals, oil and gas, telecommunications) did play a part but were dominated by state ownership, which represented continuity from the fascist era of the 1930s but which proved inefficient and unable to keep up with faster growth in productivity and innovation in Germany and the United States. Compared with both Germany and Japan, its equivalents in terms of industrial development as well as its allies during the Second World War, Italy took fewer steps to encourage domestic competition.[6]

This seemed not to hold Italy back at that time, however, especially in the industrial districts of the Centre and North-East, where small, family-owned firms proved nimble, efficient and able to collaborate with one another where necessary. Public spending on new roads and communications links, especially in the impoverished South, also contributed to growth. Yet, as Andrea Boltho

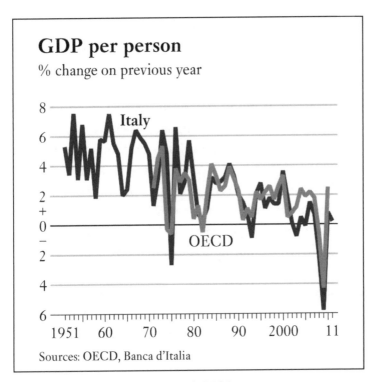

GDP per person

% change on previous year

Sources: OECD, Banca d'Italia

Italian long-term growth compared with OECD

notes,[7] Italy's moves in these directions proved insufficient, especially by comparison with Germany and Japan: it did too little to foster competition, too little 'to accompany economic changes with parallel changes in social welfare' and provided too little infrastructure. These failings were to come back to haunt it.

For then the success and growth stopped. It had slowed during the 1980s but then truly ground to a halt in the 1990s. One should not, perhaps, imagine Europe's greatest poet, Dante, pondering a matter so mundane as economics when his real concerns were love and morals, but still even love and morals do have a relationship to money, as his fellow Florentines knew all too well. So the basic Dantean question is how Italy could have moved from an economic paradise to a form of purgatory in such a short time.

It is easily, if sadly, described. During the 1970s and 1980s, public spending climbed, steadily, as welfare provisions and corporate subsidies proliferated, while tax revenues failed to keep pace: Italy ran an average budget deficit in 1973–95 of a staggering 9.8 per cent of GDP per year (compared with deficits of 2.8 per cent per year in Germany and 2.2 per cent in Japan).[8] This supported economic growth during some of that time, but also facilitated rapid inflation (10.8 per cent per year, on average, compared with 3.4 per cent in Germany) and built up the huge public debts that Italy is suffering under now. By 1994, indeed, the year when Silvio Berlusconi entered politics, Italy's gross public debt had reached 120 per cent of GDP, exactly the same level as in 2011 – a neat, but not pleasant, symmetry.

Following a financial crisis in 1992–93, and then a frantic effort to qualify for Europe's new single currency, the euro, in 1999 by cutting public spending and raising taxes to reduce that debt to closer to 100 per cent of GDP, Italy turned from still being a slight out-performer in terms of economic growth in the 1980s to being an under-performer in the 1990s. In response to that 1992–93 crisis, it also instituted a big wave of privatization, as well as pension and banking reforms, which might have been hoped to improve growth. Instead, growth became even slower, despite the benefit of the low interest rates on the new euro after 1999 – making borrowing much cheaper

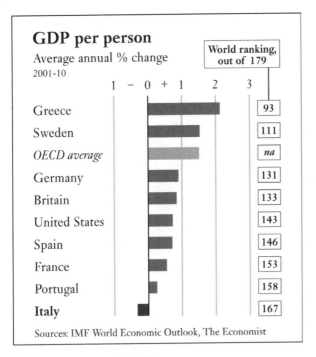

GDP per person
Average annual % change
2001-10

	World ranking, out of 179
Greece	93
Sweden	111
OECD average	*na*
Germany	131
Britain	133
United States	143
Spain	146
France	153
Portugal	158
Italy	167

Sources: IMF World Economic Outlook, The Economist

Growth in GDP per person, 2001–10

than during the era of the lira – that were making the rest of southern Europe boom.

Between 2001 and 2010 Italy's average growth rate was just 0.25 per cent a year; since its population was growing, thanks to immigration, this meant that during that period Italy's national income per head actually shrank. As *The Economist* pointed out in 2011 with rigorous cruelty,[9] this meant that of all the countries in the world for which GDP figures are published, only Haiti and Zimbabwe did worse during that decade.

Why the slowdown? Part of the answer is that no country can maintain annual economic growth rates of 5 per cent or more indefinitely. The opportunities to apply other people's technology to your own cheap labour, capital and land eventually run out, as even China will discover one day. The arrival of new 'tigers' in Asia or elsewhere naturally increases the competitive pressure, especially when they have cheaper and more abundant labour and capital than you, and enter the relatively low-technology industries in which you have prospered, such as textiles, furniture, jewellery and shoes.

Moreover, societies change in ways that affect economic dynamism: if you have a large proportion of your population aged between 20 and 35 you are likely to achieve growth rates that are much faster than for countries where the population is older. Younger workers are cheaper and more mobile, learn new things more easily, and typically work harder and for longer hours. So a country whose population structure is ageing, as is the case for both Japan and Italy, can expect to slow down, just as we all do as our hair turns grey.

However, this answer is far from the whole story. Other countries share Italy's circumstances: the Scandinavians and Germans have aged, the French have encountered stiff Chinese competition, the South Koreans have run out of cheap labour, capital and land, yet all have been faring better than Italy over the past two decades. It could have explained why Italy became merely average. It cannot explain why it fell consistently below the average for its European Union peers. For that, we need Italian explanations rather than merely demography or the way of the world.

Those explanations must focus on the burdens and obstacles that Italy placed on, and in front of, itself. Vera

Zamagni, an economic historian of her country from the University of Bologna, put it with great prescience on the final page of her 1993 book on the period 1860 to 1990:

> There are no limits to the capacity mankind has for improvement, but this is dependent on there being no obstacles deliberately placed to prevent it. Unfortunately, such obstacles do exist, and they are due to the power of conservatism and individual greed to corrupt politics and institutions, to put off fundamentally important decisions, to stand in the way of the growth of new forces, and to exacerbate the seriousness of those new problems that arise and that need to be resolved.[10]

That, in a splendid nutshell, is the story of Italy's economic purgatory ever since Professor Zamagni's book was published, but also, in reality, since the early 1970s when the obstacles began to be placed in the economy's way. It is surely no coincidence that Mario Draghi, then governor of the Bank of Italy, made the same sort of argument in his opening speech for the bank's conference in October 2011 that discussed the country's economic record since 1861:

> In the Venice of the sixteenth century or the Amsterdam of the seventeenth, societies that were then rich, a long period of great dynamism was followed by the weakening of the commitment to compete, to innovate. The forces once directed at the pursuit of growth became re-directed towards the defence of small or big

privileges, that had been acquired by various organized, social groups. In a stagnant economy, these defensive mechanisms and the promotion of special interests become reinforced.[11]

So we should now examine these obstacles, these special interests and burdens, one by one.

Burdens and obstacles: (1) Labour

Easily the most striking feature of Italy's economy is the predominance of small and (to a lesser extent) medium-sized firms. It is an appealing feature, too: the idea of an Italian army of entrepreneurs, working hard in small factories in the flat farmlands of the Veneto or amid the rolling hills and lines of cypress trees of Tuscany and Umbria is rather charming, an idea that would have gladdened Adam Smith's heart. Until, that is, he started to work out why so few of these firms ever grow any bigger. Italy's labour laws are a large part of that explanation.

Essentially, the *Statuto dei lavoratori* (Workers' Statute) of 1970, which was passed into law in the year following an intense spate of strikes and demonstrations that were popularly known as the 'hot autumn', made it illegal to dismiss workers except for 'just cause', and applied that rule to all firms employing more than fifteen workers. Below that number, dismissal is legal but requires payments in compensation. Above it, disputes over whether a cause is just are supposed to be settled in the labour courts. At the same time, the principle of tying wage increases every three months to the rate of consumer-price inflation, in a process known as the *scala mobile* (moving stairs, or esca-lator), was adopted. This highly inflationary mechanism lasted until 1992.

On its own, this legal framework might not have acted as a powerful incentive for companies to avoid expansion. But it has done so, because it was combined, in the 1970s especially, with rapid wage inflation, with an atmosphere of extreme industrial and political conflict, and with the slow, costly and unpredictable process of justice that was outlined in the previous chapter. A manager might hope to win an argument over 'just cause' in the labour courts, but it would take him years to do so, and meanwhile he would suffer strikes, demonstrations and possibly even violence.

So thousands of firms decided it was better to stay small, in two ways: by subcontracting as much as possible to other small firms; and sometimes even by remaining below the fifteen-worker threshold. It is always better to be too small rather than too large, and even better to be below the threshold altogether. This helped to produce the vibrant 'industrial districts'[12] of the Centre and North of Italy, where clusters (to use a word popularized by Professor Michael Porter of Harvard Business School) of small firms in the same or related businesses grew in close proximity to one another, subcontracting to each other, sharing marketing, research or other services, and some-times exporting in concert with one another. They often built their businesses on the basis of traditional craft skills, such as in textiles, leather-tanning or furniture-making, but also invented new ones.

The districts offer an admirably flexible and often inno-vative model, within which small firms can move nimbly in and out of markets, altering their products quickly as they do so. What this model militates against, however, is scale, which means that it also tends not to favour very research-intensive, high-technology sectors, nor sectors requiring a lot of capital investment, nor sophisticated global exporting networks that might require after-sales service or other close contacts with customers. German companies, like Italian ones, are often family-owned and highly specialized. But the German *Mittelstand* companies tend to be much larger than their Italian counterparts, to spend more each year on research and development, and to export more.

The result can be seen clearly in the average size of firms. In 1961, 26.4 per cent of Italian manufacturing employees worked for companies employing between 10 and 99 workers, compared with 18.3 per cent in Germany and 43.7 per cent in Japan (a country where small, subcontracting firms are also prevalent). By 2001, the share of manufacturing employment (which itself was admittedly declining) accounted for by firms of this size had risen to 41.8 per cent in Italy against 22.5 per cent in Germany.[13]

Meanwhile, another form of labour practice, one not directly enshrined in legislation, also acts as an obstacle to levels of employment, to economic growth and to industrial scale, not just in manufacturing but also in service industries, which now account for nearly 70 per cent of the economy. It is the system of collective bargaining between employers and trade unions. A fragmented industrial structure consisting of these clusters and thousands upon thousands of small firms might be expected, in theory, to lead to a very decentralized form of collective bargaining and wide differences in wages from region to region. In practice, it has not. Italy's bargaining system is highly centralized.

This matters in particular because Italy is still relatively highly unionized compared with other developed countries. In 2010, 35.1 per cent of employees were trade union members compared with just over 18 per cent in both Germany and Japan. Back in 1970, all three countries had a broadly similar level of unionization: 37 per cent in Italy, 32 per cent in Germany and 35 per cent in Japan.[14]

National contracts for each sector are negotiated between the relevant trade unions and employers' associations. The biggest and most powerful employers' federation is Confindustria, which boasts 146,000 members who employ 5.5 million workers between them, chiefly in manufacturing, and has a national prominence roughly equivalent to Britain's Confederation of British Industry or Germany's Bundesverband der Deutschen Industrie (Federation of German Industries, BDI). But there are also employers' associations covering service industries – Confcommercio, Confturismo and Conftrasporto – as well as groups for agriculture, handicraft firms and others. The *Contratti Collettivi Nazionali di Lavoro* (National Collective Labour Contracts) are negotiated by each association, and adhering to them is mandatory for all firms that belong to the associations.

This system grew out of successive 'social pacts' between trade unions and employers in the 1970s, 80s and 90s, in some of which governments were involved as the inflation rate was affected as well as social peace. The contracts on terms and conditions of employment are renegotiated every four years and basic wage guarantees (*minimi tabellari*) are set every two years. In principle, bargaining is also permitted at regional and company levels, but in practice the impact of this right is limited as wages are not allowed to be reduced at regional or company level below the *minimi tabellari*.

So the contracts essentially set national minimum wage levels for each industry, applicable equally in Calabria in the poor South as in wealthier Lombardy or Alto Adige in the North. Employers rarely express a desire for bargaining to become more decentralized, perhaps because they do not wish to risk confrontations with the trade unions, perhaps because they too feel pressures to maintain solidarity.

During 2010 and 2011, one firm did challenge this system, the company that had once been the greatest industrial giant of the country: Fiat. Its Canadian-Italian chief executive, Sergio Marchionne, used referendums of workers in the car-maker's factories near Naples and Turin to bring about a change in their contracts, and used the fact that the Fiat Group was anyway being split at that time into two separate companies, one making cars and trucks, the other devoted to other industrial machinery, as a means to withdraw – at that stage temporarily – from the restrictive framework of Confindustria. Mr Marchionne received little support for this historic challenge to the system of national contracts either from Confindustria itself or from other companies. Not altogether surprisingly, in September 2011 he announced that Fiat would be withdrawing permanently from Confindustria as of January 2012, which it duly did.

A similar system of national collective bargaining used to prevail in Germany, too.[15] In the mid 1990s, two-thirds of private-sector workers in the former West Germany were covered by contracts that covered their whole sector, nationwide. Now the proportion has dropped to half, and enterprises in the former East Germany have shunned national contracts altogether. Even for those companies that adopt national contracts, there are now many more clauses that allow for preferred local conditions. Essentially, Germany has moved away from national contracts and towards bargaining at regional and company level.

By the mid 1990s employment statistics in Italy showed three main features. One was a high level of unemployment, of over 12 per cent of the labour force at a national level. The second was a lower level of participation in the formal labour force than in most other European countries: in 1985–95 the labour participation rate (i.e. the proportion of people aged between 15 and 64 either in work or actively seeking work) in Italy averaged 58.8 per cent,[16] compared with 66.9 per cent in the then fifteen members of the European Union and 69.5 per cent in the thirty-member rich-country club, the OECD. The third was sharply lower participation rates for women and for the South as a whole. This correlates with a fourth feature which does not appear fully in the statistics: a large 'informal' or black economy, which is thought to account for as much as a third of workers in the South.

In 1992, Italy's financial crisis led to a sharp devaluation of the lira as both it and the pound sterling were ejected from the Exchange Rate Mechanism of the European Monetary System, the precursor of the euro. This gave manufacturing exporters a brief boost, as devaluations have always tended to, restoring their profitability as well as raising their sales volumes. The political determination to join the euro when it was first launched, in 1999, meant that this method of economic adrenalin injection by devaluation was no longer going to be available. Meanwhile, Italian wages and overall labour costs were climbing, despite the high levels of unemployment, as low rates of productivity growth led Italian industry to drift behind its European competitors.

This situation led to a big reform of the labour laws, which was made in two phases, in 1997 and 2003, and hence under two governments from opposite sides of the political divide: the centre-left in the first case, and the centre-right (Berlusconi) government in the second. Neither reform directly altered the main provisions of the 1970s Workers' Statute, however, and so left untouched the strong protections against dismissal for full-time employees on permanent contracts. What the 1997 and 2003 laws did instead was to permit a new form of employment on temporary, short-term contracts. According to the OECD,[17] over 40 per cent of new jobs in recent years (2003–07) were on this temporary, fixed-term basis. This could be counted as successful, in two senses: unemployment dropped sharply, to below 8 per cent; and labour costs for business were restrained, a little.

The reforms have been less successful, however, in two main ways. First, the intense political controversy surrounding any changes to the labour laws was brutally demonstrated by the assassinations, claimed by the modern successors to the 'Red Brigades' who had been left-wing terrorists during the violent 1970s, of a Ministry of Labour official working on the reform, Massimo D'Antona in 1999, and then an adviser to the ministry, Marco Biagi in 2002, using the same gun.

Second, the reforms created a two-tier labour market, in which the lower, less protected tier is chiefly occupied by young people and women. Known in Italian as *precari*, or precarious workers, these short-term contract workers receive less training than permanent ones and, in the case of women, in effect have no maternity leave entitlements since their contracts can simply not be renewed if they become pregnant. Their salaries are lower and their pension and other benefits are also correspondingly smaller.

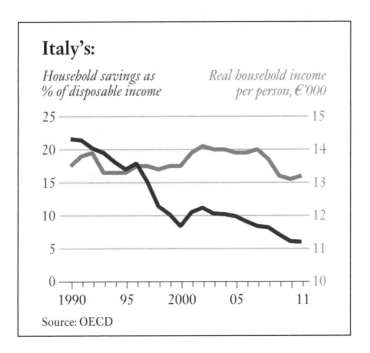

Italy's:

Household savings as % of disposable income   *Real household income per person, €'000*

Source: OECD

Italian savings and earnings

The new second tier of the labour market is certainly more flexible and has probably kept some Italian companies in business that might otherwise have either gone bankrupt or been forced to invest more in better equipment or processes in order to raise productivity. But it contributes to a widening inequality within Italian society, to a sense among the young, including young university graduates, that their opportunities are limited thanks to obstacles placed in their way by the protected older generations, and to an entrenched weakness in household consumption. Employment rose, at least until the Lehman shock brought on the global financial crisis of 2008–09, but earnings did not.

Italian households have long been famed for their high savings rates and accumulations of financial assets and property. But even with high savings, unless your earnings increase it is hard to spend more money. The savings have certainly cushioned the pain for the young, since they have enabled parents to subsidize their *precari* offspring, yet those savings are now declining. Weak consumer spending keeps economic growth anaemic, and if the young remain trapped in low-paying precarious jobs, then the country's famed household savings will decline further, for the new generation will be unable to add to them.

Already, the Italian household savings rate, when measured on an internationally comparable basis, has slid from a recent peak of 17.9 per cent of disposable income in 1986 to a mere 6.0 per cent in 2011, according to the OECD. Those numbers will surprise many Italians, who think their savings rate is in the mid teens.[18] But these figures, which include an adjustment for the change in pension benefits, less contributions, show a decline similar to that in Japan and the United States (from a lower beginning) over the same period. In Europe, the countries with high and stable savings rates are now Germany (10.9 per cent in 2011), France (11 per cent) and Belgium (11.2 per cent).

The situation of Italian households feels a little like that of the British aristocracy in the course of its long period of decline during the twentieth century: Italian families are rich, in the sense that they have valuable assets; but they are poor, in the sense that their incomes are flat or falling while their expenses are rising.

Burdens and obstacles: (2) Public finances

The idea that household savings are high has also been a comfort, perhaps a delusionary one, when it comes to the second self-inflicted obstacle, which in this case is better termed a burden: the public debt. As Vera Zamagni noted in 1993, it had been possible 'until now to finance this debt relatively easily through private domestic savings (a very small part of the Italian public debt involves foreign creditors)'[19], and that claim can still often be seen in both Italian and foreign commentary about the country's public finances.

Unfortunately, it is no longer true. A little more than 40 per cent of Italian government debt is now held by foreigners, which (according to Eurostat) makes Italy similar to Germany and Spain, though less dependent on international investors than, for example, Portugal, Ireland, Greece or even France. This is partly a result of the euro, which eliminated currency risk for investors from other eurozone countries, and partly because of Italy's own diminished savings. In Japan, by contrast, more than 90 per cent of government bonds are held domestically.

Until the world began to focus on sovereign debts as they grew spectacularly from 2008 onwards, at a time when government revenues collapsed and government spending expanded to try to fill the space being left by private spending, it had been more or less forgotten that large government debts pose both risks and burdens. That point had been well known in the 1980s, of course, but the risks were then being posed by Latin American debtors, not by rich countries. The West's sovereign debts were supposed to be risk-free, or at least low-risk assets.

Italy's own financial crisis of 1992 did highlight the risk posed by public debt, especially when combined with a floating currency, whose sinking could make those debts even harder to bear. But then came the euro, which for its members eliminated currency risks and, during its first ten years of existence from 1999 to 2009, also greatly reduced the burden of financing public borrowing as the interest rates on members' government bonds converged on the much lower rates of Germany.

This was, however, only a temporary reprieve. Sovereign debts and the risks and costs attached to them are now firmly in the spotlight. Kenneth Rogoff, a Harvard economist who was formerly chief economist at the International Monetary Fund (IMF), and Carmen Reinhart, an economics professor at the University of Maryland, published in 2009 the fruits[20] of their research into 800 years of financial crises, many of them involving sovereign debts. It turned out to be beautifully timed, not just because of the crisis but also the ballooning of rich-country public debts. Their analysis concluded that when public debt expands to more than 90 per cent of a country's GDP, and stays above that level, it acts as a consistent, long-term drag on economic growth. On Vera Zamagni's figures,[21] Italy reached that point in 1987. It has remained there or well above it ever since.

It was in the 1970s that those debts really began to be accumulated. During that decade public debt as a share of GDP rose from 34 per cent to 65 per cent. The process began at the same time as the Workers' Statute was enacted, and in response to the same pressures from social and industrial unrest, pressures that even turned into terrorism during that decade, popularly known as the '*anni di piombo*' or years of lead. A welfare state began to be built, including more generous public pensions, higher unemployment benefits (although, surprisingly, still not a comprehensive unemployment insurance system), a surge in spending on council housing and on benefits for mothers and children, and, in 1978, the establishment of a National Health Service.

The trouble is that economic growth failed to provide expanding revenues to cover the extra costs, and successive governments shied away from raising taxes to balance the books. Increasingly, government spending came to be used to try to pep up economic growth, and indeed to support state-owned industry as well as other large companies, many of which were hit especially hard by the sharp rise in oil prices after 1973 and the associated international economic crises of the following decade. The same

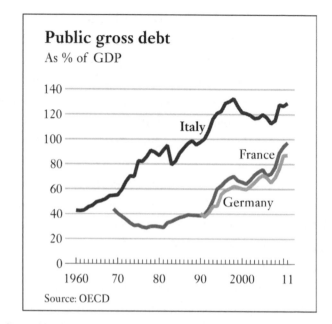

Public gross debt

As % of GDP

Source: OECD

Italian public debt as per cent of GDP, 1960–2011

political processes developed for state-owned enterprises as had done for public broadcasting: political parties vied to put their loyal friends into senior positions at those companies, and to turf out opponents' loyalists when they could. State industries as a result became more and more overstaffed with political appointees and less and less efficient.

Italians' ambiguous relationship with, and attitudes to, the state produced a strange outcome. In France or Sweden, for example, it is not surprising to see both public spending and tax revenues at levels equivalent to 50 per cent of more of GDP (in Sweden, in fact, spending peaked at more than 67 per cent of GDP in the mid 1990s). In both countries there is a political and cultural consensus in favour of a strong state, and a belief that public spending and taxation can and should be used both to deliver a wide range of services and to redistribute after-tax incomes between the rich and the poor. In Italy, only part of that consensus appears to exist: there is some belief in 'solidarity' and in the need for the state to ensure it, by providing and financing some public services, such as health, education, pensions and the management of the country's cultural heritage. But there is little trust or faith in the ability of the state to do so effectively or equitably. The state is viewed with suspicion.

The outcome of this ambiguity is a large, costly state with weak finances. It is costly both because of the provision of the aforementioned public goods and because of the politicization of public-sector employment, especially in the South, but not only there, and its use as a means to buy votes or at least reward supporters. Moreover, the generous public pension system could be, and was, used as a sort of substitute for unemployment insurance or redundancy compensation when, in the 1970s and 80s, large numbers of industrial workers were pushed into early retirement since they could not readily be dismissed.

The state has weak finances because of a narrow tax base, made that way by widespread tax evasion and the associated large black economy, which is constituted both by outright illegal activity and by tax evasion by those performing legal activities. Total general government spending (i.e. central and local governments combined) as a percentage of GDP was 52.5 per cent in 1995, just a little below France's 54.4 per cent, but well ahead of Britain's 43.9 per cent, America's 37.1 per cent and Japan's

36.7 per cent.[22] After a dip in the intervening years, it was back at more or less that same level in 2009.

Since the financial crisis of 1992–93, however, three big things have changed. One is that what was then the world's biggest privatization programme cut back the state's direct ownership of industry drastically, raising money through asset sales but also, just as crucially, stemming the annual drain on the public exchequer from the companies' losses. Having ranged from telephones to food-processing companies, the state sector is now limited chiefly to railways, the post office, water, energy and municipal utilities, with continued large (30 per cent) shareholdings in the main electricity producer, ENEL, for example, ENI, the national oil and gas producer, and Finmeccanica, a defence and aerospace giant.

The second change was that a major reform of the public pension system was begun, which was carried out by governments of all stripes during the ensuing decade. These reforms raised the retirement age, indexed it to changing life expectancy, and shifted pensions to become tied to contributions to the scheme rather than based on fixed benefits. In this one – but important – area of reform, Italy was well ahead of the rest of Europe, and succeeded in first putting a cap on the growth of its pension costs, which otherwise threatened to be explosive, and, second, in ensuring that those costs should actually fall during the next few decades, whereas in most European countries they will continue to rise. This probably wouldn't have happened had there not been a financial crisis in 1992, but some crises do have their uses.

Even so, Italy's public pensions system remains expensive: in 2010 public pension spending amounted to nearly

15 per cent of GDP, which means that it amounted to almost 30 per cent of all public spending. At 15 per cent of GDP, such spending is also the highest in the OECD,[23] about 3–4 percentage points higher than in France and Germany, where public pensions also predominate over the private sort, but almost treble the levels in America or Britain. Average spending for pensions in the OECD area is 7 per cent of GDP. No wonder that when the Monti government felt obliged in November–December 2011 to cut public spending, their main target was still pensions.

The third change was that a bigger effort was begun to increase tax revenues, in order to prevent a recurrence of the large budget deficits of the 1980s. From 1994 onwards, thanks to this and to privatizations, the government ran a primary budget surplus every year – in other words, its revenues exceeded all its spending, except the interest costs on its stock of debt. This improvement in fiscal management culminated in a big push, helped by a special tax, to get the overall budget deficit below the 3 per cent of GDP ceiling specified in the Treaty of Maastricht as the precondition for membership of the euro. Italy qualified thanks to that effort, and to the fact that the eurozone members agreed collectively not to enforce another of the Maastricht preconditions, that public debt should not exceed 60 per cent of GDP. Italy's remained a bit less than double that, but it was considered to be 'moving in the direction of 60 per cent', which it was, albeit slowly.

It isn't now: by mid-2011 it was back at 120 per cent. The reason the country is stuck with such a big debt burden brings to mind an old joke about asking an Irish farmer for directions: 'You shouldn't start from here', he is alleged to say.

Italy's starting point in the early 1990s was terrible, and no country would hope to start from there. But so was Belgium's, and by 2011, even after the global recession, that country's public debt was down to just below 100 per cent of GDP: it did better at increasing tax revenues and trimming spending than Italy, but also, crucially, its economy grew more rapidly, raising revenues less painfully. Slow economic growth makes it much harder to reduce the debt burden. But the need for high marginal tax rates to raise revenue from a relatively narrow base of taxpayers, and the cost imposed by debt servicing on the budget (which has ranged between 4 per cent and 6 per cent of GDP during the past decade) both make it harder for the economy to grow. It is a vicious cycle, or perhaps trap is a better metaphor.

That, then, is the second burden hanging around the neck of the Italian economy, trapping it in purgatory. Debt-service costs are burdensome, and carry the risk that if financial markets turn sour those costs could rise and sap the economy's strength directly, as was shown vividly during 2011. Fear of taxation, or a determination to evade it, encourages companies to remain small so as to stay off the tax-collectors' radar screen, which weakens the economy indirectly. Those who do pay taxes, either because they want to or they cannot avoid them, find themselves bearing a heavy burden.

Here is a small, but revealing, anecdote: a friend who works as a journalist for RAI television on a fixed 'precarious' contract told me that when she travels, even within Italy, to do interviews she has to pay income tax on the reimbursed cost of her travelling expenses, as if they were actually part of her income. Those who cannot escape the taxman end up being tortured by him.

Moreover, the government's ability to use its public spending to bring about needed economic reforms is severely constrained: for example, the Monti government proposed to replace the labour laws with new rules designed to reduce workers' security and increase flexibility, but also needed to offer a more comprehensive and generous system of unemployment insurance as an inducement. The present system is meagre, and relies mostly on a rather outdated idea of subsidizing big industrial firms to hold on to their workers during downturns, a scheme known as the Cassa Integrazione Guadagni and financed chiefly by levies from big firms during the good times. Yet replacing that with proper, comprehensive unemployment insurance would be expensive, at least in the short term, so the Monti proposal could not be lavish. With public debt at or near 120 per cent of GDP, the money would be hard to find.

Burdens and obstacles: (3) Competition

Or, rather, the lack of it. Times, tastes and technologies change, and economies have to change with them. Italy is no exception, though sometimes you might think other-wise if you were to listen too often to Confindustria, the employers' federation that groups together the country's main manufacturers, big and (mainly) small. The coun-try's speciality, according to Confindustria, is manufac-turing goods that can proudly be labelled 'Made in Italy'. It is certainly true that the country produces many superb manufactured goods, and that manufacturers contribute especially strongly to the country's exports. The trouble is that it is no longer true that manufacturing is what Italian business mainly does.

As recently as 1990, industry, broadly defined to include construction and utilities such as electricity and gas, accounted for 32.4 per cent of value added[24] in the economy. By 2008 the figure was down to 27 per cent, in the continuation of a long-term trend. What this means is that the vast bulk of economic activity is now occurring not in industry in general, still less in manufacturing (which is but a subset of industry), but rather in services: 71 per cent of value added was produced in this way in 2008.

This is not very different from what has happened in other mature, rich economies. In Germany in 2008 69.3 per cent of value added came from services; in Britain the figure was 75.2 per cent, in France it was even higher at 77.6 per cent. In all these economies, agriculture has been declining as a share of output for a century or more – typically its share of value added now ranges from less than 1 per cent in Britain to 2 per cent in Italy – while industry has been declining since the 1960s. So the vibrancy, competitiveness and level of innovation in service industries is now the main determining factor in national growth of productivity, of incomes, indeed of the economy as a whole.

Which is why it matters that in Italy service industries are the most restricted, conservative and often backward parts of the economy, where competition is weakest. It is also where one of the country's most puzzling and (for the young especially) frustrating characteristics can be found most prominently: its lack of meritocracy.

Most manufacturing companies sell in world markets, or at least markets that have become open to pretty free competition thanks to successive rounds of global trade liberalization under the General Agreement on Tariffs and Trade and latterly the World Trade Organization, and thanks to the single market programme of the European Union. As a result, manufacturers do mainly recruit and promote their staff on the basis of merit and open competition, with the sole (though important) exception of state-owned enterprises and family members of the founding or owning entrepreneur in private firms. But this is not as true for service industries.

It is not, by and large, that new barriers to competition have been erected. Rather, the problem is mostly that old barriers have been left in place. *The Economist* put it very well in its 2011 special report on Italy, in which it said that the country 'is a wild forest of little privileges, rents and enclosures. Each has its own lobby group; together they conspire to make reform close to impossible.'[25]

These lobby groups are descendants, conceptually at least, of medieval guilds. Virtually any profession you can think of has its *'ordine'* (order) – lawyers, architects, engineers, accountants, pharmacists, taxi drivers, even journalists – whose ostensible job is to protect the public by ensuring that everyone in the profession is properly qualified, but whose more frequent task is to make sure that newcomers do not disrupt the business, bring in fresh ideas or, most particularly, bring in more competition to push down prices or wages.

The OECD sums it up in a more rigorous or severe way: its 2007 *Economic Survey of Italy* said: 'The index of product market regulation (PMR) of 2003 ranked the stance of regulatory policies as one of the strictest in the OECD, despite some progress made in previous years.'[26] Out of the OECD's thirty members, only Hungary, Mexico, Turkey and Poland had a higher (stricter) PMR rank. In other, plainer words, competition is more constrained in Italy than in almost all of the world's other rich countries.

This is not for want of an anti-trust law, nor an anti-trust enforcement authority: the country's actually very modern competition law was adopted in 1990, and that set up its Autoritá Garante della Concorrenza e del Mercato (Authority for Guarantee of Competition and of the Market). But it is weak and has slim resources, and it does not have the power to deal with the biggest obstacles to more open competition, which are government regulations, at both national and local level, the aforementioned professional guilds and, of course, state ownership itself. So while it can punish cartels it cannot liberalize regulations. Professional services are, essentially, beyond its reach.

To be fair, things have improved. Although state ownership, through completely nationalized firms and through the 30 per cent 'golden shares' retained in Telecom Italia, the ENI oil and gas business, the ENEL electricity utility and others remains more extensive than in twenty-eight of the thirty OECD members, such ownership has declined substantially since the early 1990s. And a package of reforms introduced during the centre-left government of 2006–08 by the then Minister of Economic Development, Pier Luigi Bersani, who is now leader of the Democratic Party, attacked some of the restrictive regulations surrounding pharmacies, taxi drivers, lawyers and some other professions. This had a positive effect on pharmacies, where liberalization led to 3,000 new shops being opened, but Mr Bersani's reforms were in effect blocked by the taxi drivers. He managed to remove a minimum fee regulation for lawyers, but then remarkably the Berlusconi government that took office in 2008, standing supposedly for liberalism, reinstated it.

It is a war of thousands of cuts, thrusts and barriers. In a few cases, the barriers could be explained and justified in terms of culture or even political preference: perhaps Italians are happy to pay higher prices in small, friendly local food shops than to have their towns surrounded by superstores. But in most cases, there is no genuine cultural or national political explanation. It is simply that lobby groups are protecting their own privileges and incomes. The price of that is paid by everyone else directly in higher costs, and in the economy as a whole by a lack of dynamism, innovation and meritocracy.

Blowing up the barricades

There are plenty of other things one could cite as being weaknesses and problems in the Italian economy. The lack of world-class universities, for example, or of extensive collaboration between universities and businesses, the relatively low level of research and development spending, and arguably (though this is shared with plenty of other developed countries) outdated physical and communications infrastructure. There is also, naturally, the issue that has obsessed the country ever since unification in 1861, namely the gap in prosperity between the North and the South.

These will all crop up in later chapters, in one form or another. All are genuine problems, especially the persistent failure of the South to narrow the gap between its income per head of population and that of the North: its income per head is roughly one-third lower. Yet all these other problems can be fairly described as consequences of the problems this chapter and the previous one on politics have focused on, rather than as independent causes themselves.

Universities are weak because of weak public finances and the general lack of meritocracy in service sectors, both public and private. Research and Development (R&D) is low because so many firms stay small, for reasons of labour law and tax. The South fails to catch up because of crime and slow or non-existent justice. Southerners have done well by migrating in their millions to northern jobs, but companies have not migrated in the reverse direction to take advantage of low southern costs, preferring to migrate to Romania or Hungary instead, and there has been no flowering of local entrepreneurship in the South to create jobs and incomes indigenously. The burdens of the state and the obstacles confronting new businesses are just too great.

The outcome is not an economic catastrophe, but it is a slow economic decline. As Mario Draghi, outgoing governor of the Bank of Italy, said in his final speech to the central bank's shareholders in 2011, the result of all these burdens and obstacles is that:

In the course of the past ten years, Italy's gross domestic product has increased by less than 3 per cent; that of France, with about the same population, by 12 per cent.

The gap perfectly reflects the difference in hourly productivity – stationary in Italy, up by 9 per cent in France. Italy's disappointing result applies to the country as a whole, North and South alike.

If productivity stagnates, our economy cannot grow. The productive economy loses competitiveness; widening deficits appear in the current account of the balance of payments. Foreign direct investment dries up. In the course of a decade, Italy received foreign direct investment inflows equal to 11 per cent of GDP, compared with 27 per cent in France.[27]

It was a stirring finale by the man who had by then been chosen to succeed Jean-Claude Trichet as president of the European Central Bank in Frankfurt in November 2011. Mr Draghi played a notable part in dealing with Italy's financial crisis of 1992–93 when he was director-general of the country's Treasury, and he launched the privatization programme that occurred at that time. He is plainly disappointed that almost twenty years later his country finds itself still with its public debt at 120 per cent of GDP, still facing another financial crisis, this time as a member of the eurozone, and with its economic growth having deteriorated during that period rather than having improved.

It is indeed a dispiriting picture, especially for a liberal reformer such as Mr Draghi. The obstacles to reform, and especially to the garnering of the political will to make reforms, are great. In his speech, he nevertheless found some reassurance and inspiration by looking back to the first prime minister of the unified Italy 150 years earlier, Count Camillo Benso di Cavour, who argued then for reforms by saying 'reforms, when enacted in time, do not weaken authority but enhance it'. Moreover, as an economist and discreet critic of politicians, Mr Draghi relished the fact that Cavour said 150 years ago:

> A nation's political resurgence can never be divorced from its economic resurgence ... Civic virtues, wise laws affording equal protection to each and every right, sound political arrangements, essential to the betterment of a nation's moral condition – these are also the prime cause of its economic progress.

Dante might not have made quite that connection, but he certainly felt that his nation's moral condition was at the foundation of all its ills. Sorting out all these things, purging Italy's economy of its obstacles, improving the morals and civic virtues of its politics and government, all to move the country closer to what might in Dantean terms be described as '*il Paradiso*': it is a huge and daunting task. Contrary to what Italy's cheerleaders have often said, generally as a justification for doing nothing, Italy's economic 'fundamentals' are not strong: they are weak. And the willingness to make the changes necessary to restore their strength, to make sacrifices to reduce the public debt, to accept greater flexibility in labour markets, to remove the rights and privileges that reduce competition and innovation, is itself weak.

This is what now needs to change. The financial crisis that hit Italy in late 2011 and continued in 2012 offers at least a chance that reform could begin amid a collective, national acceptance that it is necessary. For change is not at all impossible. Little has happened at national level in recent decades but there has been plenty going on at the regional, local and company levels. It is from that that Italy needs to find its inspiration.

So this book's journey will now move out of the *Inferno* and the economic purgatory and towards more hopeful, positive places and trends. We perhaps should not call them Paradise, as Dante would, for that would be to overstate it, but they do, at least, offer clues to how Italy could move in a paradisiacal direction. What better place to start, and to be inspired by, than the city that was Cavour's home and unified Italy's first capital, 150 years ago: Turin?

CHAPTER 4

Inspirations from Turin

Once, in 1998, in the midst of peace talks to end the violence in Northern Ireland, Tony Blair provoked derision from us cynical, undeferential British journalists when he proclaimed that such a serious moment was no time for soundbites and then, seconds later, produced one of his most pompous slogans ever. 'I feel', he said, 'the hand of history upon our shoulder.'

Well, in a rather different way, I too felt a ghostly hand on my shoulder as I tucked into my *filetto di vitello piemontese*, sitting in the lovely old Ristorante Del Cambio in Turin right underneath the plaque that said that this had been the favoured table of Camillo Benso, Conte di Cavour (Count of Cavour), the first prime minister of Italy, a century and a half earlier. Cavour was not the originator of the idea that Italy should shake off its foreign occupiers (large parts of today's Italy were held then by France, Austria, Spain and, if it can be called foreign, the

Papacy) and create a single, unified, independent country, but he was the man who got the job done in 1861, albeit with quite a lot of help from Giuseppe Garibaldi and his small, brave mercenary army.

That, naturally, was why my generous host had chosen that table and that restaurant, opposite the Palazzo Carignano where Cavour had achieved so many of his political triumphs, for it was the home of what was known as the 'sub-Alpine' parliament of the provinces run by the King of Savoy, Vittorio Emanuele, and thus the first parliament of the newly unified nation of Italy.[1] Turin did not have long as Italy's first capital, for that role was soon moved first to Florence and then to Rome, and Vittorio Emanuele moved with it, to become Italy's king. But Turin remained in many ways the industrial capital of the country, especially thanks to the Fiat car company that was founded in Turin in 1899 by a group of investors that included Giovanni Agnelli.

To feel Cavour's presence was especially thought-provoking, I must admit, because it had not been very many years since I had learned who Cavour was. It is no doubt annoying to Italians, and especially Piedmontese, to find that so few foreigners have heard of the great unifier, nor realize the role that Turin played in the country's history. I blame Garibaldi for having been such a sexy, swashbuckling hero to nineteenth-century storytellers and propagandists – especially in an England which had its own ulterior motives for supporting him – that he, his splendid beard and his red shirts overshadowed Cavour.

Looking at Cavour's picture, however, I can see why he might not have caught foreign imaginations: with his plump face, little round glasses and ill-fitting clothes he looks more like a down-at-heel English aristocrat than a visionary Italian statesman. Then there is the matter of the biscuit: thanks to the smart English entrepreneur of the 1860s who swooped on his reputation, English kids still grow up nibbling Garibaldi biscuits and digesting his name, even though we liken the biscuits' filling a little rudely to dead flies. Poor old Cavour received no such honour, not even the flies.

Yet it is the foreigners who are wrong. Not only should Cavour be honoured and respected for his great achievement, but the city and the region from which he emerged should be better known too. For Turin and Piedmont offer a remarkable amount of inspiration for how to reform and modernize Italy again today. By showing what already has been done, they in effect show what could be done, at a national level.

What was it, after all, that made the Piedmontese take-over of Italy possible in 1861? It would be unwise to wade too deeply into a debate best conducted by historians and by Italians' own historical memory of the relative strengths of Savoy and the Bourbons, of Turin and Naples, of the rights and wrongs of what happened. But the basic economic and personal framework is pretty clear. In their era, Cavour and Piedmont gained their strength by being thoroughly modern creatures, with their international connections and knowledge, with their adoption of new technology (including the railway),[2] and with their acceptance of the need for openness and quite a lot of freedom if progress was to be made.

Globalized, technologically advanced, liberal: that formula, as well as Cavour's shrewd political sense and opportunism and the support of Garibaldi, is what took Vittorio Emanuele II to Rome. And today? A basic recipe for how to prosper in the twenty-first century as an already rich, mature society would be similar: be global, be technologically advanced, and be liberal enough to encourage ideas and innovations to flow freely, to be explored and exploited by new firms and institutions. You don't have to be perfect examples of any of those, and no one is, but you do have to achieve some version of it if you are going to do well and keep on evolving as times change.

For sure, neither Turin nor Piedmont is any longer the sexy part of Italy, if they ever were, any more than the Count of Cavour was much of a pin-up. But they do offer hope that, for all its problems, for all the recent ascendancy of *la Mala Italia*, reform and regeneration can in fact be done in Italy. Having been just about the dirtiest and most bankrupt Italian big city in the 1980s, with a particular reputation for industrial strife and for violence, Turin two decades later looks clean, modern, fairly peaceful and quite vital. More than that, it has pioneered reforms to its justice system, has one of the most cosmopolitan universities in the country, has rejuvenated its main museums, has become a surprising tourist destination, and is home to the internationally renowned Slow Food Movement. At least in Turin, *la Buona Italia* is on the up. It shows what can be done.

Don't let a good crisis go to waste

Turin had had a pretty bad 1970s, thanks to the oil shock, industrial unrest and the terrorist violence of the 'years of lead'[3] that hit both Turin and its larger, financial neighbour, Milan, especially hard. But by the start of the 1990s, things were still very bad indeed. Unemployment in 1991 in the province surrounding Turin was 12.4 per cent of the labour force, well above the anyway high national rate of 10.9 per cent. More than one-quarter of all youths aged between 14 and 29 were unemployed. The city was bust, with a big financial deficit. Fiat was in a state of near collapse, with its protected domestic car business being ripped open by the creation of Europe's single market in 1986–92. Turin was one of the first Italian cities to face serious social tensions over immigration. Corrupt and incompetent municipal administrations were the Torinese norm in the 1980s, as the city went through four mayors in seven years and ended with an event now more associated with southern, mafia-ridden towns, namely the dissolution of the Turin city council by the national government and its replacement by a government-appointed commissioner to run it until the 1993 elections.

In other words the city, dominated by manufacturing and especially cars, was just the sort of place you would expect to have suffered mightily in the economic crisis of 2008–10, a crisis in which demand for all sorts of goods, but especially cars, slumped after the Lehman Brothers shock of September 2008, a crisis in which the price of oil was still a painful $75 a barrel as recovery began, or three times higher than it had been a decade earlier. So what was the unemployment rate after Lehman's collapse in the province of Turin, the old rustbelt of Italy? At the end of 2009, in the thick of the post-Lehman recession, it was 8.3 per cent, almost exactly in line with the national rate. The province's economy proved quite resilient, thank you very much, by its past standards, having reduced its unemploy-ment sharply in the decade before the Lehman demise, down to just below 5 per cent at its lowest point in 2006–07. Things were not like that in Turin's 'sister' city of Detroit, where the car-makers' slump and tumbling house prices made the place look like a ghost-town.

I had never expected to gain inspiration from Turin or its businesses. To my mind, the city just meant cars, and a company – Fiat – that during my journalistic career had lurched from crisis to crisis. When I was a teenager in the 1970s, which was the last time I knew anything much about cars, Fiat and Lancia were thought of abroad as a bit of a joke. The city's image, too, was about as appealing as that of Detroit, and there wasn't even Motown Records to add a bit of soul.

Yes, Britain's deadbeat car industry was even worse, until the Japanese came along in the 1980s and showed us how to do it. The glamour of the Agnellis certainly helped lift Turin above the smell of engine oil more than any post-1945 British capitalists could manage. Yet to those who had studied it, Fiat had also been a byword for the perils of too close a relationship between a company and the state, whether under Mussolini or the post-1945 demo-cratic governments. Its protected, privileged position in the Italian car market gave it great benefits for years but did little for Italy, and ended abruptly in 1992. Fiat's share of that market slumped from 52 per cent in 1990 to 34 per cent a decade later; the car industry's employment in the city plunged from 140,000 in 1981 to just 60,000 by 2001. And Turin's dependence on Fiat had crippled its munic-ipal governments, had helped bring about that industrial and other violence, and had made the city extremely vulnerable every time an economic shock came along.

Not this time. Things have changed. The first small sign that I might be pleasantly surprised by the city came when I flew to Turin in February 2009 to take part in a big internal conference held by UniCredit Bank: not a Turin institution, but one that did have some roots there. From my hotel, I walked along the rather nondescript street towards the 'UniManagement Learning and Development Center' where the event was to be held. That very American-style name offended my linguistic pride as a writer, I admit, with its ugly capital letter in the middle of a word. Moreover, I wasn't feeling all that cheerful, on that rainy morning, having had to catch a very early flight from London to land in what I thought was a rustbelt.

But then I walked into the UniManagement building and – wow! It was as if I had landed in another world, a creative world of modern design, surrounded by video screens amid intriguing, bright-coloured walls, covered with art and photos and slogans of many kinds, with strange-shaped rooms and a much more upbeat, stimulating atmosphere than I had associated with Italy's motor city. The next day, at a reception there, I met the chairman of the UniManagement Learning Center, Valentino Castellani, and started to ask him about Turin. It was a fortunate meeting and line of questioning. For this lucky encounter, in the funky surroundings of the UniManagement building, was with the former mayor who had begun Turin's transformation in the 1990s, when he stepped into that job following a career as a professor at the Politecnico di Torino.

What happened was that the introduction of direct election of mayors in 1993 along with later reforms made it possible for new leaders to emerge in many municipal governments with new powers, leaders who did not always come from the old, discredited, self-centred, often corrupt political parties. Turin was not the only city to benefit from this, but Valentino Castellani, a scientist who entered politics, brought especially dramatic change to the city, change that was extended and preserved by his successor, Sergio Chiamparino, who came from a more conventional political background on the centre-left.

It is not too much of a stretch to liken the role of Mayor Castellani to that played at the national level by Professor Mario Monti after November 2011. This former European competition commissioner, economics professor and President of Bocconi University, was brought in as a non-political outsider to try to form a consensus, as prime minister of a 'technical government' hopefully supported by a broad range of parties, about how to reform Italy and deal with its financial crisis. So, albeit with an election, was Mr Castellani.

A crisis helped then, as perhaps now. Barack Obama's first chief of staff, Rahm Emanuel, said as they entered the White House in 2009 that you should not 'let a good crisis go to waste': it is a chance to make big, necessary changes, because the sense of crisis can make people and organizations more willing to accept change. We'll let history decide whether Messrs Obama and Emanuel wasted the economic crisis of 2008–10, but history can already see that Turin did not waste its crisis of the early 1990s.

The most important thing that the two mayors, Castellani and Chiamparino, have succeeded in doing, in response to Turin's crisis, has been both to reconnect the city internally and also to connect it better to the rest of the world. By reconnecting it internally, I mean that they managed to replace the bitter divisions of the 1970s and 1980s with a sense of common purpose. Consultations over the city's 'New Urban Masterplan', initiated by Mayor Castellani, took in people and organizations from all over the city, at every level, helped by the fact that the new mayor was directly elected, was supported by a centre-left coalition, and had a clean, independent image, in sharp contrast to his mucky, discredited political predecessors. The process was also helped by active and open communication.

The outcome was a big change in the city's appearance and infrastructure, with the railway concealed under a new road, and improved transport connections to the old industrial areas. Just as important, though, was the change of style and approach by the city government.

As a study[4] of Turin's success conducted for the Centre for Analysis of Social Exclusion (CASE) at the London School of Economics reports, Mayor Castellani recast the city government's role as a forum and a facilitator rather than a direct actor, while also coordinating closely with the provincial and regional administrations, relations with which had formerly been rather cold and contentious.

That was the simplest form of external connection, but there were also two other, bigger forms. One was the connection Turin made with the European Union, both for the use of its money and for sharing experiences and ideas with other cities all over the EU, helping to overcome a widespread Italian tendency (common in Britain as well, alas) to want all solutions to be invented at home. Barcelona has been a particularly strong influence. The second was to boost Turin's broader international and domestic connections, physically with better railway links, psychologically by encouraging and strengthening commercial and other contacts all over the world. That has been the aim of the city's broader strategic economic plan, 'Torino Internazionale', begun by Mayor Castellani and then implemented by his successor, Sergio Chiamparino, again involving a wide network of people and institutions all over the city.

This breadth of consultation and involvement is symbolized for me in two non-economic issues. The first is that despite having 8 per cent of its 2.2 million population made up of immigrants, Turin also has strikingly well-established institutions, including public bodies, churches and NGOs, dedicated to helping encourage integration and easing tensions. The big bank-related foundation in the city, Compagnia di San Paolo, has been an important source of finance for these and other charitable bodies. The future of Italian society, as Mayor Chiamparino told me, depends on immigration, but cities need to have structures and cooperation if they are to avoid conflict.

The second significant issue for me was the fact that, on 27 February 2010, a few days before we met, Mayor Chiamparino had presided over Italy's first gay 'marriage' ceremony. The event, for two women, was purely symbolic, not a proper legal marriage, for that remains impossible in Italy. But it underlined not only why I should think well of Mr Chiamparino personally but also how, as in Cavour's time, Turin is at the forefront of liberalism and modernization in Italy today.[5] It is a liberal pioneer in a conservative country.

Served in Italy as well as made in Italy

As a long-ago teenage car-enthusiast, when I came to Turin I felt a strange compulsion to visit Lingotto, in the city's formerly grimy suburbs, to walk on the famous roof-top test-track that had been featured in Michael Caine's film *The Italian Job*, and see what had happened to the old Fiat factory site that had been closed as long ago as 1983. Yet passing the vast new EATALY[6] organic food shop next door also gave me some clue as to what else might inspire me in the Piedmontese story. First, Slow Food, the movement that holds its biannual Salone del Gusto (Exhibition of Taste) food and wine fair in Lingotto itself, and which inspired the EATALY retailing, dining and cooking-school business that is now expanding rapidly around the world. But other things too: the spread of service industries as well as manufacturing, a search for traditions, a sense of place, a sense that more could be made of existing or neglected assets.

The conversion of the Lingotto factory and office complex[7] into shops, cinemas, art galleries and convention centres reminded me of what happened in Newcastle, in Britain's north-east, in the 1980s and 1990s, when a combination of shopping centres and government-funded arts centres were created to try to rescue that old, troubled industrial city. It didn't really work until a broader commercial revival took hold, along with a closer relationship between the local university and its city. It is the same in Turin. Wider connections, both national and international, are vital. So is attention both to manufacturing and to service industries.

One other manufacturing initiative by the city deserves a particular mention, however, and that is 'From Concept to Car', a project set up by the city's Chamber of Commerce in 2002. The reason why this is interesting is that it represents an effort to circumvent the traditional weakness of small and medium-sized Italian industry, namely the way their lack of scale and resources makes it harder for them to expand into international markets. This effort was born out of a desire to help the local auto components industry survive the shrinking of Fiat's local operations by finding new customers abroad, but it is also a model for cooperative attempts by 'clusters' or industrial districts to widen their markets and their contacts.

In its eight years of operation, helping to inform members about opportunities, to promote them to buyers and to provide logistical help, 'From Concept to Car' has generated 65 orders for local firms, worth a total of 40 million euros. The scheme is selective and so meritocratic, with 150 local companies picked out from among 1,400 applicants. Along the same lines, the Chamber of Commerce set up schemes in 2007 to help information technology companies in the area (extra sales so far, 3.2 million euros in 35 orders) and aerospace suppliers (8 orders totalling 11.3 million euros).

Those gains in orders are small, but helpful, and the schemes cover their costs. Just as important, they form part of a wider effort, helped also by the city's universities (especially Politecnico di Torino) to broaden the region's technological base and to improve the connections between companies and between those companies and the universities. I will return to Politecnico later in this book, looking at its 'incubator' for spin-off companies using technology created there, and at its research tie-ups with international firms. But the broad point is that firms in the city and its surroundings are making serious efforts to exploit many of today's expanding global markets, namely in information technology, health care, aerospace and biotechnology, with some help from the university.

One thing those new markets have in common is that they are neither obviously manufacturing businesses nor obviously services. The importance of services will reappear several times in this book, as it is a bit of an obsession. Probably, this is a stubborn reaction against all those who during the global economic crisis have attacked countries and their governments for relying too much on services and not enough on manufacturing. For this mantra is absurd and outdated. It is true that a reliance solely on financial services would be foolish (though such services reached only 8 per cent of Britain's GDP at their peak in 2006). But that is no more profound than saying that a reliance simply on one industry, such as cars, would be foolish – as Turin's experience had long since showed.

Taken more broadly than just finance, service industries are the very essence of modern life, ranging from education to health care, transport to tourism, entertainment and the media to marketing, from the law to design. Even in Germany and Italy, countries proud of their manufacturing industries, services account for 70–75 per cent of economic activity (including public services). Moreover, the distinction between services and manufacturing is increasingly meaningless: to which does design and engineering belong? Both, is the answer.

So if you let service industries fester, remaining uncompetitive, unproductive and unloved, you are making a big national mistake. Or, rather, you are missing a big national opportunity. As noted in Chapter Three, that is one of Italy's weaknesses: many of its service industries are weak, unproductive, not very modern and not very competitive.

That is not so true of Turin. Having had a predominantly industrial economy in the 1970s and 1980s (though even then design and engineering played a vital role), an important part of Turin's current economic and social stability has come from the steady growth of service industries in the city and region. They accounted for 67 per cent of jobs in the province of Turin in 2009, compared with 45 per cent in 1990.

The big examples remain design, engineering and other technological services. Tourism is also growing rapidly, as noted earlier, boosted by the Winter Olympic Games in 2006, and there is potential for education to do so too, if the University of Turin and Politecnico di Torino can really become world class. It was a pity, though, that the highly regarded Interaction Design Institute in nearby Ivrea, the original home of the Olivetti typewriter and computer firm, was closed in 2005 by its sponsors, Telecom Italia, after only four years of operation, and merged with the Domus Academy in Milan, which specializes in fashion – though the merger provided greater scale it was at the cost of individuality and freedom. The institute's focus on how users interact with technology was thoroughly modern; no one can look at an iPhone or iPad from Apple and fail to see the importance of that sort of design or miss the cleverness of the component design that goes into it.

Cinema, with its potential too for boosting other forms of media, is also reviving as an industry and as a tourist attraction, in its original Italian home. During the 1990s the Mole Antonelliana, a strange building that had once been intended to become the city's synagogue and had lain empty and unused for many decades, was used to house the city's large cinematic archives, and was then made the home of the Museo Nazionale de Cinema, adding another reason to visit the city and building on its cinematic legacy.

One important future task will be to improve further Turin's connections across the Alps and across Europe by building better train connections through the mountains to Lyons. At present high-speed trains come from Venice or Rome to Milan and Turin, but after Turin the lines and speeds revert to the slower, conventional sorts. A high-speed link is being blocked by fierce opposition to it in the Susa valley in Piedmont, which is in part based on environmental concerns – it is a beautiful valley – but is also attracting attention from anti-capitalist groups. No railway scheme should be supported regardless of the costs or the environmental impact, but it is odd (and a pity) how bad and slow the rail links are between both Piedmont and Liguria (the region surrounding Genoa) and France, Spain, Switzerland and beyond when their rail links into the rest of Italy are now good. Cavour would not have been impressed.

The real genius of Slow Food

He might well, however, have been impressed by Slow Food, and by its contribution to the economy and the reputation of Piedmont, as well as to Italy's reputation around the world. No doubt his enjoyment of the fare at slow, graceful Del Cambio restaurant would have made sure of that, along with the beneficial effects of the movement on the quality and income of the Piedmontese agriculture with which he was so concerned. Similarly, the gastronomic appeal of Slow Food, and of the whole idea of eating and drinking high-quality Italian products in beautiful landscapes, explains why the Slow Food Movement is so well known. Slow Food is an Italian idea, based on the traditional national regard for food ingredients and for closeness to the land, but now it is a worldwide movement based more on a philosophy than on any country's national cuisine.

Yet, and I forgive you for not believing me, it is not only or even mainly the food that interests me most about Carlo Petrini's achievement. The reason why the founder of Slow Food is an inspiration is different. It is the network, the team-building, the success in creating a national movement based on a clear set of principles and values. Italy is said (especially by Italians) to be a nation of individuals, after all, not one of teams. And it has tended to be obsessed with its particular cuisine – or even with very local dishes – rather than with principles and philosophies.

According to Italy's stereotypes of itself, Slow Food should not really have succeeded in building a nationwide network of associates, nor assembling 40,000 members in

Italy and another 40,000 worldwide. It should not have managed to persuade all the 400 local *condotte* (guides) and the 17 regional coordinating bodies in Italy to sign up to a common manifesto and a common set of values and objectives. It should not have succeeded in galvanizing support even in the home of fast food itself, the United States, which is now home to its largest membership around the world.

What should have happened, if the stereotype held true, is that the idea of Slow Food would have caught on at first, when it was launched by Mr Petrini and his associates in 1986 as Arcigola and then in 1989 was renamed Slow Food, but that lots of local or regional organizations, with their own leaders, would then have wanted to build their own versions of it, with their own manifestos and own statements of values and objectives. Progress would have been made towards lifting the quality and integrity of what is produced in Italian farms and vineyards, but it would have been modest and a bit confusing. No doubt some of that has happened. No doubt there has been all sorts of infighting along the way. There remains plenty of room for confusion. Yet it is still remarkable that Slow Food has achieved the degree of unity, of cohesion, of common purpose that it has.

If you look at all sorts of other movements and networks in Italy, they do suffer from the stereotypical Italian traits. Organizations dedicated to promoting gender equality are a good example: there are lots of such NGOs and networks, all with good ideas and good intentions, but little contact with one another and little coordination. At the last count, there were at least four recently formed organizations purporting to act as a national 'umbrella' group or coordinator on the gender issue, with hundreds of individual associations. So the objective becomes much harder to achieve, even when plenty of people are involved. Albeit in its own very special field, Slow Food ought to be a model for how to organize a national network more effectively.

How did you do it?, I asked Carlo Petrini. And what lessons are there from Slow Food's success for other sorts of movements, other sorts of networks? Mr Petrini is a tall, handsome, stylish man with a beard now peppered with grey: the beard ensures that he does not exactly look like a businessman or banker, but equally he does not really look like the leftist activist that he was when Arcigola emerged in the 1980s, nor does he look like a farmer. His answer to the question of what has made Slow Food work places him as firmly in an Italian quintessence, however, as does his stylish dress: he says that centring on food and pleasure made it easy: 'Many people find our claim of a universal right to pleasure to be elitist, but that is wrong: pleasure is not just something for those who have money. No, pleasure is essentially democratic, because it is physiological, and so everyone can try it.'

That sort of idealism and belief in Slow Food's universal application undoubtedly helped. So did the strength of its brand: a clear name, well promoted and, probably crucially, with international endorsement (even though the movement was chiefly Italian until the second decade of its life). The choice of those two English words for the name of this very Italian initiative, instantly recognizable as the intended opposite to fast food and the Big Mac, is a further explanation. One of the campaigns that helped lead to the establishment of Slow Food was an (unsuccessful) effort to block the opening of a McDonalds restaurant in the Piazza di Spagna, by the Spanish steps in the heart of Rome.

The name is not perfect – it is never ideal to name yourself in contrast to something else, rather than finding direct, positive attributes of your own – but nevertheless it grabbed attention. Another strength has been a clear philosophy that was easy for members to associate themselves with – as Mr Petrini says, something people from all walks of life could share. That philosophy, probably crucially, was not linked to any particular political party: 'Despite having always had political connotations, we have been outside the political game. Sometimes this has meant that we have been snubbed, but in the end it has proved to be an advantage as it has shown that our battles are truly transversal, cross-cutting.'

The annual Salone del Gusto, an international exhibition-cum-fair in Turin every two years which brings people together and generates lots of publicity, must also have been a big help, as was the publishing of books and guides by Slow Food Editore, which added to the brand's appeal and coherence. So, now, is the University of the Gastronomic Sciences, founded in 2004 with help from local governments, in Mr Petrini's hometown of Bra in the Piedmont countryside south-east of Turin, which provides an educational focus, an ability to keep renewing the movement's thinking and principles, and a flow every year of students likely to feel warm towards the whole idea.

It is a small university, with just 250 students at any one time, albeit from all over the world, studying food sciences but also the links between agriculture, food and tourism, for example. One of its most appealing features to the visitor is its 'Wine Bank': a store of wines from all over Italy, aimed in particular at allowing the wines to age properly rather than being sold and drunk prematurely – as Slow Food believes often happens with Italian wines, as opposed to their pricier French equivalents.

Fittingly, when asked whether he has advice for others building networks, Mr Petrini counsels for both openness and patience: 'You must always be open to new ideas and new topics, if they turn out to overlap with your traditional preoccupations. So Slow Food has also become involved with arguments about immigrants' rights when labouring in agriculture, for example, or gender equality.' Even so, Slow Food has not built such strong networks in other countries as it has in Italy and the United States: but we are not in a hurry, he says. 'This is good advice for everyone.'

Reviving the Tomb of Kha

One place that was never in a hurry was Turin's Egyptian Museum,[8] despite its long-held boast to be the world's largest such museum after the one in Cairo. That may have been true, but it was also one of the least visited. Like many older Italian museums, the collection is held in a building – a seventeenth-century palace – that is less than ideal for modern conservation. Until 2005, when Eleni Vassilika arrived as the museum's new director, amid a change in the way the organization was run and financed, it had fewer than 230,000 visitors each year. The museum's precious objects were glued on to wooden mountings and crammed into old wooden-framed vitrines with no humidity controls or special glass, there was no means to control the sunlight coming through the windows, there was no air-conditioning or ultraviolet filters, and the most notable collection, the contents of the 'Tomb of Kha' (an architect for Pharaoh Amenhotep II, in the fifteenth century BC, whose tomb features in the fictional Indiana Jones stories) were crammed into a tiny room which had no fans to circulate the air. Dr Vassilika says that among the unfortunate few who entered the tomb's display chamber, many fainted and vomited because of the build-up there of carbon dioxide.

Now, all that has changed. The Egyptian Museum in 2010 was the eighth most-visited national museum, monument or archaeological site, with more than 575,000 visitors. The Tomb of Kha is now laid out properly in a room roughly ten times bigger than its old home, since the museum's website now says that the 506 objects from the tomb, which was discovered in 1906, are 'important enough to constitute a museum in itself'. All the museum's objects are being removed from their wooden mounts and mounted instead on modern plexiglass. The museum's central courtyard, which used to function as a staff car-park, is now used for schoolchildren's picnics. Bit by bit, the old vitrines are being replaced.

Why? This change is thanks to the fact that in 2005, the year the tough-minded Greek-American Dr Vassilika was recruited as director, Turin's Egyptian Museum became the country's first, and still only, state-owned cultural institution to be transferred into the hands of a private foundation.[9] The Ministry of Culture still owns the collection, but the museum is managed by a foundation whose shareholders include a big banking foundation, the Compagnia di San Paolo (part owner of Italy's second biggest bank, Banca Intesa San Paolo), the Region of Piedmont, the Province of Turin and the City of Turin, and which put up 50 million euros to pay for refurbishment of the galleries. The Egyptian Museum was chosen as the first experiment in semi-private management because it is not classically Italian, nor does it hold Renaissance art. The idea of 'privatizing the cultural patrimony' is always controversial, so starting with an Egyptian collection was a stealthy way to show that this would not lead to anything crass, as long as the state remained in overall control. It did, however, confirm the fears of the most vocal opponents of private management: the staff trade unions.

When Dr Vassilika arrived the number of staff employed at the museum was already down from 120 to 72, but she still encountered a highly unionized and highly resistant staff. The union representative, she says, told her she 'would not last more than two years'. She says that even with 72 staff, of whom 15 were supposedly on public duty, she was lucky if she were to find as many as 5 manning the galleries at any one time. Moreover, she says those who were there had scant regard for the objects and indeed for the law. She was sitting outside in the piazza one day, eating an ice-cream, when she looked up at one of the museum's gallery windows and saw a member of staff standing there smoking a cigarette. This is illegal, and of course hardly conducive either to safety or conservation. She telephoned the museum's security office and reported this. The initial response from the office was to say no, she must be mistaken, there is no one smoking in the galleries. It was only when she pointed out that she was calling from directly outside the museum, and could see it with her own eyes, that she convinced the officials to intervene.

Her tussles with the staff unions took several years, but have now paid off. The unions no longer simply close the museum when they wish to hold union meetings, as they did before. There is no longer rubbish in the stairways, nor ancient, unmaintained fire extinguishers standing randomly about. A falconer no longer has to be brought in to get rid of pigeons. In 2006, when Turin hosted the Winter Olympics, the Egyptian Museum was not even included in the press packs because it was considered too dangerous to encourage people to visit. Now, however, not only have most of the staff been replaced, not only have visitor numbers more than doubled, but also the museum's operating income of 2.25 million euros a year covers more than 75 per cent of its operating budget, whereas most museums are able to cover only about one-third of their costs. The state's contribution is limited to 600,000 euros from the local authorities that are among its shareholders. The museum would like to do better, raising its income from entrance tickets by breaking with the tariffs fixed by the state that mean that over half the visitors pay no fees at all.

It is but one museum, in one city. But it is an important success story for the strategy of semi-privatization. Elsewhere, Italy's cultural heritage is under serious strain, and threat. Teatro Valle, an eighteenth-century theatre in Rome, was 'occupied' in 2011 by actors and other protestors keen to block the theatre's possible sale by the government. Central government spends less than 0.18 per cent of its total public spending on the Ministry of Culture, which is responsible for the country's museums and archaeological sites, less than one-fifth of the proportion devoted by France to this purpose. The cultural budget was halved during the three years 2008–11. It is no coincidence that some historic sites are in a state of decay: two sections of the city of Pompeii have collapsed in recent years, and slabs of concrete have fallen from the walls of the Colosseum in Rome. Private philanthropists are starting to fill some of the gap: Diego Della Valle, proprietor of the Tod's luxury shoe firm, is contributing 25 million euros to help repair the Colosseum; Brunello Cucinelli, the cashmere-maker who will feature in Chapter Seven, is also assisting with the repair of Perugia's Etruscan walls. The most effective change, however, would be better management of the existing budget and assets. The Egyptian Museum shows that that can be done, if the structure and incentives are altered.

The achievement of fast justice

Italy contains many mysteries for us foreigners, and long may it do so. Yet one that I hope will not remain forever mysterious is this: how is it that a judge born in Taranto in Puglia could lead a transformation of the judicial process in Turin over the past nine years, and yet this example cannot be followed in most other big-city jurisdictions?

The statistics are simple. According to the World Bank's annual survey, Italy ranks 156th out of 181 countries in terms of the average length of civil legal proceedings. Italy is just below Gabon and Guinea on the list, and just better than Djibouti. This deters businesses from investing and is manifestly unfair for citizens who have to wait years and years before securing their property rights or gaining compensations, for example.

In 2001, when Judge Mario Barbuto became president of the Turin Tribunal, he faced a backlog of 40,000 civil cases. One of them, involving a disputed legacy, dated back to 1958. That case was finally resolved in 2002, after an incredible forty-four years. More important, though, has been the general improvement. By 2006 the backlog had been reduced to 26,800 cases and in that year the European Court of Human Rights named Turin as the most efficient judicial system in the whole of Europe.

Now, Turin has just two cases that are nine years old; 1 per cent of its backlog is between five and nine years old; 4 per cent are four years old. As those numbers imply, this means that 95 per cent of civil cases in Turin are less than three years old, and in fact 65 per cent are less than one year old. Since I know that one of the only two civil cases in which I have been involved in the Italian courts, the suits for libel brought in Milan against *The Economist* by Silvio Berlusconi, is now more than ten years old at the time of writing, and still awaiting a verdict on Mr Berlusconi's appeal, I can see that these numbers are impressive.

Turin is not entirely alone in its efficiency. In rankings of the speed of civil justice, it was number one in 2007 but was pushed into second place in 2008 by Trieste, and then in 2009 came second to Bolzano. Those three, plus Trento, always take the top places, and all have improved in recent years. But these cities are unusual when compared with the big offenders, such as Milan, Naples, Rome and Bari.

So how was it done? The general symptoms of Italy's judicial sickness are well known: a huge number of cases (5.6 million civil cases outstanding at 31 December 2009, and 3.3 million criminal cases); three levels of justice in a 'hyper-perfectionist' trial system, as Judge Barbuto terms it, allowing appeals right up to the Court of Cassation before any judgment can be considered definitive; a very high ratio of lawyers to judges (44 per judge) and to citizens (290 lawyers for every 100,000 citizens, compared with 168 in Germany, 76 in France and just 22 in Britain); a lack of accountability for either judges or lawyers.

In response to condemnation by the European Court of Human Rights for what it saw as Italy's appallingly slow civil justice system, the 'Pinto Law' was passed in 2001, introducing a compensation entitlement for victims of ultra-slow justice. By 2010, more than 270 million euros had been paid out under this law. The Corte dei Conti (Court of Accounts) is entitled to ask judges to contribute personally to these compensation payments, as a way to make them accountable for unreasonably slow trials. But this has not worked, because the Corte dei Conti has not dared to apply it. For a start, that court is one of the worst offenders anyway, with some of the longest trials, so it would have to penalize itself. And anyway, the national backlog is so large that to start fining judges would be to risk a mutiny.

It sounds hopeless. But what Turin has shown is that justice can be speeded up without fundamental reforms to the judicial system, in fact without any dramatic changes. The achievements of Judge Barbuto and his colleagues are the result of applying simple management techniques, and of succeeding in creating a sense of common purpose.

Judge Barbuto drew up a set of twenty simple rules, and set targets and benchmarks for all of the teams of magistrates. They set to work to compile a catalogue of all the cases outstanding, labelling them according to the year in which they had started – a surprisingly innovative move in a country which has no national catalogue of cases. And replacing the common instinct in Italian courts to deal with easy new cases first, leaving old and difficult ones to fester, Judge Barbuto set a rule that the oldest cases must henceforth be cleared first.

The most important element was persuading judges and lawyers alike that speed and efficiency were important: that justice delayed was justice denied. Lawyers, who stand in principle to benefit from delay, might have been expected to try to block the process. So Judge Barbuto went to the local Lawyers Association,[10] stated his objectives, presented his proposed rules, and asked the Association to nominate a special commission from among the members to review them with him. After the review, the Association agreed to support the process. And in fact, a fast process has turned out to be good for the lawyers too, since more cases are brought to court rather than being settled privately, and because payments come sooner, improving the lawyers' cash flow.

It would be even better if a national reform of procedures and of the judiciary itself could occur. But with an almost complete loss of trust between the government and the judges, each of which accuses the other of malpractice, political bias and much more, this is impossible. That was one of the biggest costs of the Berlusconi period in government, since it pitted judges and ministers against one another when the nation needed them to be working together.

What it took to revolutionize civil justice in Turin was leadership, the setting of clear objectives and a common purpose, peer pressure and an emphasis on performance and merit. Teamwork plus leadership, in other words. Impossible in Italy, shouts the chorus. It is hard to see why. That is what Italians expect from their soccer teams in every match (though as the 2010 World Cup showed, they don't always get it from the national team).

'La Vecchia Signora'

For one final (for the time being) positive observation about Turin, I am going to step on to dangerous territory. Talking about justice or food or politics is all very well. But talking about *calcio* (soccer) is much more serious. In British newspapers, a journalist making a point like that would almost certainly rush straight for a footballing cliché: he would quote the late Bill Shankly, manager of the great Liverpool teams of the 1960s and 70s, who said 'Some people say that football is a matter of life and death. It's not. It's more important than that.'

That is no doubt why, when I mentioned to Italian friends that I was thinking of including Juventus among my positive tales about Italy, they mostly snorted with derision. You cannot be serious, they said. Juve has had a terrible season. Yes, it is true that they bounced back from their demotion in 2006 to Serie B after the match-fixing scandal, winning that division despite starting with penalty points. Yes, in their first season back in Serie A they came third, and then second in the second season. But that's history. The only thing that matters in soccer is whether you are winning now, and at the time I was consulting my sneering Italian soccer-fan friends they were not: they came seventh in Serie A in both 2010 and 2011, which means they failed to qualify for the Champions League in either year. That is costly: the lost revenues from failing to qualify amount to at least 25 million euros each season, which is about 10 per cent of the total.

So, yes, I accept that things have not been going all that well recently for Juventus, a venerable club owned by the Fiat Group and known semi-affectionately as 'La Vecchia Signora', the Old Lady, although in the 2011–12 season the club fared much better, being at or near the top of the league. But, just as I am not really interested by Slow Food because of food and drink, it is not strictly the soccer that interests me at Juventus. It is the business model, the club's commercial approach, and especially the club's approach to its fans.

Soccer is more, I realize, than just a matter of profits and losses. But without them it is unsustainable and often unfair. That is why the new UEFA 'financial fair play' rules,[11] confirmed in 2010, will exclude from UEFA's Europa League and Champions League any club that does not at least break even, so as to avoid clubs simply being subsidised by billionaire owners. The new regime will begin in 2015 but will be phased in during the previous three seasons. The rules also put limits on investments made during the transition years.

Juventus had already adopted that policy of aiming always to break even, and so at least in principle is some way ahead of others in preparing for UEFA's rule change. Every Italian fan surely knows of the millions lost by other clubs every year, thanks to their benefactors. That era is coming to an end. Juve made a small profit in 2008/09 and in 2009/10 broke even after tax, though it made a small loss thanks to a real estate transaction. This was despite not having a very good season on the field, at least not by Juve's old standards.

In a sport in which the extraordinary cocktail of television rights and billionaires' vanity has sent players' earnings into the stratosphere, the rule of thumb is that if the cost of players exceeds 60 per cent of revenues the club will lose money. In order to avoid that, especially if you do not always qualify for the lucrative Champions League, two things are necessary: a big investment in spotting and developing young talent to avoid just buying it in at high prices; and putting fans sufficiently at the centre of the business that revenues from them are robust.

That is what Juventus has tried to do with its Primavera ('spring') youth team, which has been doing rather better in the youth competitions than the main team, and its football school. Just as important, putting the fans at the centre is what the club is trying to do by building a new stadium in Turin, which was formally inaugurated in September 2011.

British soccer was transformed during the 1990s as new stadiums were built, turning the sport from a rough and violent affair into something closer to a family experience, and creating other sources of revenue from use of the facilities when games were not being played. Italian stadiums are not as bad as the British ones of the 1980s, but they are nevertheless far from modern compared with those in the UK or Germany now. The last new stadiums to be built in Italy were constructed for the World Cup in 1990. And all of those were paid for with public money. Juventus's new stadium has been entirely privately financed, at a total cost of 175 million euros.

The new stadium is also a symbol of how things can get done in Turin at speeds that are rarely matched in other Italian cities. Despite all the familiar worries about official authorizations and building permits, and despite being a fan of Juve's arch-rival, Turin, the then Mayor Chiamparino helped the project to proceed rapidly and a scheme approved by the club's board of directors only in 2008 was begun in June 2009 and was then ready for use within two years. With design by two firms made famous for their automobile creations, among other things, Pininfarina (the inside of the stadium) and Giugiaro (the outside), Juve has made sure it is a thoroughly Italian project, one linked to the motoring history of the region, and is intended by the city to be something of a showcase for Turin.

Fast justice, Slow Food, a transformed city, a new soccer stadium: of course these are only possible in the peculiar air of Cavour's old city. Or are they? There is one other club in Serie A which is now also planning to build a new stadium, using the same architect as Juventus, and using private financing. Indeed, it is a club that finished two places higher than Juventus in Serie A in 2010. It is Città di Palermo, the club of Sicily's biggest city. So let us go there, to Italy's South, a place which brings to many northern Italian minds the lines that in Dante's poem were emblazoned at the entrance to Hell: '*Abandon hope, all ye who enter here*'.

CHAPTER 5

Hope in the South

It was only after I had handed over the money that it occurred to me. By buying a red T-shirt at the Fiera Addiopizzo (Addiopizzo Fair) as a gift for my companion, might I be subconsciously paying homage to Giuseppe Garibaldi, another visitor to Sicily from afar, who had arrived in Palermo a century and a half earlier, almost to the day? Well, red was no doubt more suitable anyway for a woman than the macho black version I was buying for myself, which was why she chose it. And we were neither invaders nor liberators, nor, despite my previous visit to Turin, collaborators with Cavour and the Savoy king. But both shirts were nonetheless modest contributions in support of a new struggle, one at least as challenging as that of Garibaldi's redshirts of the *Spedizione dei Mille*[1] in 1860. This is the struggle by young people against the mafia.

The T-shirts carried versions of the original slogan of the group of seven young friends who in 2004 had started the movement now called Addiopizzo:

UN INTERO POPOLO CHE PAGA IL PIZZO E UN POPOLO SENZA DIGNITA

Or, in rough English translation, 'A community that pays protection money is a community without dignity'. The group of friends – lawyers, doctors and others, all in their 20s – had been thinking of opening a bar together in Palermo, but it then occurred to them that they might be asked to pay protection money – *pizzo* – by local gangsters. What would they do if they were asked? Fighting the mafia as individuals is suicidal. That, certainly, is what Libero Grassi found in 1990 when he, a small clothing manufacturer in Palermo, publicly refused to pay the *pizzo*, even going on national television to explain his refusal. Shunned by a local business community who denied that the *pizzo* even existed, and given no support at all by Confindustria Sicilia, the local business confederation, this brave 67-year-old was gunned down in the street in August 1991. His crimes were to have stood up for his freedom and to have told the truth. Only in 2006 were his murderers brought to justice.

The would-be bar owners came up with a different approach, a new way to tell the truth, a new way to encourage collective action. They printed stickers carrying their slogan and, in the middle of the night, pasted them up all over the city. It caused quite a stir: no one knew who was doing it, for the stickers were anonymous and no organization had been formed. The *pizzo* was still a taboo subject, just as it had been in Libero Grassi's day. For the best part of a year, the group just kept on leaving stickers around the city, until eventually they got bolder: they put a banner in the soccer stadium saying the same thing, and then started an anonymous publication.

It is what in the internet age is known as 'viral marketing', the use of word-of-mouth, or 'buzz', to create interest and momentum, even if the Addiopizzo organizers did not really plan it that way. A movement needs some structure and purpose, however, as well as 'buzz'. So in 2005 Addiopizzo (goodbye, protection money) was set up formally as an association, with two related ideas for its agenda and purpose: to start a campaign to persuade consumers in Palermo to buy goods and services only from businesses that do not pay the *pizzo*, and to publish a list of non-paying companies.

The biggest local newspaper, *Giornale di Sicilia*, gave them two free pages to publicize their campaign of 'Consumo Critico' (critical consumers) by printing a list of 3,500 people who said they wanted to buy only '*pizzo*-free' goods. Armed with that display of support, they began going from shopkeeper to shopkeeper inviting them to join and reject the *pizzo*. By May 2006 they were able to publish their first list of *pizzo*-refuseniks, with a hundred companies. And a few days later they held their first Fiera del Consumo Critico, or Fiera Addiopizzo, for extra publicity and to put the refuseniks in touch with one another. They never got round to opening their bar, by the way.

The fair I attended, at the end of May 2010, was the fifth, and the event has expanded from one day to three, with debates and concerts as well as shopping and exhibits. It was a jolly affair, attended by quite a big crowd of people, in the grounds of Villa Trabia. Working on one of the shopping stalls was Pina Grassi, Libero's widow. A slender, dignified lady, she told me how happy she had been to hear of Addiopizzo's founding, thirteen years after her husband's murder, and how much change the new movement had brought to Palermo. But she also had a bitter comment. In three days of the fair, no one had attended from any of the governing institutions – not the city, nor the province, nor the region. The citizens, she said, are still alone. 'This government', and she meant both the national and the regional administrations, 'has done nothing against the mafia.'

It is certainly arguable that the government has done too little, though 'nothing' is a bit unfair. But I can understand Pina Grassi's bitterness. Meanwhile Addiopizzo is making its own progress, step by step. Its list of *pizzo*-refuseniks is growing by about 100 a year and had by late 2011 reached 690. It is generally accepted that about 80 per cent of Palermo businesses pay protection money. Many of the firms that first went on to Addiopizzo's public list were probably from the 20 per cent that were not being asked to pay it anyway, and have now gone public in order to deter gangsters from asking them in future. More recently, however, there has been an increase in the number of businesses reporting mafia approaches to the police and naming the gangsters. In a trial in April 2010, a mafia *pentito* (literally penitent, but essentially informer or turncoat) named Giuseppe Di Maio delighted the Consumo Critico campaigners when he was quoted as saying 'If a shopkeeper joins Addiopizzo or an anti-racket association we will not go there any more, we will not call them any more.'[2] It has become too dangerous to approach such firms, he added. There is now also an Addiopizzo association in Naples, in whose region one of the other big mafia groups, the Camorra, operates.

Addiopizzo is being greatly helped in Sicily by the existence of another charitable group, Libero Futuro, set up three years ago and named after Libero Grassi. It employs lawyers and other advisers to help companies that want to denounce extortionists, so that they need not feel alone or so vulnerable. And Libera Terra, an offshoot of a nationwide anti-mafia association originally founded in Turin in 1995 by a priest called Don Luigi Ciotti, uses confiscated land and other former mafia assets to create new legal businesses and jobs, especially by using vineyards and farms in all the southern regions, helping to increase the number of opportunities for people, especially the young, to make a living independently from organized crime.

I visited one wine cooperative founded by Libera Terra, called Centopassi. It was named after Marco Tullio Giordana's 2000 film that told the story of Peppino Impastato, a young campaigner killed by the mafia in 1978 and who lived 'cento passi', 100 steps, from his murderer in the town of Cinisi, just outside Palermo. Peppino Impastato, who used local radio and other media to campaign against the mafia, was notable, in part, because his own family had been linked to the mafia: his uncle was a local boss who had been killed in 1963. He was a rebel from the inside. Peppino's brother, Giovanni, was one of the first businessmen to join Addiopizzo's list in 2005.

These movements are now being supported by Confindustria Sicilia and, to some extent, by local businesses – unlike in Libero Grassi's day. Officially, Confindustria Sicilia is standing against the *pizzo* and ejecting from its membership any firm being found to pay it. The *pizzo* is just the tip of the mafia iceberg – it is essentially used as a tax and as a form of territorial control – but rejecting it is of high symbolic importance. In 2007, a venerable Palermo dining institution, Antica Focacceria San Francesco, hit the headlines when its proprietors not only denounced the mafiosi who first tried to take control of the restaurant and then to charge it *pizzo* but also gave testimony in open court and identified the culprits publicly.

After the two brothers who run the restaurant, Vincenzo and Fabio Conticello, took this dramatic action, you might have expected them to get plenty of support from the town. Their restaurant dates back to 1832, after all, and was even visited by Garibaldi and his redshirts in 1860. During five generations of family ownership, it had never been targeted by mafia clans until 2005, when the family inadvertently hired an ex-convict. Having got inside the restaurant, he started, in effect, to take it over, replacing its old suppliers with his own network. When the Conticellos decided he had to leave, the gangster arranged for a mafia associate to come and demand *pizzo* from the restaurant. Fortunately, the Conticellos had already contacted the Carabinieri, and two officers happened to be eating at a table nearby when the approach was made.

The successful conviction in 2007 of the would-be extorter and his two accomplices, coupled with long prison sentences did, it seems, help to encourage other businesses to denounce extorters or to join Addiopizzo's list. When one of the Conticello brothers was interviewed about the case on (state broadcasting) RAI's TG1 evening television news by its then director, Gianni Riotta (a Palermitano), President Giorgio Napolitano telephoned TG1 afterwards to say how moved he had been by the interview. In September 2011, President Napolitano also met, during a visit to Palermo, a group of anti-*pizzo* campaigners, adding his growing lustre and reputation to the cause.

Yet despite such national support, life was certainly not easy for the Conticellos or their restaurant. They had to have twenty-four-hour police protection for three years. During the trial, seven of their workers resigned, including three cooks. And use of the restaurant by Palermitanos declined for two to three years, possibly out of fear, possibly out of disapproval. Support, Fabio Conticello told me over dinner at Antica Focacceria, came chiefly from younger people, especially students, and, often unknowingly, from tourists. Only by 2010, when I dined there, was business back to a more or less normal level. Even so, Mr Conticello says he is preparing options in case the mafia take revenge or renew their pressure: he is opening a branch in Milan, and is willing (reluctantly) to move there himself if he has to.

Revolutionaries of normality

Yet that would not necessarily be an escape from organized crime: Milan, according to Aldo Pecora, president of Ammazzateci Tutti, another anti-mafia association, is now the true headquarters or at least main stronghold of the Calabrian mafia, the 'Ndrangheta, which prosecutors say is the most powerful of all Italy's four main organized crime groups – stronger than the Cosa Nostra in Sicily, stronger even than the Camorra in Naples, made internationally infamous by Roberto Saviano's book *Gomorra*,[3] much stronger than the small Sacre Corona Unita in Puglia. That power and the strength of the 'Ndrangheta in Lombardy was confirmed by the dramatic arrests on 13 July 2010 of 305 alleged 'Ndrangheta mafiosi, including a man said to be their boss of bosses – with more of the arrests being made in Genoa, Turin, Milan and elsewhere in the North than back home in Reggio Calabria. All of the mafia groups exercise their territorial control by methods such as the *pizzo*, but make their real earnings in vastly more profitable ways, including drug-dealing, the construction and waste management businesses, illegal sweatshop production of textiles and garments, smuggling, and sundry other trades. They are not just national but international businesses.

These strugglers against the mafia – Saviano, Pecora and the founders of Addiopizzo – also have something in common, something particularly heartening. It is that they are all young. Roberto Saviano was 27 when he published *Gomorra* in 2006. The Addiopizzo founders were all between 26 and 30 when they started printing their stickers in 2004. And when Aldo Pecora founded Ammazzateci Tutti in Reggio Calabria in 2005 he was barely 21 years old.

The full slogan, and name, of his association[4] is 'E Adesso Ammazzateci Tutti', or 'Now kill us all', and it was the first group to use the internet as one of its main means to encourage young people to collaborate with one another in the fight against the mafia. It was founded as a more or less spontaneous reaction to the murder on 16 October 2005 by the 'Ndrangheta of Francesco Fortugno, a vice-president of the regional council of Calabria who was investigating mafia involvement in health-care contracts. He was the twenty-fourth 'Ndrangheta victim that year. At the funeral in Locri, in the suburbs of Reggio Calabria, some boys unfurled a banner proclaiming the slogan that one of them, Aldo Pecora, had written. Soon, the group had 2,000 members, mainly students aged between 15 and 20. A few weeks later, they organized a demonstration attended by more than 15,000 people. Now, more than six years on, Ammazzateci Tutti is a nationwide organization with 100 core organizers, with 500 coordinators at regional level and 8,000 members in all.

All of Italy's mafias continue to thrive and even grow, and are not going to be defeated either by demonstrations or by the arrests of some of their members and leaders. But these movements are important nevertheless, because if they themselves can survive and thrive, they will gradually undermine some of the basis for organized crime.

Paolo Borsellino, the judge who was assassinated in Sicily by the mafia shortly after his colleague Giovanni Falcone in 1992, once said that 'If the youth refuse their consent, even the almighty mafia will vanish like a nightmare.'

It is on that inspiring idea that Ammazzateci Tutti has focused, gathering together the young and sending them into schools, especially in Calabria, to talk about the 'Ndrangheta, about freedom, and especially about the importance of the rule of law, as often as possible taking with them witnesses who have denounced the mafia in trials. They are seeking to be, in Aldo Pecora's words, 'the revolutionaries of normality', for in Italy, he says, 'normality is revolutionary'. These revolutionaries do not, however, take any public money, as they 'want to be free'.

Each August they hold a three-day event in Reggio Calabria called 'LegalItalia', attracting primarily young members, journalists, lawyers and others from all over the country to discuss the rule of law and the fight against the mafia. It opens on the anniversary of the killing in Calabria of Antonino Scopelliti, an anti-mafia judge who struggled against pro-mafia bias inside the judiciary itself, on 9 August 1991, the same month that saw Libero Grassi murdered. All this sounds potentially political, and in a sense it is; but one thing that my conversation with Aldo Pecora made clear was that, as a young activist, he is deeply opposed to judges themselves going into politics. He had, he told me, been having a big argument about exactly this point with a judge who has now become a Member of the European Parliament. Judges, in his view, do their most valuable work in the courtroom, not in parliament. I must admit that I agree with him.

One important thing that Aldo Pecora has learned personally is that collective action is a lot safer than the individual sort. In Calabria, anti-mafia campaigning still draws local hostility. He told me that initially his work with Ammazzateci Tutti caused him no problems with the 'Ndrangheta, who ignored the group. As he has become better known as the organization's president, however, things have changed. His car tyres were slashed at his home in Reggio Calabria, and later the wing mirrors were removed, as a sort of metaphorical warning that there is nothing to protect him. He says that most local people seem to hate him, many treating him as an enemy. But things got even worse when he worked as a journalist on a local paper, *Calabria Ora*, and began to investigate links between the 'Ndrangheta, freemasonry and journalists, including some on his own newspaper.

He says that out of the blue he received a phone call at 1.00 a.m. from an uncomfortably senior executive from his newspaper, a man to whom he had never previously spoken. Professing admiration for his work, the caller offered him a job on a new venture the firm was starting, while also telling him a long story about how he needed protection. Believing this was at best an attempt to buy his silence, at worst a threat, Aldo Pecora quit his job and moved to Rome to study. That is why when I interviewed him we met in Rome, not in Reggio Calabria.

Mr Pecora, who is a very eager, strong-looking and idealistic young man, told me about another frightening experience which happened shortly after he had moved to Rome. On 5 March 2008, he was driving south from Rome, along the autostrada near Naples, when he was overtaken by a fast car which cut sharply in front of him. Then it fell back and soon afterwards cut in front of him again. As he was leaving a tunnel it did so for a third time, forcing him to skid and causing a big accident. Aldo was in hospital for a week. He has now concluded, understandably, that investigating mafia crimes is a job for judges and not for a 25-year-old.

Buying their own paper

When, as a middle-aged journalist, you go round inter-
viewing young people, especially at Sunday fairs in
Palermo at the end of May, you expect to find them
wearing jeans and T-shirts. Sitting cross-legged on the
ground, trying to look comfortable while actually in pain,
and trying in such awkward conditions to write notes that
will still be legible when you get home: well, that is all part
of what we journalists call 'colour'. However, when you
visit judges and prosecutors, and find them also clad in
jeans and T-shirts, working in small, crowded offices piled
high with paper, that is not 'colour' but information. More
information also comes from seeing the Carabinieri
guarding every door, the video cameras checking on visitors outside each office, and the two-man police escort
who drove me and Judge Antonio Balsamo from the windy
basketball court where we had begun our conversation to
a quieter and more comfortable local café.

And what information did all this convey? That, quite
rightly, a lot of public resources go into keeping anti-mafia
judges and prosecutors alive but, unfortunately, too little
money goes into ensuring that they can do properly the
job that Mr Pecora rightly thinks is theirs to do. This is
slowing down or even endangering the undoubted progress
that is being made in fighting the mafia.

One of the surprisingly informal but still beleaguered-
looking public prosecutors that I met was Mrs Lia Sava in
Palermo. She has been in the city for the past thirteen
years, having previously worked as a prosecutor in Brindisi
(a port city in Puglia, Italy's heel), and before that she sat

as a judge in Rome. In some ways, she said, her task has indeed become easier, thanks to the growing public support for the magistrates on the island. Instead of jeering during arrests of mafiosi, police and prosecutors are now as likely to be greeted by applause.

The day before we met, one mafioso had been denounced by a business he was targeting, and in other cases an impressive 150 million euros worth of mafia assets had recently been confiscated. The judiciary's own efforts in schools, talking to children about legality and the mafia along the same lines as those of Ammazzateci Tutti mentioned earlier, are paying off, she said. Mrs Sava cited the case in 2004 of Carmela Rosaria Iuculano, a wife who was persuaded to give testimony against her husband, Pino Rizzo, and his brother, by their daughter, who had come home from school saying how ashamed she was at not being able to write the anti-mafia essay assigned to the class by her teacher. Now, Carmela Iuculano is under police protection and her daughter has gone to university.

But – and there is always a big 'but' – Mrs Sava told me of how the prosecutors' and judges' jobs is made much harder by a shortage of resources. She says they have no money to buy petrol to go outside Palermo, have to buy their own paper and notebooks, and have no money even to have hearings transcribed. As in other parts of Italy, justice itself is not computerized, and anyway the computer I saw in her office was a very old model. She carries her own files to hearings as she often has no administrative clerk. Everyone thinks they need or deserve more resources, of course. But it is clear that Palermo is short of both judges and prosecutors, as well as the resources for them to do their jobs. This is, to say the least, surprising given the supposed importance of the fight against organized crime, both for the nation and the region. Let us be frank: money is short for all public services at present, given the pressure of Italy's huge public debts and the lack of help from its slow rate of growth; but also there are plenty of politicians, at both local and national level, who do not want the judges and prosecutors to be too successful in punishing the mafia. There is a lot of what Italians call *connivenza*, which in English would be complicity or connivance.

Antonio Balsamo, a senior anti-mafia judge, was rather more smartly dressed when we met; he was also under police protection. The reason we sat at first on a windy basketball court was because we met away from his office, at the oratorio where later that evening he was attending a service. I appreciated Judge Balsamo's willingness to talk to me regardless of comfort and convenience, which would not be true of many judges in London, who tend to be rather self-important. I also appreciated the lift given by his police escorts from the basketball court to a nearby café, since to this nervy outsider it felt a bit safer than simply chatting in the open air or walking to the café.

Judge Balsamo still sounded beleaguered, however. A member of the board of the National Magistrates Association, which is in effect the judges' trade union, he said that recent years had been very difficult for the judiciary, a moment when their independence and legitimacy was being threatened– by which I took him to mean the assaults on the judiciary's motives and methods that came from the Berlusconi governments in 2001–06 and

2008–11, the challenges to judicial independence. Some of those assaults have caused direct damage to anti-mafia investigations, in particular a change in the law preventing the use of previous statements by witnesses as evidence in trials. A law to control phone interceptions, the 'Legge Bavaglio' (Bavaglio Law), was a big threat to anti-mafia investigations, until its provisions were watered down in 2010.

'A large majority of Italian judges', Judge Balsamo said, 'agree that judges should be non-political.' Meanwhile, what has been under way, in his view, is a 'delegitimization of the judiciary'. It all reminded him, he said sadly, of the efforts used during the 1980s by many establishment figures against the anti-mafia pool led by Giovanni Falcone and Paolo Borsellino. Now, with the arrival of the Monti government, at least the head-on assault can be said to be over. But it might equally just prove to be a ceasefire.

The shaking of consent

In 1991, when Libero Grassi went on national television, on *Samarcanda*, Michele Santoro's then-show on the public television channel RAI 3, his words were calm, brave but also moving and direct. He said:

> Legal supremacy, political supremacy, moral supremacy … but above all supremacy over consent, that is the true weapon of the mafia. Moral values, dear judges, are transient, they form themselves, but no law is valid forever. Politicians make the laws, but they do so by reference to consent. If the consent is bad, the laws will

be bad. So now we must take care of, concentrate on, the quality of the consent...[5]

In his day, the consent that allowed organized crime to flourish and dominate Sicily was the consent of the young, which Paolo Borsellino emphasized, the consent of politicians, both national and local, but also the consent of businesses. The silence of Confindustria Sicilia was one of the forces that signed Grassi's death warrant.

How much has changed in the past twenty years? To try to get an idea, I went to the home of Rita Borsellino, sister of the murdered Paolo, now a member of the European Parliament, and sat with her on her porch. Her encouraging view is that since the killings of her brother, of Giovanni Falcone and of their accompanying guards in 1992 a lot has indeed changed. The strong popular reaction shown then against the mafia has proved to be durable. The activities of Libera since 1995 (when she co-founded it, in effect, with Don Luigi Ciotti) and, in the past six years, of Addiopizzo and Ammazzateci Tutti have had a big impact and do represent a cultural change, especially among the young, who are now able and willing to create their own networks to exert pressure or just to get things done.

The problem, however, is that there has been too little sustained support from political institutions, she said, which are still characterized by connivance and clientelism. 'Sicily,' she said, perhaps being loyal to her island, 'was always against the mafia, but the problem was that it was alone. The mafia had the support of political forces and of business.' Some of that has changed, but efforts against the mafia have not been continuous, said Mrs Borsellino.

There are impressive and successful blitzes such as the 305 'Ndrangheta arrests in northern Italy in July 2010, but there has not been enough of a broad, sustained effort by government institutions. Too often, politics has returned to connivance. And the present government has 'made the work of the judiciary more difficult, for example by relaxing legal provisions that had prevented communication by jailed mafiosi with their clans outside'.

Giovanni Impastato, Peppino's brother, told me much the same thing: in his view the anti-mafia investigations and the pressure from groups such as Addiopizzo have improved things, but have also led the mafia to change, become more bourgeois, more intertwined with professions such as lawyers, doctors and engineers, and always much more intertwined with politics.

Local glimmers of political hope

One potentially positive political development, according to Mrs Borsellino, is the emergence of independent, non-party candidates in municipal elections in Sicily, who are beginning to break the old party grip of local politics. In June 2010 the commune of Pollina elected Sicily's youngest ever mayor, Magda Culotta, a 25-year-old, on an independent centre-left list. This is not the first time this trend has happened: when Peppino Impastato was killed in 1978 he was a candidate for a city council seat for a similarly non-party list. And when direct election of mayors was introduced nationally in 1993, many young women and other outsiders were elected, before the mafia hit back with threats, and before some popular fatigue set in and the old party-dominated politics came back. But, with young people now actively getting organized outside the old political groupings to fight the mafia, the trend might have a better chance to spread.

On a bigger scale, in the other mafia-plagued regions of the South, there has also been the emergence of city mayors who are relatively independent of the political parties. Vincenzo De Luca in Salerno (Campania) and Michele Emiliano in Bari (Puglia) were two I encountered. Both are nominally members of the centre-left Democratic Party, but both are highly critical of it and pretty independent minded. Both have cleaned up town centres that for decades were riddled with crime and unsafe to enter, especially after dark, and as a result are seeing the rebirth of their cities as tourist attractions, as cultural centres and as places in which citizens again want to live. I was captivated by the old historic town and the waterfront of Bari; a decade or two ago, I might well have been hospitalized if I had walked through there at night.

Both men, like Mayors Castellani and Chiamparino in Turin, are essentially managerial figures rather than ideological ones. Salerno, just 40 minutes by car from the garbage disaster that is Naples, is now Italy's top town for recycling: Mayor De Luca claims that 75 per cent of the total rubbish collection is recycled, and his town is working on infrastructure to deal with composted waste too.

On asking a nominally centre-left mayor about how he had handled a different sort of garbage – gangsters and other criminals – it was a bit shocking, I must confess, to hear Mr De Luca respond approvingly with the word 'repressione', or repression: 'We are the only centre-left reality where the word "order" is not feared,' he added. The fact that he said this in his large office in the City Hall of Salerno, a rather impressive Art Deco building built during the Mussolini era, made his tough approach feel even more unnerving. Nevertheless, Salerno certainly looks a happier place for it, and will be even happier once the large, noisy and ugly container port right in the middle of town is moved around the bay during the next few years. Mayor De Luca wants Salerno's waterfront to be like Barcelona's, he says, and certainly he has a better chance than Turin of achieving that, and of attracting many more tourists.

In Bari Mayor Emiliano, a big bear of a man, is a former anti-mafia prosecutor, so he already knew a thing or two about battling against criminals. As in Sicily, he has invested in schools programmes to try to persuade kids not to join the mafia clans. Like Mayor De Luca, he talks a lot about efficiency: he claims that municipal costs in Bari are 30 per cent lower than the average for Italian towns, and cites proudly a survey in the *il Sole 24 Ore* business daily that ranked Bari highly for its municipal administration. Where Mayor De Luca has stayed well clear of the national Democratic Party, considering them basically to be political dinosaurs, Mayor Emiliano cuddled up to them when he ran for a second term, having previously bragged of his independence: he needed their protection, he says, though he plainly does not think much of them as national politicians.

Nichi Vendola, a real southern anomaly

Protection from whom? Well, Mayor Emiliano didn't quite say, but I took him to mean from Nichi Vendola, his local rival and the man who, as regional governor of Puglia, has also achieved quite surprising results. His results are surprising in part because Mr Vendola is such an unusual character to be running a southern region, being a homosexual former communist who is also a devout Catholic.

With help from his regional government, Puglia outpaced its southern neighbours in terms of economic growth and the reduction of unemployment in the three years (2005–08) until the global economic crisis intervened – though not by as much as Mr Vendola likes to claim, of course. And not all the results are good: Puglia has, in particular, suffered from huge financial deficits in its health system.

So what is special about 'Nichi', this poet who hopes to be one of the next great personalities in Italian politics? In practice, it is, first, that he won on two occasions, in 2005 and 2010, against opposition from the old dinosaurs of the Democratic Party, who in a sane form of left-wing politics would have been his supporters. Second, it is his charismatic appeal. Plainly, he is one of the few Italian politicians who has the oratorical ability and the imagination to be able to mobilize mass support, rather in the style of Barack Obama – or, dare it be said, Silvio Berlusconi. He is not 'the Italian Obama' in terms of having similar policy ideas, and he will find it hard – probably impossible – to build broad coalitions in the manner of Mr Berlusconi. But he can carry that title for being, like President Obama, the sort of outsider, from an often suppressed minority, who is capable of creating the sort of dreams and enthusiasms among both young and old in Italy that Mr Obama did in America during 2008.

So I was intrigued to be able to visit Mr Vendola in his beautiful Bari office, looking out to sea. Unexpectedly, for someone of his background and popular appeal, he was very smartly dressed, in a dark suit and tie. As I walked in to his office, three images immediately caught my eye: the photograph of President Napolitano, of course; but then a religious icon on the shelf just behind the governor's desk; and, third, a prominent photograph of Mr Vendola meeting the Pope.

Our meeting was less a conversation than a speech by Mr Vendola. In response to my opening question, his answer essentially took up the next 90 minutes. He began this piece of oratory by explaining why Puglia had, historically, been very different from the rest of the South: it had 'no parasitical ruling class', unlike Sicily; unlike Campania it had not been dominated by Hispanic influence which had 'put corruption in the DNA'; unlike Calabria, it had not been 'feudal'; power was 'not built on organized crime', unlike in those other regions. Instead, Puglia was more 'Levantine in its spirit', more international, much fuller of curiosity and openness. 'In a way,' he said, it is 'the Lombardy of the South'.

Well, perhaps, I thought, but in that case why has it remained so poor for so long – even if not as poor as Calabria? Being a politician, Mr Vendola's answer was, in effect, that this was because he had not been in charge until recently. Puglia had all that potential, all those virtuous traditions, but the politicians had forgotten about them. So Mr Vendola's team had to revive or invent them all over again. His vision, he said, was for a Puglia that 'is not afraid of globalization; is curious about China rather than fearful of it; that welcomes people rather than being xenophobic; that is a laboratory of social reform'.

That is certainly a vision that appeals to me personally, as a convinced globalist. Mr Vendola's speech also implied that he has largely reconciled himself to capitalism as a necessary support for his social objectives. He divided his approach into the need to deal with Puglia's three big weaknesses: social fragility; economic fragility; and environmental fragility. His social language was intelligent – about seeing people not as problems but as resources, whether they are immigrants, the disabled, women, unmarried couples or the poor, and about reallocating resources in order to help them in new ways. Those ways, he said, should not follow the right-wing approach of offering 'the minimum', nor the old 'paternalist' style of the left. Still, it costs money: social spending per citizen has been raised sharply from 2 euros per head in 2005 to 20 euros per head this year.

To pay for that, Puglia would need a rather stronger economy than it has. Acknowledging this reality, Mr Vendola talked about boosting broadband internet access and about big infrastructure investments in railways, seaports and airports – in 2005, Puglia had only one properly functioning airport, he said, the one in Bari, but now had four (or at least, four in preparation) in Bari, Brindisi, Foggia and Grottaglie-Taranto. This will be very helpful in boosting Puglia's already impressive record in tourism, in which in 2011 it became Italy's most visited region.

Recognizing the fragmented nature of Puglia's companies, 95 per cent of which have less than ten employees, Mr Vendola also talked about encouraging mergers between small firms to help them cope better with international markets and competition, about boosting industrial clusters of related firms, about special efforts to encourage creative industries such as film, music and the arts, and getting government out of the way of their progress. Except, of course, with his third Pugliese fragility, the environment, which is one of his signature national issues too: he has created fifteen new protected 'regional parks' since 2005, claims to have tightened pollution controls on heavy industry, notably the steel plants in Taranto, and has pushed hard for national investments in solar and wind power. The Taranto steel plant achievement must, however, be viewed rather sceptically, since magistrates in that city counter-claimed in 2011-12 through a study by independent chemists that the ILVA steelworks is poisoning its neighbourhood with dioxins and other pollutants. Noting the failure of politicians and official agencies to force ILVA's owner, the Riva Group, to clean up the pollution and to compensate the victims, magistrates opened a major case against the firm in February 2012.

Overall, the speech was encouraging – though for each area of regional government spending or of the solicitation of national and European funds my antennae started twitching at the thought of potential corruption and clientelism, as well as waste. Moreover, I remain unconvinced about how far Mr Vendola's conversion towards capitalism and globalization has really gone. Since our interview in mid 2010 he has taken a strongly pro-union and anti-business position on a number of issues, placing himself firmly on the left rather than staking a real claim to the centre of politics. The party he has formed, Sinistra, Ecologia, Libertà (Left, ecology, freedom) is positioned to the left of the Democratic Party (PD), while seemingly being willing to join a coalition led by the PD. Yet one last note of encouragement, for now, is that when I asked the president of Confindustria Puglia, Alessandro Laterza, what his main worry about Mr Vendola was, he said this: his worry was 'that Mr Vendola might now focus too much on his national ambitions and neglect his own region'. I can think of plenty of businessmen, especially in the South, who would be only too happy to be neglected by their regional governors.

Needed, a business revolution

The rise of more mayors like Mr De Luca and Mr Emiliano, in more towns in the South, would be a hugely positive sign, as would the spread of pro-capitalist sentiment among more regional governors like Mr Vendola. Pending that, however, the most notable change, alongside the youth movements, has been the change in business, especially in Confindustria Sicilia.

Where that institution was silent about the mafia in 1991, it is now vocal. It condemns payment of the *pizzo*, seeks to expel from the employers' association any firm proven to be paying it and, in the words of Ivan Hoe Lobello, president of Confindustria Sicilia, is working to break down the social bonds between mafia, business and politics. Mr Lobello describes the work of Addiopizzo as 'revolutionary', partly because young people are now organizing themselves in a new way, but partly too because the battle has shifted from morality to economics – which is a field on which Confindustria can also fight.

This, though, also reflects a broader change. In the 1980s and early 1990s, the chairmen of all the nine provincial associations that make up Confindustria Sicilia, as well as of the regional federation, were either from construction companies or were in the public sector. The economy of Sicily, like those of Calabria and Campania, was dominated in the 1960s, 70s and 80s by state money and state companies, especially by spending on public works schemes, by urban development in the bigger centres such as Palermo and Catania, with no rules and no planning, and by big capital-intensive state-run projects such as oil refineries and petrochemicals plants. Such gigantic projects, typical of regional development schemes all over Europe in those decades, produced few jobs once the installations had been built, but a large flow of cash. There are no prizes for guessing which groups got their hands on much of that cash.

This era of abundance is long gone. Where once capital spending on buildings, roads and other infrastructure acted as the main financial fuel for the private sector and for Cosa Nostra, now 98 per cent of the Sicily regional government budget is taken up by current spending, chiefly on salaries. In the 1970s, only 40 per cent was current spending and 60 per cent went on capital projects. This still leaves the economy disproportionately dependent on public money, however: more than 30 per cent of the island's annual GDP comes from state spending, says Mr Lobello, compared with 13.5 per cent in Lombardia. If you add state investments in private companies, the figure rises to 40 per cent. 'We have a little socialist republic in Sicily,' he says.

It is the same in Calabria and Campania, though less true in Puglia or Basilicata. An essentially parasitical economic model, one hostile to the market, has been created, in which politicians, mafia, trade unions and businesses collude to build monopolies, to rescue friends and supporters, and to draw an income from the public purse, all in effect regulated by the mafia. It is rigid as well as being short-sighted. Old practices die hard. Palermo, for example, now has a garbage crisis matching that in Naples in 2008: the company responsible is bankrupt, rubbish is piling up in the streets. So what do the politicians do? They employ 2,000 more people in the garbage company, to absorb unemployment and to help their supporters, despite the fact that this has made the garbage firm even less financially viable and has no impact on clearance of the waste. In Puglia, Nichi Vendola described this sort of system to me, the state system of the South, as 'Brezhnevismo', conjuring up the doomed conduct of the former Soviet Union. His candour and realism were refreshing.

Mr Lobello has no doubt that the 'socialist republic' of the South is changing, and has been ever since the national financial crisis of the early 1990s started to cut the flow of cash. Businessmen in Sicily increasingly accept, he says, that the market is their future, rather than the state. In fact, they realize that they have a great conflict of interests with the state, because they want less interference and parasitism, and more spending on infrastructure, education, research and development and rule-enforcing services such as civil justice.

The past problem for the state is that parasitism and such spending have gone together. The future problem is that the state's money has run out. A popular remedy for these public sector problems, especially among voters for the Northern League, has been fiscal federalism: making southern regions more responsible for raising their own taxes and thus for keeping their own spending efficient. At least as far as Sicily and Sardinia are concerned, this is likely to be beside the point. Their special status under the 1947 Constitution already gives them full control over all the VAT and income taxes paid on their islands, but that hasn't obviously provided a great incentive to be responsible.

In any case, however, money is not really the issue, even if theft or the waste of it naturally causes great anger. It is really the same issue as is being argued about on a global scale with overseas aid: there is no country, anywhere on the planet, which has achieved economic development chiefly thanks to receiving aid money. Economic development, whether in South Korea, China, India, Ireland, Sicily or Calabria, is not a matter of how much money you have or are given: it is really a matter of how money is used, the quality of institutions, the incentives and opportunities for citizens, whether the policy environment is disciplined and dependable, the property rights people have.

Ireland is a good European example: it joined the European Union in 1973, but wasted ten to fifteen years of European funds through its own fiscal profligacy. By the early 1980s, its government was more or less bankrupt. Only from the late 1980s onwards, once its own governing institutions became more efficient and less profligate, did it achieve rapid growth. European funds for infrastructure helped facilitate that growth but did not cause it.

The Bank of Italy held a big conference about the problems of the South, also known as the Mezzogiorno, in November 2009.[6] As its then governor, Mario Draghi, said in his opening address, the fact that the South continues to lag well behind the Centre and the North in the provision of essential services for citizens and firms is not caused by a lack of spending. 'In many cases – a typical example is health – the gap clearly depends on the lower efficiency of the service rendered.' Very similar inputs of public spending, measured as spending per head of the population, produce much worse results in the Mezzogiorno than they do in Lombardy, Tuscany or the Veneto: much slower justice, worse educational test scores, worse health care, worse public services.

Consequently, it is not at all obvious that giving more responsibility to local and regional governments who now use the money badly will make them use it more efficiently in the future. Scarcity might have some good effect, but it cannot be relied on by itself. Nor, as Governor Draghi said, does the solution lie in more special regional development policies initiated from Rome, since those too have failed in the past. The focus, he went on to say, 'should above all be on general policies, whose objectives concern the entire country, and on the local conditions that make their application more difficult or less effective in certain areas'.

In other words, national programmes for education, health and justice – which are the most critical ones anyway for the region – should include measures and requirements to ensure that they are implemented properly in the South, including corrective mechanisms to be used when they are not. Such an approach implies more central control and interference, not less, albeit through rules, measures and sanctions rather than simple flows of cash.

That is easier to say than to do. But it must be the right approach. As Governor Draghi pointed out, regional grants are in any case far smaller than the spending devoted to national public programmes: just 5 per cent of the money flowing to the South. So it makes much more sense to focus on making the 95 per cent of public spending more effective than to play around with the 5 per cent.

In what promises to be a coming decade of fiscal austerity, of cutbacks in public spending all through the nation, the South will be hit especially hard because of its greater dependence on the public sector for jobs and output. Mr Lobello fears that this will bring about an 'implosion of the economic and social system'.

Bad Sicily, Good Sicily

I heard the same fear when I visited the grand old man of industrial development in Sicily, Domenico 'Mimi' La Cavera, who at 95 years old had lost none of his passion and anger.[7] Mr La Cavera was a farmer's son and former public official who then worked in Sicilian industry in the early 1950s, and began a long campaign to try to secure regional and national policies that would favour local entrepreneurship, rather than the old, statist policies of the past.

In his early 40s Mr La Cavera did the job Mr Lobello does now, as president of Confindustria Sicilia; he and the island's spurt of growth in the 1950s even prompted an article in *Time* magazine in December 1957 headlined 'Success in Sicily'.[8] It reported that 'long-neglected Sicily has suddenly started racing ahead far faster than the rest of Italy – or for that matter almost any other part of Europe'. Mr La Cavera, then 41 and described nicely as 'slim and dynamic', was quoted by *Time* as saying that 'My heart beats with joy. I am vibrating with enthusiasm.'

As history shows, the subsequent fifty years have been as much heart-breaking as heart-beating. Still, let us be clear: although the gap between Sicily and the rest of Italy has remained disappointingly wide, Sicily itself, like the rest of the Mezzogiorno, has become hugely better off in the intervening period.

I naturally asked Mr La Cavera how he thought things were now on his beloved island, fifty-three years later. He had some good words to say about Mr Lobello, and about Confindustria Sicilia's attitude today. But he was still angry, about many things. After railing at Confindustria Sicilia's past follies, especially its silence over Libero Grassi, railing at the island's return to statism and neglect of the market over that half century, railing too at what he saw as the Berlusconi government's attitude towards the mafia and the judiciary, Mr La Cavera paused, as if for dramatic effect. Then he resumed: this is, he told me, 'the worst period for the island' that he can remember.

Can this really be true? I have seen so much of the Good Sicily, fighting to push back the Bad Sicily. I have seen the greater optimism of Puglia, the feeling there among businesspeople such as Mr Laterza that progress is being made. I have felt the desire of young people to refuse their consent to the mafia, the understanding among businesspeople such as Mr Lobello that Puglia's example needs to be followed, that the market now is the path that needs to be followed, not the state.

Mimi La Cavera can be forgiven for his pessimism, for it was based on a lifetime spent in his native Sicily, struggling to run his businesses successfully but also struggling to encourage his island and the rest of the South to develop more rapidly. In that 1957 article in *Time* magazine, after all, he was quoted as saying that 'All it takes is will and work, intelligence and initiative. In ten years, we'll catch up with the rest of Italy and then we'll push ahead.' He knew whereof what he was speaking. The same cannot always be said of northerners and even national government officials when they speak of the South. They use it, essentially, as an excuse for failings elsewhere.

The clearest example that I know of that habit came from a very senior official at the Italian Treasury, who I cannot name because the statement I am about to quote was made 'off the record' at a seminar for British journalists held in Venice in January 2011. His statement, however, found its way into an article on the Italian economy in the magazine of which I was once editor-in-chief, *The Economist*, so it naturally caught my attention. He told the journalists (one of whom was the European editor of *The Economist*, John Peet, who took notes and is my source for this story) that the Italian economy could be summarized as consisting of the North, which grows by 3 per cent a year, and the South, which shrinks by 2 per cent a year, producing the apparently weak annual average growth rate of about 1 per cent.

This statement is nonsense on every level, but it is damaging, distracting nonsense too. It is nonsense in mathematical terms: since the South has a smaller GDP than the North (24 per cent of the national total, against 76 per cent in the Centre and North) it would take much more than a 2 per cent annual shrinkage to neutralize the national effect of 3 per cent growth in the North. But it is also nonsense in factual terms: during the past decade, the South's GDP has shrunk only twice: by a tiny amount in 2003, and then in 2008–09 it actually shrank by less than the North did[9]. In no year of the past decade did the Centre and North grow by more than 2 per cent. (Italy, by the way, is not easily divided into North and South for there is a centre too, which includes Tuscany, Umbria, the Marche and Lazio, among other regions, so the normal way to divide the country statistically is between the Centre–North and South.)

Now, this is not to deny, for one moment, that the South is a problem. Its economic growth ought in fact to be faster than that of the North, since its labour costs are lower and it has so much room to catch up. Over the past forty years, especially, the economic performance of the South has been disappointing: while GDP per head in the South had risen gradually to become 67 per cent of that in the Centre–North by 1971, up from half in 1951, it then slipped back to 58 per cent by 2001 before narrowing the gap a little during the ensuing decade. But northerners often overstate the South's failure nonetheless, in order to avoid paying too much attention to the slow rate of growth in the Centre and North of Italy, to all the obstacles that block growth, to the responsibility for the country's huge public debts that come from public spending for the bulk of the population, that is, in the Centre and North, rather than in the South.

Local glimmers of corporate hope

Still, the South must be seen as a failure, in recent decades, both of public policy and of private enterprise. The sense of that combined failure no doubt explains why Diego Planeta, one of Sicily's most successful entrepreneurs, also voiced pessimism to me when we met. But it still came as a blow when he did. There we were, near Menfi in the south-west of Sicily, sitting on an idyllic sun-dappled terrace, looking out at vineyards and the occasional gently turning wind turbine, and this sprightly septuagenarian had just invited me to lunch. For a moment, it had been hard to imagine that life could be any better than this. But I suppose it was my fault. I asked him what was going to happen in Sicily now that public money is getting scarce.

'There will be a revolution,' he said, quick as a flash. It was a prediction laced with a clear, bitter contempt for all the politicians on the island. For years, in his view, politicians have governed simply by buying the next election. The regional governments, he said, 'have been terrible for more than ten years, and today's is the worst of all', having changed its agriculture minister three times in the past year, with none of them knowing anything at all about agriculture. What's next?, I asked, slightly dreading the answer. 'Misery, a misery that will affect us all,' said Mr Planeta. And this was a year before the financial crisis surrounding both Italy and the euro became truly manifest, and before it became clear that public spending cuts and other austerity measures were going to be necessary, for many years to come.

This was not a very cheerful start to our conversation. Had it taken place in the evening, I imagine he might have added 'have another grappa', to comfort me. And yet the story of Planeta itself is extremely cheerful, inspiring even. So I forgave him rather quickly for forcing us to encounter the harsh reality outside.

Diego Planeta is the creator and driving force of one of the island's most successful wine-makers and president of the Settesoli wine cooperative, which is Europe's biggest co-op and, if you add together all its members, an employer of 20,000 people on 6,000 hectares of vineyards. The Planeta story shows how a private company can exploit one of the great potential assets of the South, namely its land and its viticultural productivity; it shows how the brand of Sicily can be shaped and exploited internationally; it shows how an initially small Sicilian firm can operate successfully in international markets; and it shows how Sicilian wines can be sold at premium prices, with a premium brand. Planeta provides an example that could be followed by many more private entrepreneurs, in many industries.

It even made me think: yes, there could be a revolution in Sicily, not a nasty, bloody one but a commercial revolution, a revolution of the market. Rather than a comforting grappa, it seemed more fitting to raise a glass of Planeta Chardonnay to toast that optimistic thought, which we indeed did over lunch.

The viticultural revolution that Mr Planeta led was launched in 1985, but as wine requires long-term investments it got under way really only in the 1990s. His family owned land and farms, which produced grapes among other things. Sicily had long been a big producer of grapes but had mainly sold them in bulk through traders in Marsala on the island's western coast. The population of Menfi, the village near where we met, had grown and shrunk according to the vagaries of that business: 13,000 in 1900; 9,000 in 1939; 12,000 again in the mid 1950s; but then, as the big Marsala trading houses started to collapse, 3,000 people emigrated in the mid 1960s. The first response to that was the Settesoli cooperative, of which Mr Planeta became president in 1972. His second response was the first Planeta winery in 1985.

It was a period when the global market for wine was changing rapidly, with new technology, new varieties of grapes, and a wave of new competition for European wines from Australia, New Zealand, Chile and California. Sicily, however, was poorly placed to respond to those changes, with parochial attitudes, a tradition of low-priced bulk sales reinforced by European production subsidies, and a viticulture dependent on oenologists from northern Italy or from France where the climate and soils were very different from those of the island.

What Mr Planeta brought was two things: a very international view and a modern, businesslike approach. The international view arose in part because he had travelled a lot as a young man, even marrying an Englishwoman. It was reflected in what he describes as a stroke of luck – the fact that he had heard of a first-class Italian oenologist from Piedmont who had been working in Australia for fifteen years and who thus had experience of the sort of hot, dry conditions typical of Sicily. Most vineyards in Sicily had hitherto used wine-makers familiar with more northerly regions such as Tuscany, the Veneto or even Bordeaux. Mr Planeta flew to Australia and hired Carlo Corino to come to develop the Planeta vineyards and wine-making. And later this international perspective was implemented using modern market research to see how Sicilian wines might best be positioned and sold abroad.

What the research, which was conducted in several countries but in particular in Britain, showed was that Sicily was one of only two Italian regions that was then widely recognized abroad (the other was Tuscany). Fully 85 per cent of those interviewed had heard of it; and for them the name conjured up positive images of history, sun and unspoiled, rustic traditions but not, perhaps surprisingly, the mafia. Only 7 per cent associated it with wine, however, despite Sicily being Italy's second-largest wine region, with 120,000 hectares in total under vines. Here, he thought, was the marketing opportunity: to fit wine into the image of an island that was thought to be 'unspoiled, rustic and sunny'.

The Planeta winery was developed in a very Italian manner, nevertheless, as a family enterprise. At the time when the idea of building a boutique winery emerged, Mr Planeta's nephew, Alessio, was 21 years old and Diego's daughter Francesca was 16. Alessio was sent to France to work for small wineries and learn the business there. When she was old enough, Francesca was sent to London to study communications, after which she worked for Nestlé, the Swiss confectionery giant. So when the first Planeta vintage was ready in 1995, the family had been as well nurtured as the vines, especially for selling to an international market.

Now, Planeta sells 60 per cent of its wine abroad. This helps spread the firm's risks but also fits its chosen strategy of selling high-quality, quite expensive wines. The market for such wine is more easily found in London, New York and Tokyo than in Reggio Calabria, as long as the wine can be presented as being special, of high quality, even exotic, and not just a typical supermarket plonk. Many of the Planeta wines are marketed in a manner more reminiscent of the 'new world' wines of Australia and California than in the traditional European style, with simple labels and with the grape variety prominently displayed, but are positioned as 'premium' or luxury products.

Could this example be followed by others? In wine, the idea of strong branding and premium pricing is being followed already, not just on the island but elsewhere in Italy. Sicily, as Settesoli and Planeta have shown, is an island where a surprisingly wide variety of grapes can be grown successfully, but it is not an island well suited to mass production and mass marketing of the sort practised by large Australian wine conglomerates. Asked about the prospects, Mr Planeta divided the island's wine-makers into three types.

First, there are the small private producers, the most well known of which are Planeta, Donnafugata and Tasca d'Almerita. In 1985 there were only two; now there are hundreds, of which Mr Planeta says perhaps about 25–30 are truly successful. He expects consolidation and a shake-out, at the end of which there could be 50–60 good boutique wineries.

Second, there are a few big-volume, lower-priced producers, including Settesoli and Corvo, often buying grapes from farms rather than having their own vineyards. He reckons they have a good chance of prospering, as their ratio of quality to price is good, they are well organized, and the name of Sicily is becoming stronger as a brand.

Finally, however, there is a large group of about eighty cooperatives which have been dependent for years on public subsidies, especially from the European Union, which has led to a vast amount of over-production and scant attention to marketing or proper organization. Many of their grapes go for distillation. With the public money gone, these, he says, are 'dead co-ops walking'. Out of the eighty, no more than five can survive, he thinks.

This sort of analysis can also be applied to Sicilian agriculture and to much else on the island. There is no chance of Sicilian farmers or food companies competing in world markets as low-priced mass producers – which is the sort of approach that EU subsidies and political interference have tended to foster. Firms dependent on that approach and on public money are likely to die. Higher-quality foods, sold under labels that convey both the quality and the Sicilian origin, stand a much better chance of being profitable. Some consolidation is also needed to enable small producers to become capable of handling international sales and marketing.

I asked Mr Planeta whether he thought this approach was catching on. The answer brought us back to politicians. Recognition of this opportunity was growing, he thought, but it takes time. The best development in every industry in Sicily, he said, in fact in any walk of life, comes where there is no powerful politician to get in the way or to try to take control and exploit what is being done. The cleanest and most efficient towns and villages are those which have had communist mayors, not for ideological reasons but because they have been starved of public money.

Flying out of Naples

In the north of Italy, said Mr Planeta a little ruefully, entrepreneurs are politically important. They can see the regional governor whenever they want to. Not in the South: his part of the world is driven by politics, not business, and politics is driven by public money. Entrepreneurs are unimportant, as far as he can tell. Just outside Naples, not far from Caserta, the managing director of Tecnam, Paolo Pascale Langer, made a similar point to me. His local town is Capua, but he has never met the mayor. He didn't really sound as if he wanted to, actually. Being outside the system – of local politics, of the Camorra mafia – is one of the things that has helped this aircraft-maker thrive.

Tecnam, which was originally in Naples itself but moved to Capua in 2004 to gain access to more land and a local airport, is hard to find. There are no big signs proudly directing visitors to the company, just a few small discreet clues. The factory and offices are surrounded by a high fence, with tall electric gates. I was glad my taxi driver from Caserta's railway station knew where the company was, since otherwise I might never have found it. But the drivers have good reason to know: a stream of international visitors attests to the fact that Tecnam is the number one producer in the world in its market, namely ultra-light sport aircraft.

A maker of smart, sporty, rather sophisticated aircraft in Naples, a city infamous for rubbish and chaos, and near to Caserta, a town made better known by Roberto Saviano's *Gomorrah*? It was a surprise to me that it was there, I must admit, though when I arrived I realized that there are several aeronautical manufacturers in the area, and a government aerospace research institute which shares a landing strip with Tecnam. I had, it is true, been reading a lot at the time about Fiat's negotiations with the unions at its Pomigliano d'Arco factory in the outskirts of Naples, so I ought not to have been surprised to find fairly advanced manufacturing in the area. Still, stereotyped images are hard to shake off. And, as I realized as my morning at Tecnam developed, they are not entirely misleading, either.

The company is a very Italian miracle. It is a miracle that it has survived and prospered in and now near Naples, well away from Italy's industrial heartlands and in what is a hostile environment. It is, as so often in Italy, a miracle created by a man, or rather in this case two brothers, Luigi and Giovanni Pascale Langer, lovers of planes and of flying, who started the company in 1948. Luigi Pascale Langer is still the company's chairman and chief design-engineer, and comes into work every day at the age of 86. Paolo, the managing director, is his nephew. But it is also, for all its miraculous features, a company whose size and growth have been constrained by the combination of Italian employment law and its difficult location. As Mr Pascale Langer the younger told me, the company had an opportunity to move to America in the 1970s, but his father and uncle felt they were even by then too old to move countries. 'We may have lost a good opportunity,' says the nephew: in America, they might have become world leaders in a much broader range of aircraft. It is thus a miracle the firm is still there, in Campania.

Tecnam's success, even at its limited size, arises essentially from its design skills – which chiefly means Luigi Pascale Langer's skill and reputation as an engineer who is also a pilot. Manufacturing skills matter too, though about 40 per cent of each plane is made by outside subcontractors, most of them in Campania. Tecnam insists on keeping an eye on the quality systems used by all those subcontractors. All the research and development is done inside the firm, chiefly in a team centred on 'the professor', as the older Mr Pascale Langer is known. The firm produces nearly 300 aircraft every year, at prices ranging from 70,000 euros for the simplest single-engined plane up to 300,000 euros for a new, larger, twin-engined model. They are sold all over the world, from China to California, especially to flight-training schools but also private owners.

Having chosen not to move to America, the sole step of international expansion Tecnam has taken since then was a purely opportunistic one, when it bought a Spanish aircraft-maker more than three years ago that had been 80 per cent owned by the regional government of Aragon, in north-eastern Spain. It had 125 employees, had lost lots of money, but, most important of all, had a huge airport next door that had been built by the regional government. The firm was of interest because of that airport and because its aircraft are made using composite carbon fibre rather than aluminium, the material with which Tecnam has previously worked. In taking over the Spanish firm, Tecnam showed some ruthlessness: it interviewed all 125 existing employees, but in the end kept none of them as it felt they did not have the right skills. It now employs just 30 workers at its Spanish plant.

Such hard-headed management is not possible at Tecnam's Italian factory. Paolo Pascale Langer described it well: 'In Italy you are married to your employees, but they are not married to you.' Rigid employment laws are, he says, a big barrier to the firm's growth. Given the training, the skills and the quality control inherent in aircraft manufacture, 90 per cent of Tecnam's workers at Capua are regular, permanent employees and only 10 per cent are contracted from agencies.

The Camorra are another constraint: a few months before my visit, a local clan had attempted a shake-down on Mr Pascale Langer the younger, who had to be accompanied for a month by a special Carabinieri unit. In the end, the Camorra were scared off when they narrowly escaped arrest after their pay-phone conversation with Mr Pascale Langer was intercepted. But this doesn't alter the fact that, based where it is, the company has to keep a low profile. If the firm were in Milan, says Mr Pascale Langer, it would probably be double its present size. Even so, this miracle is doing perfectly well and is riding out the recession.

Ancient labour practices or modern ones?

Perhaps the most important question for the future of the South is whether the environment there could now start to become less difficult for business and thus for investment. One way it could become less difficult would be if organized crime could be beaten back. Another is if politics could become less clientelistic and parasitic. A third way, though, which would perhaps be easier to achieve, would be for trade unions to collaborate with companies to bring working practices in the region more into line with those in the rest of Europe – and indeed in the world.

As was outlined in Chapter Three, the deal struck just before the summer, in 2010, between Fiat and the main labour unions at its production plant at Pomigliano d'Arco near Naples to reform working practices there is a vital test case. Despite continued opposition from one of the unions at the factory, agreement by the other unions to the new practices has encouraged Fiat to proceed with a €700 million investment, bringing production of the new Fiat Panda car to that plant rather than building it in Poland.

The statistics are chilling as well as telling. The Pomigliano d'Arco factory employs 5,200 people who in 2008 built just 78,500 units of three Alfa models. In 2009, thanks to the worldwide slump in demand for cars, output at the plant fell to 36,000, leaving only one-third of the workforce being used (the rest were on temporary lay-offs under the *cassa integrazione* job-subsidy scheme). But whatever the external economic environment, the internal environment is highly uncompetitive. Fiat's 6,100 employees in Poland, just 17 per cent more than Pomigliano, produce 600,000 cars a year – more than seven times as many. The firm's 9,400 workers in Brazil produce 730,000 cars a year. Taking all Fiat's five Italian factories[10] together, the 22,000 employees produced only

650,000 cars in 2009. Even on the company's ambitious recovery plan, their target is to produce only 900,000 cars in Italy as a whole in 2012.

To produce cars and commercial vehicles with such low productivity is not just uncompetitive, it is unsustainable. Britain has no auto manufacturer to compare proudly with Fiat: our own equivalents essentially died in the 1970s. But Britain is a bigger automobile producer than Italy, thanks to American, Japanese, French and now Indian and Chinese companies: unbelievably, Britain produces 1.5 million cars and commercial vehicles every year. Whatever the unions say, and whatever Italy's government does to try to intervene, if Fiat's Italian factories remain so terribly unproductive then all will eventually close and all cars sold in Italy, under any brand-name, will be assembled abroad, whether in eastern Europe or elsewhere. That would be a pity, for it is not as if Italy is generally bad at making things in factories. What it is bad at doing is making things like cars in big factories, dominated by the trade unions.

An average 30 per cent of Fiat's Italian production workers are involved in unscheduled stoppages every day. At Pomigliano, absenteeism has been a huge problem: Fiat cites days on which 470 doctors' certificates have been presented simultaneously to justify absences, or months when 1,500–1,600 workers were missing because of elections. The new working practices are intended to cut this absenteeism drastically by putting the onus on the unions to find ways to make up for lost production when stoppages occur, as well as by cutting the amount of break-time workers are entitled to during each shift. If the agreement holds, the company's stated aim is to build 300,000 Panda cars per year at Pomigliano d'Arco, well over treble the 2008 output of Alfas.

If this project succeeds, which means if the company and the main trade unions truly forge a new partnership that makes the Pomigliano factory internationally competitive, it would be enormously encouraging to other potential investors in the south of Italy, its so-called Mezzogiorno. In fact, it could be a big encouragement to businesses all over the country, whether Italian or foreign.

CHAPTER 6

Enterprise Obstructed

In the admittedly emotional wake of the western financial and economic crises since 2008, many of us who have felt disappointed or disillusioned with our unstable, unequal, often short-sighted forms of capitalism have groped for alternatives. Not alternatives to capitalism itself as some of the 'Occupy Wall Street' style of campaigners have demanded, for that is futile, since the use of competitive, commercial activities, dividing our labour, investing our savings and taking or avoiding risks – which is all capitalism means – is simply an essential and inevitable part of human life. But rather the groping has been for alternatives to the forms of capitalism that have recently come to predominate.

We have hankered after banking systems that are more closely regulated and supervised than those of boom–bust America or Britain, that depend more on stable deposits than on flighty wholesale funds and that are less speculative. We have hankered after companies whose owners are closely connected with their firms and who take a long-term view, rather than the remote, disconnected, disinterested shareholders that are epitomized by the big pension funds and life insurance firms that dominate British and American markets, that buy and sell their shares according to formulas, equations and computer programmes.[1] In our dreamiest moments, we have even hankered after companies that take a responsible, quite paternalistic approach to their employees, treating them as partners and real assets rather than simply as tools to be bought and sold at will. After all, the greatest management writer of the twentieth century, Peter Drucker,[2] pointed out in his pioneering study of the General Motors car company in 1946, *Concept of the Corporation*, that the corporation had by then become the principal social organization of the age and, if anything, that has become even more true in the more than half a century since. If such social organizations act towards their employees as if the laws of the jungle prevail, then the result will be an unproductive and conflict-ridden disaster. Moreover another concept popularized by Drucker, that of the 'knowledge worker' and the 'knowledge economy', surely requires a more cooperative rather than adversarial relationship between owners, managers and other employees.

The funny thing is that answers to all of these dreams, these hankerings, can be found in Italy. Its banking system may have all sorts of flaws, but speculative and flighty it is not, and since the big banking reforms[3] of the early 1990s, to which are generally attached the name of a two-times prime minister, Giuliano Amato, those banks have no longer been simply small, fragmented, local banks under local political control but rather more consolidated and large-scale, with considerable (if sometimes inadequate) independence from the local banking foundations that now own many of their shares. Two banks, UniCredit and Banca Intesa San Paolo, are now among Europe's biggest. Their shareholdings have proven to be a tad flighty since the global crisis began, but that is not true of Italian companies in general, where family ownership and a clear entrepreneurial control remains the rule.

Italian capitalism is not about 'punters' or gamblers, about which Rupert Pennant-Rea presciently wrote a critical survey article in *The Economist* in 1990,[4] rather it is chiefly about the 'proprietors' that he contrasted with them, admiringly. One of those proprietors admittedly has been the state, though its ownership has declined. In a system prone to high levels of interference by political parties, using state-owned companies as vehicles for patronage and power, such state proprietorship has generally been neither far-sighted nor productive. But most of the great Italian corporate private names have also had clear proprietors – Fiat, Ferrero, Prada, Illy, Barilla, Tods, Benetton, yes Mediaset, and many more – generally with long family heritages and with much more far-sightedness. And the entrepreneurial instinct remains alive and well in Italy, with each new generation seeking either to take over from their parents and grandparents, or to found their own new companies. Let's be honest: even the mafia clans, whether the Camorra, 'Ndrangheta, Cosa Nostra or Sacre Corona Unita, are essentially family entrepreneurs, now on a larger and larger scale, even if they also use decidedly illegal and distasteful methods to advance their businesses.

So here's the funniest thing – though it isn't a laughing matter if you are an Italian, young or old, looking for a job. It is that these virtues are not currently working to Italy's overall benefit. That much is obvious if you look at the stagnation in economic growth since the mid 1990s, or at the country's failure to create productive, well-paid jobs for its new generations either of school-leavers or university graduates. In Chapter Three, we looked at the broad economic reasons for this failure, including labour laws, taxation and low levels of competition enforcement. We now need to apply these reasons at corporate level, to see why a capitalist system or model that in some ways looks so right actually is turning out so wrong, or at least so disappointing.

There are three parts to this explanation-cum-description. The first concerns the problems, poor overall performance and poor incentives faced by small and medium-sized companies. The second concerns why even successful, global companies so frequently fail to grow to an adequate, even market-dominant scale. And the third applies to all sizes of company, and concerns why Italy's record of innovation in science and technology has become so poor. All the explanations lead to two basic points: one is that far from small being beautiful, as in the famous 1970s phrase of a British economist, Ernst Schumacher, small is ugly in today's open, globalized economy. The second is that without competition and a high value being given to merit, mediocrity will be the inevitable result.

The middle-Italy puzzle

What the existing data shows is that for Italian industry as a whole, productivity growth fell behind the European average during the first decade of the twenty-first century. Productivity is notoriously difficult to measure, especially when trying to do so across a wide variety of types of business, in which labour is important in some and machines or other technology is important in others. Still, even after several revisions of the data by the experts at ISTAT, the Italian official statistics institute, in response to criticism, the picture remains the same: especially since 2000, Italian firms have been falling behind, and have not been reacting as well and as quickly to the impact of new Chinese, Indian and East European competition as, say, German firms – even ones of a similar size.

One can argue with definitions of productivity, but the fact remains that the point of productivity growth is to produce consistently rising wages and profits, and neither has been seen in Italy in the past decade or more. And one can find all sorts of other countries where productivity performance has also been poor. But for Italy the most apt comparison is also the most damning one: with Germany. For both countries have been characterized by relatively enduring manufacturing sectors, by a preponderance of small and medium-sized family-owned companies, by a greater reliance on bank finance and internally generated finance than on stock market flotations, and by historically strong positions in the sale of capital goods and components on the one hand, and goods with a strong design and engineering element on the other. German industry has prospered from the growth of China, for instance. Italian industry, by and large, has not, at least not to anything like the same scale.

Why not? As part of a five-year, wide-ranging enquiry, the Bank of Italy conducted a survey of 40 Italian companies, mostly small and medium-sized manufacturers, based on in-depth personal interviews with the owners or chief executives.[5] What they found was a widespread reluctance to modernize and restructure, despite growing competitive pressures, and in particular to introduce new information technology such as 'enterprise resource planning' software, which automates accounting and process management. Salvatore Rossi, then chief economist of the Bank of Italy, told me that many firms appeared to resist this because it would require them to flatten the firm's hierarchies, altering all sorts of personal relationships, might lead to battles with unions, and might – if productivity were to jump in response to the new technology – oblige the firm to grow rapidly in order to make full use of its employees.

The success stories of restructuring, however, had an important and interesting feature in common: all had 'invested in activities not directly involving production', according to the bank's report. These include research and development, design, advertising and marketing, reorganizing using new information technology, and boosting sales networks. In other words, in improving services associated with the business rather than manufacturing itself.

An earlier study by the Bank of Italy,[6] based on surveys of manufacturing firms by Mediocredito-Capitalia in 1995–2003 (now part of UniCredit), looked at a further question, one that will also be relevant later in this chapter, on innovation: is the slow productivity growth of Italian manufacturing mainly a result of a lack of innovation, or has it been caused by the way rigid labour markets discourage or prevent firms from reorganizing themselves and reallocating workers? The conclusion was straightforward: it is the fact that Italy's labour laws are far more rigid than those in Germany that explains most of the poor Italian record on productivity.

The second broad finding from the existing economic data is that industrial districts, the great creative force of Italian industry since the 1970s, especially in the Centre and North but also in Puglia, have been big losers in terms of competitiveness, as well as being eroded by the emergence of alternative production sites in central and eastern Europe. In principle, industrial districts might be expected to be rather well suited to adapting themselves to changes in global competition and technology, for being comprised of small firms they should be extremely flexible. Smaller firms are also less constrained by the labour laws. However that has not proved to be the case, especially since Italy's membership of the euro removed the advantage and competitive fillip that had been provided by frequent devaluations of the lira.

A study by Alessandro Spaventa, then of Leonard Business Consulting, and Salvatore Monni, of University of Rome Tre, in 2007 showed how low-technology districts in the Veneto were being hollowed out by competition from Romania.[7] In the late 1990s, many manufacturers in the region transferred their lower-technology production abroad, often to Romania, in order to import semi-finished goods back to the Veneto for completion. This has proved to be quite a substantial and successful move by such firms: by 2004, the study reports, there were 15,302 Italian–Romanian firms registered in Romania, with investments totalling nearly 560 million euros. These are particularly concentrated in traditional 'Made in Italy' sectors such as textiles, furniture, shoes and food. This outsourcing, however, has not proved to be a long-term survival strategy for the Veneto districts themselves: it has resulted, say Messrs Spaventa and Monni, in new districts forming in Romania, around the Italian investments, and thus in more and more of the activities moving to Romania along with them. Simply cutting production costs, in other words, has not given the Veneto districts a new future. To achieve a new future requires a move more sharply up-market.

This fits with the first finding. Insofar as those traditional 'Made in Italy' industries are surviving in Italy as pure manufacturing businesses, they are being taken over by immigrant entrepreneurs willing to do things in new ways. Mature businesses, in the second generation, are surviving and even prospering only by increasing the element of design and service in their products.

A company such as Morellato, a third-generation (or, rather, second generation of a second family) business in the Veneto making watches and jewellery, is a good example. The core of its business is no longer manufacturing or traditional Italian craftsmanship. It is design and innovation, following fashions but also creating them. GEOX, a successful maker of shoes and clothes, makes its shoes and clothes abroad, but the design, sales and advertising are all handled in Italy. The Poltrona Frau Group, a set of international, up-market furniture designers assembled in 2005 by the holding company of the family of the chairman of Ferrari, Luca Cordero di Montezemolo, Charme Investments, is another case of how a traditional sector must – and can – change in order to modernize, in its case by seeking greater scale through mergers and acquisitions.

The third general finding from the data is that although this need to move up-market, and towards more intensive use of design and technology, exists all across Europe, Italy stands out in another way too: unlike firms in neighbouring countries, Italian companies have not generally responded by becoming bigger as well: Poltrona Frau is an exception. If you go back thirty or forty years, Italy had a fairly similar industrial structure to those in France and Germany, with giant corporations and conglomerates in fields such as chemicals, oil, utilities, cars, steel, aerospace, telecommunications and computers. Yet Italy today has fewer big firms, in proportion to its economic size, than it did thirty or forty years ago, while France and Germany have more. In those economies, one of the chief ways in which firms have reacted to intensifying competition and technological change has been by consolidation, building up more scale through mergers and acquisitions. Except in banking, this has not happened in Italy.

Vittorio Terzi, managing partner of the McKinsey & Co. consultancy in Italy, told me that a few years ago his firm mapped its future potential clients by counting the number of 'large global enterprises' in each country. He said they compared Italy, Switzerland and just the city of Dallas in Texas. They found fourteen 'large global enterprises' (on their definition) in the Dallas area alone, seventeen in Switzerland but only eight in the whole of Italy.

There are, no doubt, many reasons for this – some to do with particular chances or accidents, some systemic. We know or at least believe that Italy's continued foundation is small firms, and the entrepreneurial spirit of its people. Yet along with these small firms, there seem to be plenty that do grow to middle size. Surprisingly few, however, then go on to grow much bigger, to join the ranks of the top global companies in their fields. Why? It is not because they are unprofitable, make unpopular products, or products that are of little international appeal – far from it. Can this really be for cultural reasons, an Italian entrepreneurial preference to stay small, as so many Italians tell me? Somehow, I doubt it. I am like Hermann Goering in that respect: as he is supposed to have said, 'When I hear the word culture, I reach for my gun.'[8]

The big-Italy puzzle

One company that has grown to dominate its market all around the world is Luxottica, Italy's huge maker of spectacles and especially sunglasses, that is still controlled by its founder, Leonardo Del Vecchio, but has raised capital through a listing on the New York Stock Exchange. There will be much more about Luxottica in Chapter Seven. But for now, let us note a comment made to me by Luxottica's chief executive, Andrea Guerra, a man who by Italian corporate standards is unusually young for that post (46), and is a manager, not an entrepreneur. His comment was that what Italy needs is more ambitious business owners.

This is not to say that all entrepreneurs should dream of world domination. To want to occupy a small niche, or even quite a large niche, is a perfectly sensible and understandable approach. Some sizeable Italian firms, however, seem deliberately to curb their own ambitions. An intriguing example is Tod's Group, the leatherware firm run by Diego Della Valle and his family. It is in its third generation of family leadership, and has grown hugely from its humble shoe-making origins. It has done well, with sales in 2009 worth 713 million euros, which is big by many standards. But it is not big by global or, especially, American standards. It is revealing to compare Tod's with an American competitor, Coach Inc.: in 2009 Coach's sales were $3.2 billion, or about 2.5 billion euros, more than three times as large as Tod's. This is especially intriguing given that the Della Valle family have succeeded in transforming their firm essentially by creating non-Italian brands, notably Tod's and Hogan, in order to be able to sell worldwide and to escape narrow Italian stereotyping. This would suggest the firm could have used that approach to become a lot bigger than it is and to fight Coach head-on for leadership in a broader market. Perhaps it will in the future, but for the time being it seems to have decided not to.

To remain medium-sized and profitable is a legitimate decision. The important question for Italy and its future, however, is whether the decision is always freely made, or might often be constrained in some way. Italy may not need all of its entrepreneurs to be super-ambitious. But if it is to prosper, Italy needs to be sure that any of those capitalists who do want to expand and lead the world are not being artificially prevented from doing so. Or, to put it another way, it needs to be sure that if they have such ambitions, they do not all have to leave Italy to realize them.

Are they being constrained? Talking to entrepreneurs all over Italy, from Sicily to Piedmont, it feels abundantly clear that they are. The business owners that I have met have all been hard-working, clever, innovative, creative and humane managers, who have not lacked either international awareness or ambition. The constraints, it seems to me, can usefully be divided into two broad categories: temptations and burdens.

The basic temptation is to create a firm as a kind of walled garden, a protected private reality. This quite traditional Italian instinct became a common response to the dangers of the 1970s, when terrorism and industrial turmoil led many entrepreneurs to choose to hunker down and keep a low profile, to avoid being attacked. But since then the situation has changed, as the terrorism and turmoil have ceased.

The temptation in the 1980s and the decades since has been different. It has been the temptation to build a business by finding, creating or exploiting a right, privilege or flow of cash granted by the state, by politicians or by a restrictive guild. State ownership, a legacy of Mussolinian corporatism and of the post-war spread all across Europe of socialist ideas, has declined since the 1980s, but state influence and power, and dependence on the state and thus on political parties and their patronage, have not.

Those companies that are living off state contracts and licences or depending on regulatory entitlements are essentially a type of farmer, harvesters of a source of profit granted to them by a government institution, or more often by local or national politicians, and by established laws and regulations. Such businesses may farm well or badly, but their chief task is protecting the source of their profit, the 'rent' as economists call it, from assault by others. They do not have to, or particularly want to, think about building a competitive global business.

Fiat, during the long period when it enjoyed a protected car market in Italy, was a prime example. The temptation of living cosily behind protective walls is a pretty good explanation for why Fiat failed to become one of the world's top car-makers, and the loss of those walls in the early 1990s explains its struggles for survival ever since. Only now, with Sergio Marchionne's gamble on merging with America's Chrysler and the bold release of the energies of younger executives at the firm by giving them early promotion, is Fiat really trying to join the top ranks of the global car industry.

Mediaset, Silvio Berlusconi's company, is a contemporary example. Commercial television, with the associated advertising sales company of Publitalia, is a rich business that most entrepreneurs would love to own and dominate, as Silvio Berlusconi has, no doubt with great skill and energy. But Mediaset's creation depended chiefly on gaining licences from the government and now depends on maintaining barriers against the entry into commercial television by others, such as Sky Italia in pay-TV and many budding web-TV firms. Mediaset is not going to be a source of growth for the country, nor, most probably, of innovation. At one point Mr Berlusconi toyed with the idea of turning Mediaset into a big international media company, but beyond one foray into Spain's Telecinco, and then a co-investment in a Dutch reality-TV production company, Endemol, he has done little. The power over licences that he gained through his ties to Bettino Craxi's governments and of course through his own governments, were not reproducible abroad. Nor, though, are they likely to be sustainable once his political power has definitively waned. His son, Piersilvio, will face a big problem in keeping Mediaset alive. During the next few decades, Mediaset promises to be the Fiat of its era.

All the parasitical companies of the Mezzogiorno, especially but not only in construction, reflect this rent-seeking temptation, as do real estate developers all over the country (Mr Berlusconi's original business). Another big, broad set of examples is the privatized but protected monopolies held by electricity, rubbish collection and other local and national utilities, which keep prices for those services high and their delivery often inefficient. The temptation to create your own privileges is also, however, reflected in the work of guilds and associations of groups such as taxi drivers, lawyers, doctors and even journalists to restrict access to their professions and so avoid competition.

This interplay with politics and protections produces a second level to the temptation. In an environment in which rents or profitable privileges are so important, it is tempting for a business owner or manager to seek political status, in order thus to hope to ensure further protection or to prolong it. Managers typically do this by investing their time in achieving high office in industrial associations, with Confindustria at the top of the pyramid, and in belonging to networks of all kinds, rather than in building their businesses and dominating their global markets. This seems to be much more prevalent in Italy than in Germany, France or Britain.

Meeting managers and entrepreneurs during my years as a journalist, I have developed a rough inverse indicator for their likely success. The more interesting they are talking about politics and global affairs, the less likely they are to do outstandingly in their business. Those who are obsessed with their business, even to the point of being boring, are likelier to expand, make money and in the end dominate. My top examples are Bill Gates, Steve Jobs and Rupert Murdoch. None of these was ever much interested in talking about global or national affairs, except insofar as it affects the software or media businesses directly. The more lively types, fascinated by politics, keen to boast of their recent visits to the Elysée Palace, the White House or Number 10 Downing Street, seemed to me likeliest to have taken their eyes off the entity that had brought them to prominence, namely their business.

Those temptations essentially constitute diversions and disincentives. Rather than emulating Steve Jobs or the Toyota car company in trying to become global leaders in their markets, too many entrepreneurs and managers in Italy find other, more limited ways to prosper. Other entrepreneurs, however, carry heavy burdens that hold them back from becoming bigger. Chapter Three outlined such burdens in direct, economic terms. But there are also other quite explicit burdens on the shoulders of corporate Italy.

The most dangerous sort of burden is naturally the need to deal with, or preferably avoid, organized crime, as for my southern companies. Another is dealing with corruption, though that is principally a feature of the rent-seeking sectors, for where there is a rent to be granted there is typically an official or politician demanding a slice of that rent as a bribe. Corruption is anyway more objectionable in moral and political terms than it is in business terms, for as long as it is fairly predictable, the need to pay bribes can be built in to business plans. If there is some off-setting gain from the privilege thus obtained, the bribe may make little eventual difference to the company, although for the economy it is likely to be yet another facet of the lack of open competition and legality.

There is also the need for businesses to avoid becoming a target for draconian taxation, given that the Italian tax base is so narrow; the need to avoid becoming a target for trade unions; the need, above all, to avoid drawing the attention of local or national politicians to your company as a source of cash and, even more important, of patronage. That political control sometimes comes through the banks, which helps explain why so many Italian entrepreneurs are wary of them. For, despite the remarkable and successful reforms brought in by Giuliano Amato in the early 1990s and outlined earlier, smaller and medium-sized banks and the associated foundations that own and control them, often remain political tools. The Northern League, in particular, has discovered the potential of using bank foundations as political instruments in its region, and others dabble in this too. All these reasons often explain why company owners prefer to hunker down rather than achieving too high a profile.

Then, however, there are more conventional burdens, all of which in effect raise the cost of doing business in Italy. One example is the high prices for utilities, already mentioned under the category of rent-seeking temptations. One of the biggest burdens is the labour law and its rigid basis in the Constitution, and the near-impossibility of dismissing permanent workers, even with compensation, which discourages so many companies from expanding. Another important burden is outdated infrastructure.

At the Bank of Italy's annual shareholders' meeting in 2009, Governor Mario Draghi said:

> In the last twenty years the gap between Italy's infrastructural endowment and that of the other leading EU countries has more than tripled ... The list of high-priority strategic infrastructures, originally 21, has now swollen to over 200. The time and costs for high-speed rail lines and motorway network extensions, and even for short road links and bypasses, are far greater than in other European countries. A kilometre of motorway can cost over twice as much as in France or Spain.[9]

A more general form of tax that holds back many entrepreneurs is the unproductive and uncompetitive nature of the service sector. All companies, whatever business they are in, need to purchase services. As well as infrastructure and finance, Italian firms pay heavily, compared with their European neighbours, for logistics, transport, marketing, legal advice, and information and communications technology.

As was indicated earlier in the section about the Bank of Italy's corporate survey, if you compare the success with which German small and middle-sized enterprises have adapted to the trends and challenges of globalization with the record of their Italian equivalents, part of the difference can be explained by the existence in Germany of a more advanced and productive sector offering business services. And Germany is not even a country famous for its competitive and advanced services sector, unlike Britain or, to a lesser extent, France. Nevertheless, in Germany modern, efficient, productive business services have supported the restructuring and growth of its exporting companies, while in Italy that sector has acted like a tax, a burden.

It is a huge missed opportunity. A country famed for creativity and design, especially in fashion, food and film, ought to be among the most advanced in developing efficient and modern services. If you look at the structure of Italian industry, and especially at the sources of entrepreneurial success in the past, it is just this sort of constraint that needs to be removed if companies are to survive and thrive in a more globalized, more technologically advanced era. If it were to be removed, if services were to become more innovative, productive and entrepreneurial, then the whole of Italy – households, manufacturers, the government, other service companies – could take a big step forward.

There is a broader point, too, that applies to all companies, whether they think of themselves as manufacturers or as service-providers. It is that what is most needed for a vibrant entrepreneurial future in Italy is a new generation of businesses founded directly on ideas, knowledge, science, creativity, innovation – call it what you will – that could be applied throughout the economy. Those traits, those features, are quintessentially Italian, in the minds of most outsiders, but they are not quintessential parts of contemporary Italy. They are traits that brook no neat distinction between manufacturing and services, and that flourish typically when there is open competition and a broad exchange of ideas.

The innovation puzzle

'The shock of the new' was how Robert Hughes, the great Australian art critic, described the impact of modern art during the twentieth century, in his book[10] and TV series of that title. Innovation can be shocking in all walks of life, disrupting old ways of doing things or old ways of thinking, but it can also be invigorating and refreshing, providing new opportunities, new ways of doing things, new ways of thinking. That is ever more valid in this era of globalization and rapid technological change, the most rapid the world has ever known, which means that it is ever more necessary for countries – especially rich, mature ones – to find ways to innovate, to apply new technology, to exploit their brainpower. For that is their main – perhaps only – asset.

Italy is not typically a country that likes to be shocked, however, and certainly not by the new. Moreover, many inclinations and arrangements in business and in public organizations discourage innovation: the emphasis on loyalty rather than performance or merit, the strength of family, of vested interests and of patronage, and the widespread distaste for competition. So a search for innovation in such a country was always likely to test even my eternal optimism.

In this case, the critics are correct. Everything that is said about Italy's conservative nature, and about how that and the country's industrial and social structure discourage innovation, is surely true. This is not an innovative country. At least, it is not innovative in a straightforward way, according to the conventional measures of innovative capacity.

Overall spending on research and development is well below the European Union average, as a proportion of GDP, and by far the lowest of any of the big western European countries. It was a mere 1.18 per cent of GDP in 2008, even before the Lehman shock pushed the world into economic crisis and a deep recession, compared with 2.02 per cent in France, 2.53 per cent in Germany, 1.88 per cent in Britain and 1.35 per cent in Spain.[11]

Italian universities are essentially nowhere to be seen in any of the main league tables of the world's top academic institutions, published by Shanghai Jiao Tong University, the *Times Higher Education Supplement* (*THES*), and the University of Leiden, among others. In the *THES* ranking in 2011,[12] Italy's highest-ranked university was Bologna at number 226. Defenders of this poor record argue that as Italian universities do not care about attracting foreign students, they make no effort to climb the rankings to do so – an argument which unfortunately would also apply to quite a lot of universities in other countries (e.g. Japanese ones) where similar attitudes to foreign students prevail, but whose colleges still comfortably outperform Italy's.

Some also argue that many of the top Italian colleges suffer in these rankings from their sheer size, which lowers their average result, but say that they contain particular departments with great research excellence. That may well be true – people I interviewed cited excellent departments in robotics, nanotechnology and medical research, among others – but still does not make Italian colleges capable of acting as pioneers or innovation leaders for the country as a whole. Leiden University's rankings[13] measure research citations by other scholars, which should make them capable of detecting these departmental centres of excellence, if there were enough of them to count. Yet Leiden found in 2000–07 that just three Italian universities were in the world's top 100 by volume of citations (Milan, La Sapienza in Rome and Padua), with none higher than 42nd. Adjusting for the size of universities and their specialties to calculate their impact, Leiden found that Milan came 72nd in the world, followed by Bologna (84th), Padua (85th) and La Sapienza (91st).

The more accurate explanation is that Italian universities' non-appearance in the rankings is explained by the fact that professors' performance is not measured by research output, teaching quality or any other test of merit (nor indeed measured at all, by and large), and that financing has not historically depended on these either. Nor are most students selected on merit.

The Italian state university system, in other words, is a system expressly designed to achieve mediocre outcomes, overall – or, to say the same thing more neutrally, it is not designed with excellence in mind. It may be designed to provide a broad education in a fairly egalitarian way, as some defenders certainly argue, but it is not designed to be world class, nor indeed to foster the idea of meritocracy among its students. And the situation is very unlikely to change, except in isolated and short-lived instances, for as long as universities remain governed by a rector elected by the faculty and hence chiefly accountable to them, and financed with scant connection to quality or performance in research or teaching. This is a system controlled by and run in the interests of the professors, not the students or the nation as a whole. Reforms that play around with structures but leave that form of governance and account-ability intact are unlikely to achieve any fundamental improvements.

Then there is the awkward, headline-grabbing matter of Nobel prizes. Italians have won twenty Nobel prizes since the awards began in 1901, six of them since 1980. But the only two received since 2000 were given to Italians working in America (Mario Capecchi at the University of Utah in medicine, and Riccardo Giacconi at Johns Hopkins in physics). The only Italian Nobel in the 1990s was the literature prize for Dario Fo. Franco Modigliani, who won the economics laureate in 1985, had left Italy in 1939. Carlo Rubbia, who won the physics prize in 1984, did so for work at CERN in Switzerland. For the last Nobel given to a scientist or economist working in Italy for a substantial part of their life one must go back to Rita Levi-Montalcini in 1986, though even she did most of her Nobel neurological work in St Louis in the United States. The Nobel most recently awarded for work actually done in Italy was Giulio Natta's prize in 1963, for his work on the chemistry of polymers. Since 1980, Germany has won twenty-six Nobels, France fourteen and Switzerland eight. Most have been for work done in domestic research institutes, not in the United States.

Attend a global celebration and exploration of new ideas, such as the 'TEDGlobal'[14] forum that is held each July, and Italians are hardly anywhere in evidence, at least among the speakers. Check the number of new patent families filed every year: on that measure Italy does beat Spain but at 769 in 2007 was well behind Britain (1,666), France (2,462) and Germany (6,283).[15] Look at the amount of public and private investment that is devoted to information and communication technology (ICT): 10.6 per cent of non-residential investment in Italy went to ICT in 2006, compared with 14.1 per cent in Germany, 16.1 per cent in France and 23.8 per cent in Britain.[16]

You may think, nevertheless, that Italians are exceptionally creative, for that is what the national image claims. And yet, taking the country as a whole, it seems that you would be wrong on this measure too. A consultancy called the Creativity Group Europe (CGE), which is dedicated to defining and studying 'creative classes' all over the continent, reports that Italy's such class more than doubled in size between 1991 and 2001, reaching 4.3 million people.[17] This doubling is in line with a broad western trend, and is chiefly the result of CGE's definition, in which access to and use of technology plays an important part: the 1990s saw the flowering of the internet and of ICT more generally. Yet Italian creatives make up only 21 per cent of the workforce – a smaller proportion than in other western European countries or in the United States, where they constitute around 30 per cent, according to CGE.[18]

Creativity is hard to define. CGE's measure is derived from educational qualifications, the aforementioned access to technology and the nature of the environment in which people live and work – technology, talent and tolerance, as it terms it. If you prefer instead to count what CGE calls 'super-creatives', highly qualified professionals who are engineers, architects, mathematicians, doctors and similar, Italy's proportion of such stars is 9 per cent of the workforce, against 18–20 per cent in Belgium, Switzerland and Ireland, and 13–14 per cent in Germany, Spain and Greece.[19] It is especially in these professions that one finds Italians living abroad, where their opportunities to flourish in those fields are greater, for in Italy barriers and protections for privileges make it hard to become a 'super-creative', and not just for reasons of merit.

This judgment that Italy is well behind its European neighbours is confirmed by a more neutral measure: the proportion of Italians who have had university-level education. Tertiary education is a general measure of people's capacity to participate in creative or knowledge-intensive work: in 2007 only 13.6 per cent of Italians aged 25–64 had had tertiary education, which is comparable to Portugal but lower even than in Mexico. It compares with 24.3 per cent in Germany, 26.8 per cent in France, 31.8 per cent in Britain and 40.3 per cent in the United States.[20] For those aged 25–34, the number rises to 18.9 per cent, but that is still only half the level in the other big western European countries for that age group. The judgment is also confirmed by the OECD's data on the number of research professionals in Italy compared with other countries: just 3.8 researchers per 1,000 people employed, compared with 8.3 in Britain, 7.3 in Germany and 8.4 in France.

Again, we can try out a few defences. Some of these measures might be misleading, because of differences in Italy's industrial structure and taxation system: research and development spending in private companies is undoubtedly understated by the OECD data because Italy has so many small and medium-sized enterprises, in comparison with other countries. Smaller firms tend not to organize or account for research and development as a separate activity, and the tax system encourages firms to treat R&D as an expense rather than counting it as capital investment. Moreover, countries with large pharmaceutical sectors, such as Germany and Britain, tend to have a lot of formal R&D spending and a lot of research professionals, whereas in Italy the pharmaceutical sector is fairly small. In mechanical engineering, which is Italy's strength, R&D is done not so much in specialist laboratories but by people improving the processes and techniques used on the factory floor.

This is plausible, but is not enough to explain the size of the gap. It also has elements of circularity: why do so many small enterprises stay small? One reason may be that they cannot organize R&D effectively at that scale. Nor does this sort of argument alter the other measures, especially those concerned with human capital: the number of graduates, the quality of universities, both of which constrain the 'creative' or 'innovative' input available to firms. Once upon a time, this could be mitigated by the notion that new graduates received intensive training when they joined companies, but the rise of short-term contracts has destroyed that defence. Most young Italians are building their human capital neither in universities nor in companies.

Nor do such defences alter the facts of Italy's relatively low expenditure on information and communication technology, which is today one of the basic fuels of innovation, rather as electricity was in the past. Measured by the number of households with access to a home computer, or with access to the internet, again Italy is a laggard, with, in 2008, no more than two-thirds the level of access reached by France, Germany and Britain. In 2008 less than half of all Italian households had access to the internet. And this is not just a case of the backward South distorting the numbers: the South brings down the average, as it also does on tertiary education, but not that far. Only on mobile phone subscriptions is Italy ahead of its neighbours.[21]

It is not a pretty picture. At least, it is not pretty if you think that Italy's future needs to be shaped and revived by technological innovation, by a new wave of scientific discovery, or by a new generation of young Italians being educated to advanced, globally competitive levels by domestic universities.

So on this point, I concede defeat. Italy is not, and cannot soon be, on the technological or innovative frontier. The pessimists are right. But that does not mean that Italy does not or cannot contain innovators. The raw material, after all, is there. How could Italy fail to be innovative if it is also a country so rich in entrepreneurs? Unless they are all really running bars or bakeries, the very essence of entrepreneurship is innovation. After all, you cannot usually start a successful business just by doing what other businesses are doing. To survive and thrive, you have to think of something new – even if, occasionally, that involves bringing someone else's idea to a place or industry where it has not yet been applied.

Moreover, in its frustrated, partly dispossessed younger generation, forced to work on short-term contracts or not at all, deprived of traditional openings and opportunities, Italy has just the sort of group of young trouble-makers that could prove motivated enough to try new things, to come up with new ideas, to start to shake the country out of its conservative slumbers. Some may choose to do so in Paris, London or New York, but not all of them, surely.

The potential is there, and the next chapter will take a look at some examples of it. But for the moment it remains just that: potential. There will need to be a substantial reform programme to remove burdens, to reduce temptations and to change the incentives towards merit and high performance if that potential is to be released, on a national scale.

CHAPTER 7

Potential Displayed

Antonio Gramsci said that he was 'a pessimist because of intelligence, but an optimist because of will'.

I rather doubt if the great Marxist philosopher would approve of a quest for optimism about his country that was founded on global capitalism, on the will that capitalism requires, and on the belief that this globalized capitalism is one of the main places in which the Good Italy resides. Gramsci's way of thinking and his pessimism, which is forgiveable given his experiences with Mussolini, would surely lead him to pour scorn on such a quest and on such a belief. But apply a bit of will, Antonio, please. For the global capitalists you are about to encounter are humane to their employees, are kept under pressure and surveillance by international customers and capital, are conscious of their community responsibilities, and help to give Italy a good name around the world.

They are, in other words, signs of the country's potential. Greeted by stagnation, by political paralysis, by the tragi-comic opera of the Berlusconi era, by frequent evidence through strikes and demonstrations of the resistance to change, it is all too easy to think that a country has lost its spark altogether: that genteel decline must be all that awaits it; that bitter divisions between the dispossessed young and the selfish old are going to scar the face of society forever. Well, of course, such outcomes are possible. But if vitality, enterprise, humanity and ingenuity can be seen even in the obstructed, stagnant, disappointing times, then there must be some hope of a better outcome if some of the obstructions, temptations and burdens could be lifted. So, to feed this hope, this chapter will offer some case studies of existing success and progress: four examples that could broadly be described as in the 'middle-Italy' category outlined in the previous chapter; three examples of international ambition; and some glimmers of hope in universities and innovation.

The philosopher-entrepreneur

Brunello Cucinelli won't have sold many of his exquisite cashmere garments to communists like the latter-day Gramscis, at least not to real ones. Arriving after the short drive from Perugia at Mr Cucinelli's restored castle in the small hilltop village of Solomeo, with his own lovely villa nearby, the initial impression was distinctly and inevitably feudal. The castle contains his offices and some workshops, with a much larger modern factory in the valley below. It is not surprising that the *New Yorker*, whose journalist visited the firm a few months before I did, headlined their long article 'The Prince of Solomeo',[1] for that is just what he appears to be, a thoroughly benign monarch. If Gramsci were to visit, and to see the grand theatre, library, workers' restaurant and music room that Mr Cucinelli has built in the village, he might well conclude that his concept of 'cultural hegemony', of ruling classes imposing their values on workers, was being further confirmed. Yet this would be unfair.

The initial feeling may be feudal, but the welcome is warm and egalitarian. Mr Cucinelli moved far more quickly than most Italian entrepreneurs do to calling me 'Bill'. We conversed in French, thanks to our mutual frailties in each other's native languages, sitting casually by the long, simple, wooden table in his office high up in the castle. His dress too was comfortably and elegantly casual, in the manner of the menswear collection that he designs and sells, his jaw unshaven, displaying the soft stubble that is often favoured by men in fashion and the arts. His explanation of his company and his objectives featured very few numbers and little mention of marketing, brands, or positioning. Much of it, in fact, was about philosophy, supplemented by writing lists and diagrams in pencil on blank sheets of paper. Characters who featured in our conversation included Marcus Aurelius, Saint Benedict, Adam Smith and – though not quite a philosopher – Barack Obama. Just as important, though, was Mr Cucinelli's father, Umberto.

For this is not a typical, second- or third-generation, Italian family fashion business, founded on a dynastic capitalism that Gramsci would presumably consider bourgeois, and anathema to working-class interests. It is a first-generation business, founded by the son of a farmer who moved to Perugia to work in a cement factory. Umberto Cucinelli's work was miserable and, in his son's view, meaningless. So in 1978 Brunello, at the age of 25, founded his own company. His initial idea was to do with cashmere roughly what Benetton was doing with wool, namely to sell cashmere clothes in bright colours, rather than the more normal neutral shades. Almost immediately, he became an exporter, initially to Germany, later to the United States. Once he had made a success of this, branching out into selling a wider range of his own clothing designs, he set out to build what he sees as a 'humanistic' company, centred on the *castello* in Solomeo (his wife's home village), which he bought in 1985.

Mr Cucinelli's company may be headquartered in a castle but what is notable to me about it is that it is open, not closed. It is completely exposed to international competition, international trends and international ideas. Moreover, it is perfectly possible that this will be a one-generation family business. He has two daughters, but neither is closely involved with the company. With his theatre and, soon, a spiritual 'sacred park' as a retreat for ecumenical religious contemplation and discussion, one might imagine him to be building an entity that is expected to last for centuries, a permanent enclave for his family. Perhaps it will last, but not necessarily as a Cucinelli family enterprise: the 59-year-old Brunello says he sees himself as just a 'custodian, not an owner'.

One of the quotations with which Mr Cucinelli summarized his management philosophy during our conversation was from Saint Benedict: 'The Abbott shows himself to be simultaneously a severe, gentle and very demanding master, and a very caring father.'[2] That combination of discipline and gentleness or humanity is rather appealing as a way to run a capitalist business but also to build a sustainable community based on capitalism. So are the 'moral sentiments' of cooperation and fellow-feeling that Mr Cucinelli quoted from Adam Smith, and which featured in Chapter One of this book. Smith would agree: the clear motives of self-interest are what drives capitalist productivity, efficiency and innovation, but they also need to be placed in a social and moral setting if they are to thrive and survive.

Mr Cucinelli believes, he says, that the way to profit is through 'ethics, dignity and the morale of employees'. He describes how he divides the profit into a slice for the factory, a slice for Brunello, a slice for *i ragazzi* (the guys, in Italian slang, which means both men and women) and a 20 per cent slice for 'humanity', in other words for charitable projects, often in Africa though also in Umbria. Following the example set by Diego Della Valle, owner of Tod's shoes and other high-fashion brands, who is paying tens of millions of euros for the restoration of part of the Colosseum in Rome, Mr Cucinelli announced in mid 2011 that he will be paying in a similarly philanthropic way for the restoration of some of the Etruscan walls of the Umbrian capital, Perugia.

This philosopher-proprietor plainly believes in open communication and collaboration, albeit in a company in which everyone knows who is the boss. Every two months he holds a general meeting for all the employees in

Umbria, at which they discuss the business, its plans and products, philosophy and even politics. At one of those meetings, in September 2008 at the height of the global financial crisis, he told his employees that he did not and could not know what was going to happen, but that he could assure them that he had enough money to keep the factory open for the next one-and-a-half years, regardless. After that, he said, he could make no guarantees.

As it turned out, Brunello Cucinelli did remarkably well during the crisis – remarkably, given that the firm's products are high-priced, luxury fashion goods, of just the sort that you might have expected people to stop buying, at least for a while, when the crisis hit. Growth in sales did slow from 32 per cent in 2007 to 19 per cent in 2008 and just 7.5 per cent in 2009 (to 154.69 million euros), but then picked up speed again in 2010 (28.7 per cent growth) and 2011 (18 per cent growth to 241 million euros). Profits, before tax, have at times been lean, but rebounded in 2011 by nearly 70 per cent to reach 30m euros.

Mr Cucinelli owns 100 per cent of his business, though he has plans for a stockmarket flotation. He gives shares to no one, but nevertheless seeks to treat employees as partners. The firm now employs 710 people, up from 393 in 2007, and in addition uses about 350 subcontractors, mostly in the area around Perugia. The employees are paid, according to the firm's own estimation, salaries that are about 20 per cent above the market rate.

Such an approach is possible when the profit margin is high, which in the fashion business occurs when a product is of high quality, rather special design and well marketed. Mr Cucinelli likes to describe his output as *costoso*, and hence expensively luxurious but with a feeling of value for money, rather than simply *caro*, or costly. He also drew for me on one of his blank sheets of paper a distinction between his approach and that of what is now a more typical Italian fashion business, GEOX. Careful to describe both approaches as *bella*, he listed GEOX as epitomizing the new idea of designing products (in GEOX's case, shoes) in Italy, but manufacturing in Romania to maintain price competitiveness. The Cucinelli approach is to design in Italy but also produce there, using the traditional seamstress and tailoring skills of Umbria, and promoting that provenance in its advertising. This is also, though, probably why his business is only about one-third the size of GEOX and his profits about one-quarter as large. But that is fine for him, and perhaps appropriate for the pricing and exclusivity of his designs.

Although their business models are different, GEOX and Brunello Cucinelli do have one crucial thing in common: their sales are resolutely global. Only 31 per cent of Mr Cucinelli's sales are in Italy, and that share is declining. Just over half are in America, Japan and the rest of Europe, often through shops with his own name over the door. A rising proportion look destined to be in 'emerging economies' such as China, India and Brazil, which, as with many firms these days, he sees as his new emphasis. That global destiny, or rather the ability to seize it, is increasingly what will separate successful Italian companies from nice, but essentially local, 'walled gardens'. The growth of those successful globalists will increasingly determine whether or not Italy prospers, too.

Playful openness

After leaving Mr Cucinelli in his hilltop redoubt at Solomeo, I drove out of Umbria and across eastwards into the Marche to visit another, rather different company, making a different sort of product, in flatter lands near the coast and close to Ancona. As soon as I arrived at the Loccioni Group, I was asked to play a game.

In the company's main lobby area stands a low platform, at one end of which are a pair of footmarks, to tell you where to stand, and at the other is a round tub filled with water, rather like a small child's paddling pool. I began to worry that I might be expected to jump into it, but fortunately not. Next to the platform is a screen, on which are projected the instructions: READY; STEADY; GO! When GO comes up, you are supposed to throw a ball quickly into the pool, as close to the centre as you can make it. Then as you wait for your accuracy to be measured, the platform and screen convey the effect of your ball's impact: a shake of the platform, a little like an earthquake, according to the waves you produced, film of your ball entering the water, and a graphical display of the ripples. Then your score is shown, and the game is over – unless you would like to try to do better, as of course I did, being a competitive sort of person.

The game and the whole set-up encapsulates Loccioni rather well. Labelled 'Play Factory' and 'Play 40', the display was erected to mark the firm's fortieth birthday in 2008. It is the work of a Japanese designer, Isao Hosoe, who has lived in Milan since 1967, and who also designed a set of playing cards for Loccioni, based on a word-association game. The notion is that it is through the free association of ideas that true creativity arises, and that is what Loccioni wants from its staff. (Or, as my former *Economist* colleague Matt Ridley, now a successful independent science writer, has written in his recent book,[3] human progress is made 'when ideas have sex'.) And it is in the measurement business that Loccioni makes its money: hence, in the ball-throwing game, the swift detection and interpretation of the player's impact in terms of vibrations, waves and accuracy.

Enrico Loccioni, the firm's 63-year-old founder, does not look like an especially playful fellow. He is friendly and informal, greeting me at his company wearing a simple, rumpled blue sweater, but is also quiet and reticent. This is a typically small, family firm: his wife is in charge of finance and administration. Mr Loccioni's achievement since starting his firm in 1968 (at the remarkably young age of 19) also strikes me as a microcosm of Italian industry, and of the choices many firms face now.

Loccioni is simultaneously a highly open company and a very local one. It makes sophisticated measuring and testing devices, generally for use by other manufacturers, often in the domestic appliances or automobile industries, such as Germany's Bosch or Mercedes-Benz. Hospitals are also important clients, since precise measurement, without risk of human contamination, is often vital in medicine. All this work now takes Loccioni into sophisticated technologies, including artificial vision, robotic sensors, lasers, breath-analysis and a robotized system for the preparation of anti-cancer drugs (fifty-five of which are now installed in hospitals around the world). Its products are mostly custom-made for each client. The firm has been exporting ever since 1976, at first serving Italian firms abroad but then foreign ones too. Now 40 per cent of the firm's sales are outside Italy, with the main foreign markets being Germany, France and America.

Loccioni does much of its research in-house, relying on the creativity of its own technical staff (one employee in eight works in research), but also works in collaboration with universities, including La Scuola Superiore di Sant'Anna at Pisa for robotics, and local universities such as Ancona, Urbino and Perugia, from which it also recruits its employees.

Most of all, though, Loccioni is open by virtue of its attitude to spin-offs and other entrepreneurial activities among its staff. Mr Loccioni says he likes his firm to be small as that produces 'a climate favourable for development, one in which people know each other and work together in a creative and fertile way'. But he also sees it as 'a laboratory for the future', a place in which it is important to allow employees to 'create new opportunities, new businesses, different competences'. This is shown by the fact that, in the past thirty years, Loccioni has given rise to eighty-two spin-off companies, which has turned the firm into the core of a network of small businesses, a little akin to Slow Food.

In addition, the Loccioni family has invested in ten more closely related businesses through a holding company. It has also, since 1998, held a 'master class' on entrepreneurship for new employees, generally once or twice a year. In addition, the firm receives visits from local schools and universities on a daily basis, and runs several other educational programmes. When Mr Loccioni teaches a class about the company and about business, he typically opens by asking 'So who wants to be an entrepreneur?'

Thus the firm is highly sophisticated, highly creative and highly open. It is also, however, extremely local and extremely careful. All its work is done near the town of Rosora, near Ancona, and all its 350 or so employees are recruited locally and live nearby. That does not make them parochial, of course: the head of communications, for example, told me she had returned to the area after several years studying Native American poetry in California. It makes Loccioni very concerned about the local community and the local environment.

Enrico Loccioni told me he has always wanted to expand 'step by step', in partnership with whoever is the best customer or collaborator in each field, and emphasizing quality rather than quantity. This has worked well, making the firm profitable and growing steadily, but keeping it medium-sized: its annual turnover in 2011 was 60 million euros, and pre-tax profits 4.5 million euros. Taken all together, the 82 spin-offs add up to roughly another whole Loccioni Group: about 300 employees and more than 50 million euros in annual sales.

Mr Loccioni told me that his model for the culture of his operation has always been Adriano Olivetti[4] and his humane, open, creative form of management – just as, presumably, Olivetti's philosophy could be a model for Brunello Cucinelli. His model for the aims and development of his business, though, is German: Siemens. That is a model of quality, technology and global reach that would imply a much greater size than Loccioni has so far achieved.

Might the firm grow further? Mr Loccioni says he feels the global economic crisis, combined with concerns over the environment, has produced a new period of opportunity. It is an opportunity to become a lot more international, but also to extend and expand the business in new areas, especially in human care (food security, safety, health and medical) and for needs connected with sustainability, such as energy efficiency and waste. How far might this extend? Mr Loccioni is reluctant to venture a forecast. The new internationalization of the Loccioni business will be run by the family's second generation, namely his son Claudio. In 2011 he took a first step in this direction, by opening a commercial and service centre in the United States.

Wellness and ambition

Not far up the coast from Ancona stands a company faced with a similar question: how best to become truly international, while retaining control and without losing the essential source of the firm's success. The firm is Technogym, and its headquarters are at Gambettola, near Cesena, just across the regional border in Emilia Romagna. Walk into its premises there and you instantly feel a little tired and unfit, bombarded as you are by pictures of healthy-looking people dressed in lycra sports clothes and by the sight of rows and rows of fitness machines – albeit rather plush and smartly designed machines – for that is what Technogym makes and sells.

This firm is larger than either Brunello Cucinelli or Loccioni, with 1,750 employees around the world, of whom about 1,000 are in Italy, and annual turnover of 400 million euros. It is also even more international: 90 per cent of the sales, by value, are made outside Italy, with Britain currently the largest market. That is no doubt why all the signs in the offices are in English, even though the staff are Italian. More disconcerting was the fact that in the meeting room where I had my initial briefing from the head of communications, Enrico Manaresi, there were not chairs around the table but rather the sort of large inflated balls that people use for exercises and to help avoid back-strain.

The founder, however, is instantly reminiscent of other Italian entrepreneurs. Nerio Alessandri launched his firm in 1983, at the age of 22. He had graduated as an industrial designer and was working for a local company. Happening to visit the local gym, he noted that the equipment was extremely basic, reflecting the fact that most European gyms were used by body-builders rather than by ordinary people or sports-players. He designed a new, safer and more comfortable piece of equipment. And so his business was born, and as it grew up so the European market for fitness-centres left the body-building niche and became much broader.

At first sight, Technogym is just a classic 'Made in Italy' business, melding together skills at manufacturing in fairly limited quantities with modern and often beautiful design. The machines are the epitome both of good looks and of the latest consumer-electronic technologies, laden with screens and with docks for iPhones, iPads or iPods. The top-end machine, the Kinesis, takes 60 hours work from craftsmen in Florence applying gold leaf. Mr Alessandri told me that his inspiration is Giorgio Armani: he designs 'look goods' while Mr Alessandri designs 'feel goods'.

Nevertheless, it is noteworthy that the name he chose for his company is international, not Italian. Mr Alessandri felt, he said, that an Italian name would have had 'no credibility'. In fact, contrary to the usual assumption, he says that for his firm 'Made in Italy is actually a disadvantage', not a strength. It implies, one supposes, products that look terrific but are not necessarily practical.

That observation is interesting enough. But the company is also more interesting than the standard design-plus-manufacturing model in two main ways. The first, and principal, way is that Technogym has turned itself into a service company as well as a manufacturer – indeed, its conception of itself emphasizes the service aspect more than the manufacturing one. Since 1992 it has described its business as being in 'wellness'. Mr Alessandri's business card introduces him as a 'wellness designer'. Much of what they sell may be manufactured, but what they want to position themselves as offering are facilities to promote wellness. And you will note the choice of 'wellness' rather than 'fitness': this broadens the image away from sport and towards health, but also opens up the possibility of entering other fields, such as nutrition.

Also, however, an increasing part of Technogym's business – now 30 per cent – comes directly from offering services to customers. It will do interior design for gyms, will give advice on how to install gyms at home or in the other main client-base, hotels, provide education and training to gym staff (including at its own school, 'The Wellness Institute'), offer access to an international network of personal trainers, and manage facilities for big corporate customers. Some of this is high-profile and good for the firm's international image: Technogym has been the official supplier of fitness facilities for the Olympic Games in Sydney (2000), Athens (2004), Torino (2006) and Beijing (2008), and was picked for the same role in London in 2012.

The equipment is the base of the business but design and services are what build Technogym's competitive advantage. Mr Alessandri told me that Steve Jobs is his true hero and inspiration, for the key development in Apple's success with its iPods and iPads was the merging of its gadget business into what is a service business, namely iTunes. Technogym, he says, must offer not a product but an experience, in which the service and the wellness is the 'content', the equivalent of Apple's music or its software 'apps'. All of this, along with elegant design, enables the firm to achieve premium prices and a margin on sales of about 15–20 per cent. When they provide financial services as well, the margin can rise by a further 5 per cent.

I was glad to see that the lunch kindly offered to me in his office by Mr Alessandri was light and nutritious. That wasn't, however, the second way in which Technogym is interesting. That lies in its ambition to become a global market leader in its field and the Alessandri family's decision to sell 40 per cent of the company to a British private equity investor, Candover, in 2008. This, as he explained, is intended to be the first step towards a full stock market listing, as well as to provide the capital for international expansion.

At the time of our interview, in October 2009, Mr Alessandri said that Technogym's worldwide market share was roughly 20–25 per cent. But it is hard to define the market, for it keeps changing and broadening. He considers that his competitors – which are chiefly three American companies – sell fitness equipment, while Technogym is the only one offering 'wellness'. His firm's approach could potentially prove the best one for the future, and the most profitable, but Technogym at present is the market leader only in Europe. So Mr Alessandri has plans for expansion.

He believes, he told me, in a 'three-hub model' for globalization, and thus wants to build strong local businesses in the United States and Asia to supplement his existing business in Europe. The question is how. When we spoke, Mr Alessandri said that his time horizon was to create the American business during 2010, probably through an acquisition, and then to move on to Asia during 2011. The idea would be to create local factories, because the cost of transporting fitness machines around the world is too high. However, as 2012 dawned, this plan had not been carried out. The notion of an Asian hub had been put on hold, said Technogym's Mr Manaresi, while the hunt continued for a suitable American facility.

Clearly, these have not been easy economic times for any business. Nevertheless, Technogym's turnover has continued to grow, reaching 350 million euros in 2010 (15 per cent higher than 2009) and 400 million in 2011, amid especially fast growth in North America. Instead of taking the plunge with overseas factories, Mr Alessandri has preferred to concentrate on consolidating Technogym's four Italian factories and ten warehouses onto one new site, with improved scale and logistics, along with all the research, design and other activities, in a new 'campus' designed by a noted Italian architect, Antonio Citterio, and costing 60 million euros. The new campus will open in September 2012. After that, America is still intended to be the next step.

Currency movements and economic crises may well be part of the explanation for this slower than predicted move overseas. For the full explanation, one probably should add the inbuilt caution of the Italian family entrepreneur. I would bet that Mr Alessandri will eventually build his businesses in America and Asia. But he will take his time.

Somewhere, over the Rainbow

It is proving quite appealing, this area in the centre of Italy: having journeyed from Perugia to Ancona and to Cesena, we can now return southwards to just past Ancona to take a look at another small, appealing and highly creative Italian company, one that is again of quite recent creation by a young, first-generation entrepreneur. It is called Rainbow and it would not be too far-fetched to describe it as the budding Walt Disney of Italy.

Rainbow's core business is writing and creating children's cartoons. Its most successful creation has been a set of characters called 'Winx' – young, pretty, pre-teen girls, dressed somewhat racily in mini-skirts – who get up to all sorts of adventures. They are in fact fairies, and so their adventures generally involve magic of various kinds, rather like a less gothic Harry Potter. Unusually, for animated characters from continental European countries, they have been designed and conceived with a view to reaching worldwide audiences, not just Italian ones, which is vital if high production costs are to be recouped. Following the Disney model, the Winx are not just available on television, DVD and in cinemas: they are the centre of a big merchandise branding business, with Winx school backpacks, Winx dolls, books, games, toys, indeed everything else you can imagine that young daughters might demand that their parents buy them, as well as websites to go with it all. Moreover, in May 2011, the Winx also became the centrepiece of the most Disney-like venture yet: Rainbow opened a big theme park in the outskirts of Rome, called 'Rainbow Magic Land', which cost 300 million euros in investment.

As with all good tales, a bit of history is required. Rainbow was founded by a comic-book designer called Iginio Straffi in 1995, when he was just 30 years old. At first, the firm worked as an animation studio for other film-makers, but then began to create its own characters and, like other animation businesses in Europe, subcontracted much of the basic animation work overseas to cheaper locations. As Mr Straffi says, the most important and valuable element is the story and the character, not the animation itself. In Rainbow's new and very modern headquarters, there are quite a few animators, but they are chiefly either creating the original brands or working on some of the more sophisticated developments and animations.

Rainbow's first big success was with a cartoon for boys called *Tommy & Oscar*, who are rather like young do-gooding James Bonds or Batman and Robin. Making them a success was a struggle, as so often for small companies: in 1998 the firm encountered a financial crisis when its Singaporean co-producer suddenly terminated their agreement. Mr Straffi managed to survive by raising new capital, however, and then took over the international sales effort himself. *Tommy & Oscar* became an international business, distributed in fifty-six countries, though still not very profitably. According to a case study on Rainbow produced by the London Business School in October 2010,[5] the firm made a cumulated net profit of just $20,000 in the seven years from 1995 to 2001.

It was a result of that international sales achievement, but poor commercial results, that persuaded Mr Straffi to change his business model by developing the approach that has now flourished with Winx, not only promoting characters internationally but also turning them into merchandise brands, in the Disney manner. The unusual thing about Rainbow as an independent animator, according to Mr Straffi, is that it creates and develops its characters, series, films and products just like a 'major' film company, doing all its own testing and development. Then to make that work as a relatively small independent firm, it needs partners for the various specialized parts of the business, such as the theme park and the merchandising. Moreover, he says, it is rare to have a film company with a creative person as its CEO – Mr Straffi was personally the creator of Winx in 2004 – rather than, as is more normal, a lawyer.

It was with Winx that Rainbow hit the big-time. Mr Straffi's intuition was that most cartoons involved boys and so left a gap in the market for one that could appeal directly and especially to young girls. Some mothers worry that the Winx characters are too sexy and might encourage girls to emulate them and, in effect, to grow up too quickly, and Mr Straffi acknowledges that in some countries this perception has proved an obstacle. But he argues, firmly, that the Winx characters are morally good even if they dress sexily, so that the educational content is positive. Winx achieved its launch and its popularity through several series broadcast on RAI public television, and has since been broadcast on more than a hundred television networks worldwide.

I asked Mr Straffi the question I have been asking many entrepreneurs: what are the obstacles to success that arise from being Italian, or being located in Italy? His main answer, apart from the usual groans about poor infrastructure, was essentially one of isolation: that there are practically no investments by television channels in children's programmes, and there is really no entertainment industry in Italy either, and (unlike in France) no public subsidies. So Rainbow had to become international very quickly, in order to raise finance and earn enough money to fund investment in the next series, and had to buy in knowhow, mainly from abroad, on areas such as licensing, branding and merchandising.

To an outsider familiar with Italy's great cinema heritage, displayed proudly in the national cinema museum in Turin as well as in the famous, if now dilapidated, cinematic production centre in Rome, Cinecittà, this is rather surprising: a creative, artistic country without a real entertainment industry. But it is true. And it is the result of two things: the dominance of entertainment by American giants, which affects all national industries, and which has also driven down the prices paid by television networks for content; and the near monopoly in Italy held by Silvio Berlusconi's Mediaset channels alongside the public broadcasting services of RAI, which has choked off most innovation since Mediaset blazed its way to success in the 1980s through reality TV, game shows and semi-naked showgirls.

This unhelpful situation culminated, in 2010, in Mr Straffi's biggest, most momentous decision yet: to go into partnership with Nickelodeon, the children's cartoon arm of the American entertainment giant Viacom, which also bought a 30 per cent stake in Rainbow from Mr Straffi's original private partner. This is the first time that Nickelodeon has agreed to take content from an outside firm. They are co-producing the sixth series of Winx, as well as helping develop and promote some new characters. Mr Straffi's plans are ambitious: a full cinema movie ('Gladiator'), more theme parks, an ice show ... For this he needs support, partners and capital. Hence Nickelodeon. Scale is not easy to achieve, for Italian companies.

The future's so bright, I gotta wear shades

Some do achieve it, however, and here are my three chosen examples of international leadership and scale: Luxottica, Ferrero and Autogrill.

Luxottica is a lot larger than either Loccioni or Technogym, with 60,000 employees worldwide (of whom 8,000 are in Italy) and annual sales of 5.8 billion euros (in 2010), nearly 60 per cent of that in North America, all making it the world's top eyewear company. It is also one of the few examples in the past twenty years of small and medium-sized Italian companies becoming not just dominant but genuinely large. It is not, in other words, the typical 'pocket-sized multinational', as Italian firms going global have been called.

The company is extraordinary in business terms for still being so vertically integrated – in other words it controls every stage of a pair of glasses from moulds to frames to retail distribution, to opticians' tests, and even to insurance. Most companies decide that they are good at only part of that chain of processes, and hand the other part on to others. So Luxottica is a designer, a manufacturer, a retailer, a provider of financial services. But for my purpose its main relevance lies elsewhere. For this is a success story of Italian globalization that flouts all the simple stereotypes about why family entrepreneurs in Italy supposedly cannot achieve global scale and dominant market positions.

You say that their English isn't good enough? Leonardo Del Vecchio, who founded Luxottica in 1961, speaks barely a word of it and yet has always been an eager internationalist. You say that they cannot raise enough capital to build scale, without losing control? His firm went public in 1990, through a stock market listing not in Milan but New York, listing in Milan only a decade later. But Mr Del Vecchio still owns 70 per cent of the shares.

You say that they cannot find the right overseas acquisitions and then find it difficult to manage them or integrate them effectively with their core Italian business? Well, helped by that stock market listing and the resulting ability to use its own shares for acquisitions, Luxottica has bought more than ten substantial foreign companies, including Ray-Ban, Sunglass Hut, LensCrafters and

Oakley, giving it a big retail presence in Anglo-Saxon markets such as America, Britain and Australia, as well as mainland Europe, without encountering big integration problems. Submission to American accounting standards gave Luxottica and its shares global credibility. The acquisitions have given it brands and, most usefully, those retail chains all around the globe.

You say that Italian firms cannot operate well in far-flung, growing but difficult markets such as China? Luxottica has two factories in China (along with six in Italy and one in America) and has even bought two companies there, to give it optical retail chains to help it to match those it has in America and Europe.

You say that they cannot find and trust good managers to professionalize the business, as the founder gets older and the company gets larger? In 2004 Mr Del Vecchio recruited as chief executive Andrea Guerra, who had been running Merloni, the domestic appliances firm, since 2000. At Merloni, he became the youngest CEO of any major Italian company, taking that role at 34 years old. Now that he is at Luxottica, he is still the youngest Italian CEO of a big listed company, which tells us something, unfortunately, about the lack of meritocracy, risk-taking or perhaps trust in many other big Italian companies. Certainly, Mr Guerra struck me as not only young and eager but also exceptionally plain-speaking and clear-minded. Some owners might find it hard to share power with such a forceful character.

Admittedly, exceptions often confirm the general pattern, rather than showing the way to a different possibility, because their differences from typical firms outweigh their similarities. Yet, as Mr Guerra told me, in some ways Luxottica is also typical. The firm's success is the result of individual leadership by Mr Del Vecchio during almost fifty years, rather than the creation of a self-sustaining management system as would probably have occurred at an American company. Mr Del Vecchio happens to have been an individual who had very big global ambitions.

That individual leadership, as at Brunello Cucinelli, Loccioni and Technogym, is both an Italian strength and a weakness. Mr Del Vecchio is 77 years old and still owns 70 per cent of the company. It remains unclear what will happen after he leaves the scene. By arranging the transfer of management to Mr Guerra, he has answered part of that question, but by no means all of it. Just as with Mr Cucinelli, he may take the view that he is the custodian of his firm, rather than its owner, and be content to have his great creation taken over by others, helped by the management system and structure now being built around Mr Guerra. But the point is that neither we, nor his employees or minority shareholders, can know. He may not even know himself.

A chocolate surprise

Over in Piedmont, in the region of the Langhe that is most famous for truffles and for wine, there is another globe-spanning firm that is in a rather different business to that of Luxottica – confectionery – but which nevertheless shares some of its characteristics. It is Ferrero. The most obvious feature it shares is that while being thoroughly international in its business and even in its way of thinking, its growth has been driven and masterminded by a man who speaks barely a word of English: Michele Ferrero, who is now 86. The richest man in Italy is often mistakenly said to be Silvio Berlusconi, but in fact it is Michele Ferrero, who would probably be even richer if his private company were to be floated on a stock exchange. The two men, however, could not be more different.

Ferrero was founded in 1946 by Michele's father, Pietro, who concocted a creamy chocolate spread, based on the hazelnut chocolates, or Gianduja, for which Turin and the Piedmont region have long been renowned. Initially, the spread was thus called Pasta Gianduja, but Michele Ferrero modified the recipe and the branding in 1964 and called the resulting product Nutella, the spread for which Ferrero is now best known. The choice of that name, Nutella, indicated Michele's essential business strategy.

Rather than being an Italian maker of Italian chocolate products, he decided that Ferrero should be an international firm with international brands. Did you know that Ferrero also now makes Kinder Surprise chocolate eggs, Kinder Bueno chocolate wafers, Mon Cheri liqueur chocolates and Tic-Tac mints? Probably not, because the firm's intention with such products is to play down their national origin and ensure they have a broad appeal. The name Kinder Bueno, note, combines a German word and a Spanish one, with no Italian in sight.

Ferrero employs nearly 22,000 people in eighteen factories around the world now, of which two produce all the company's products: the original one in Alba, and one in Germany. The rest specialize in one or two products, and use raw materials and semi-finished products shipped from Alba and Germany. Strict control is maintained over the processing of those raw materials (chiefly hazelnuts, cocoa, milk and sugar) and their manufacture into confectionery, both as regards quality but also secrecy. Access to the firm's factories is tightly controlled. This fits also with Mr Ferrero's attitude to publicity: he wants none. He has never given a press conference and appears in public settings as little as he possibly can.

Ferrero managers feel about their recipes and product rather like a more complicated version of Coca-Cola: you may think chocolates are easy to replicate, but our formula and techniques are secret, and we aim to keep them that way. The managing director of the factory in Alba, Giovanni Di Palma, explains the basic philosophy as being never to make any product that is easy to make, and to avoid being in direct competition with other companies' products. Touring the production lines for Nutella and the famous Ferrero Rocher chocolates, I could see what he means: the light Rocher chocolates look simple when you unwrap them, but actually are made through a pretty intricate process, since this praline chocolate has a hollow wafer ball at its core, filled with pieces of hazelnut sitting in a bed of Nutella cream, and is then coated twice with chocolate and hazelnut chip layers.

Enough salivating, though I did plenty of that while visiting Alba. Ferrero's distinctiveness, as indicated earlier, is both that it is a private firm and that it is firmly international in scope and ambition. It makes a narrower range of goods than the global giants such as Kraft Foods, Mars (also private) and Nestlé, but according to *Candy Industry* it is nevertheless ranked fourth in the world in net confectionery sales, behind those three giants, with $8.76 billion worth in 2010. That makes it larger than Hershey Foods ($5.7 billion) or Lindt & Sprungli of Switzerland ($2.6 billion).

One final way in which Ferrero stands out is in its attitude to the communities within which it operates. This sense of what is known in the jargon as 'corporate social responsibility' is not uncontroversial, for alongside the company's generous, humane activities many would place the fact that Michele Ferrero lives in Monaco, thus as a tax exile. He is too private to be quizzed about this, and on the other hand seeks little or no publicity for the firm's community activities. The Ferrero Foundation in Alba is open to every Ferrero employee who has worked for the firm for twenty-five years or more, and exists to find ways for these retirees to do voluntary work of various kinds, such as with local schools, or running an arts centre or, after the 2008 earthquake in Abruzzo, serving meals to evacuees, or even coming up with ideas and products for new businesses. In 2009–10, 1,551 Ferrero employees reached that 25-year point. Similarly, Ferrero has set up 'social enterprise initiatives' in Cameroon, South Africa and India, countries where it obtains raw materials, as well as selling chocolate. The plan is that these initiatives in developing countries should grow, be added to, but also should spawn a lot of new local enterprises. But little detail is given by Ferrero, for, once again, the firm shuns publicity.

In an airport near you

The archetypical Italian company is a manufacturer, generally with some snazzy design attached. Many Italians that I meet seem to consider services to be not entirely respectable activities, particularly when they are conducted abroad. Give us good solid artisanal manufacturing any day, they seem to be saying, or mechanical engineering, or fashion, or food businesses. Yet here is a notable exception, perhaps a portent for the future: Autogrill.

This firm had its humble and not very notable beginnings as a privatized spin-off of food and drink businesses in 1995 from the state conglomerate IRI. Unlike Luxottica, it is not the work of one individual, but is a firm that has been controlled since privatization by Edizione, the financial holding company of the Benetton family, which retains 59.3 per cent of the shares. Like Luxottica, however, it floated itself on the stock exchange (Milan, in its case) in 1997, and made a series of acquisitions in France, Belgium, the Netherlands, Austria, Germany, the United States, Switzerland, Spain and more. The group now operates in forty-three countries, with less than 25 per cent of its revenue derived from Italy. Like Luxottica, it is run by a young-ish professional chief executive, Gianmario Tondato da Ruos, who started his career at the Mondadori publishing group, moved to Benetton, joined Autogrill in 2000 and then became chief executive in 2003 when he was 43.

The business is not glamorous: it mainly runs restaurants on motorways, in airports and at railway stations; duty-free shops in airports; shops at petrol stations; and inflight retailing. Its purchase of Host Marriott Services, now renamed HMS Host, in 1999, made it the leading food provider in American airports. Its purchase in 2008 of World Duty Free made it the biggest retailer in British airports, with eighty-four outlets in all. The company's restaurants are not exactly trailblazers for the greatest Italian cuisine, though they are not McDonald's, either. But like McDonald's they are trailblazers for success in branding, logistics, standardization and quality control, in the setting up of systems to create and manage that success in very different countries and over long distances. That all adds up to a number one slot for Italy: Autogrill is the world's biggest company in what is called the 'travel dining' sector – restaurants for people on the move.

The acquisitions have also been managed in an unusual way. Mr Tondato told me that when Autogrill bought HMS Host in 1999 the parent's own management was relatively weak, so it chose to maintain and promote managers from within the acquired company. It has followed that method with subsequent acquisitions too. As Mr Tondato said, 'when an Italian company buys a foreign firm, they normally send a team of five Italian managers to run it, and then wonder two years later why they have failed. Instead, we make changes in the companies we buy, but find people inside the firms to run them.' Now, seven of the ten managers who report directly to Mr Tondato are non-Italians. Foreign management expertise and talent has served to strengthen and influence the Italian parent, while the main Italian contribution, Mr Tondato says, has been its knowhow in managing operations.

Naturally, being in retailing and restaurants, Autogrill employs a lot of people: it has 62,500 employees in all, of whom about 10,000 are in Italy. That, note, makes it larger than Luxottica. Autogrill's sales also put it on a par with the sunglass kings: 5.7 billion euros in 2010. Just over 1 billion euros of those sales derive from the Italian business.

Those numbers, it is also worth noting, make Autogrill's sales almost three times larger than those of Benetton itself, whose sales in 2009 totalled 2 billion euros. In 2009, however, it was not as profitable as either Benetton or Luxottica, with its after-tax profit dropping to just 37 million euros from 84 million euros in 2008, while Benetton's remained robust at 122 million euros. Autogrill's profit did, however, rebound in 2010 to 103.4 million euros. What this underlines is that the branded clothing business has higher profit margins than do airport restaurants, and that the catering and retail businesses are more cyclical than selling brightly coloured sweaters. But it also reflects the drive for growth at Autogrill, which its main shareholder endorsed: the big acquisitions in recent years meant that it had a big amortization charge of 'intangibles' in its profit and loss accounts during this period. Autogrill's post-tax profits in 2007, before the crisis, had been a comfier 172.5 million euros.

Since then, the global economic crisis has been felt most keenly in rich developed countries, in consumer spending and in travel: in other words, all the things Autogrill depends upon. Surprisingly, though, Autogrill was helped by having expanded in retailing immediately before the global recession began. Before buying World Duty Free and ADEASA, a Spanish airport retailer, Autogrill was the unsuccessful bidder for another travel dining chain. This was lucky – or good judgment, given that its bid was low – since retailing is much less capital-intensive than the restaurant business, and so was more stable during the downturn. You still have to devote capital to refurbishing kitchens and premises in restaurants even when business is poor, whereas retailing just needs shelving and displays. Now, Mr Tondato says that Autogrill will still seek growth, but less through acquisitions than through partnerships and alliances. His main target for growth will be in the emerging economies of Asia and Latin America.

Just because a business has been hurt by the recession, that does not mean it is not a good sector to be in for the future, especially if there are still big countries and territories available to expand into. Given the drop in travel and in consumer spending in 2009, and then the disruption caused when European airspace was closed for fear of volcanic ash in April 2010, Autogrill has done well to avoid suffering big losses. That makes it a more stable company and industry than, for example, car-manufacturing, where the global economic crisis pushed firms as varied as Fiat, Ford and Toyota into big losses in 2009, or aviation, where the losses have been huge.

Did those losses make the car industry an obviously bad business to be in, for the longer term? Few countries seem to think so, given the efforts they have made to support their car industries through scrappage schemes and the like. Italy doesn't appear to think so either, given the fuss made in politics and the media about plans by Fiat to produce new vehicle models in Serbia rather than in its Italian factories, and fears that it might move its corporate headquarters to Detroit. Moreover, if Alitalia, the troubled national flag-carrier airline, had achieved even half the international success that Autogrill has, it would have been feted as a great national achievement. Not that Autogrill needs or wants the sort of help and attention given to Alitalia, but I make the comparison just to illustrate the strangely fuzzy nature of nationalist thinking. Alitalia is just a service business too, providing transport and inflight catering, inside a metal tube manufactured by Airbus Industrie.

The struggle to innovate

Whether in manufacturing or in services, a critical test in any country is whether new ideas, new technologies and new business models can emerge or at least be tried. As Chapter Six argued, Italy has a particularly poor record in university quality and in science and technology during the past several decades, thanks to a distinctly anti-meritocratic university system, one that is also quite closed to foreign faculty and new ideas, and to a lack of scale in many Italian companies. But there are glimmers of change. Here are two examples: an incubator and investor in start-ups just outside Venice, and the efforts by universities in Ferrara and Turin to emulate Stanford in America and Cambridge in Britain by spinning off new high-technology companies and profiting from them. The first, indeed, is such a sower of new seeds that it describes itself as a farm.

The farm is near Treviso, just outside Venice. It is in a delightfully quiet area, so different from the cramped industrial development of much of the Veneto in Italy's north-east. From where I sat, at a table under the trees with one of the founders, Maurizio Rossi, the fields spread out as far as the eye can see. But this is no ordinary farm, and nor does it produce ordinary crops. It is called H-Farm, and it is an incubator, a germinator, of new companies.

Although the firm's logo includes an old-fashioned tractor, the 'H' in its name stands for humans, and the idea is to foster innovation centred on the way in which human beings interact with technology, especially through mobile phones and other gadgets. Mr Rossi describes the twenty-first century as having brought the 'first generation of digital natives', but also a 'merger of design thinking and technology'. Humanity's agricultural era was, he argues, 'the last time humans and technology were united'. I suspect Karl Benz and Henry Ford might disagree, believing the motor car to have qualified for such a description, or Thomas Edison might put in a claim for electricity. But I see his point: the digital era is a time when use of, and contact with, technology is becoming ubiquitous, and fundamental to the way we live and work. So the search for ways to improve that contact and exploit the new opportunities it creates is one of the principal arenas of innovation.

The innovation at H-Farm takes two forms. It occurs, by the way, not actually in the fields but in a series of low buildings, the views from which and the atmosphere in which are made more tranquil and serene by the rural aspect. It is, Mr Rossi says, a better place in which to think disruptively than Milan. The first form of innovation is in H-Farm's own approach, which is to be both an investor in start-up companies and to act as an incubator for them – in other words, to provide them with premises, services and support to help them to grow, but also to provide some of their capital.

Normally, investment and incubation are done separately – that is certainly the practice in the world champion of innovation, Silicon Valley in northern California. But in Italy, there are fairly few providers of venture capital – large-scale equity financing, with some management support, offered in return for a stake in the company, on the understanding that when the company is sold or floated on the stock market the venture capitalist will take their profit and leave. So when they founded H-Farm in 2005, Riccardo Donadon and Mr Rossi decided that they had both to invest and to incubate.

Mr Donadon's background was in e-commerce, developing Italy's first online store with Benetton and then his own web-design agency, E-TREE, which he sold in 2000; Mr Rossi had worked in his family's shoe firm, Rossimoda, now part of the French LVMH group, directing the development of a sports-clothing division. Thus, they had experience of business development and of web-related commerce, some capital of their own, and a sense that with smartphones and other new devices emerging, now was a moment of opportunity.

The second form of innovation is in the start-up companies themselves. They are all, in their different ways, concerned with the new opportunities provided by the internet, many with the 'social' character of the web, in other words with the way in which the web facilitates collaboration. One, Thounds, is aimed at musicians, enabling them to exchange musical ideas and compositions with one another rather as Facebook enables people to exchange photos and articles. Another, Zooppa, offers a venue through which companies (such as Google, BMW and Universal Studios) can invite people to bid for contracts to produce advertising videos and other material. LOG607 has come up with a new sort of travel book, which enables tourists to design their own tours around cities led by SMS messages and codes in the book.

So far, in its seven years of existence, H-Farm has worked with twenty-five start-ups. None has failed yet, so it has not had to write off any of its investments. Five have already moved to what venture capitalists call 'exit', or sale. Among these was H-Art, a web-based marketing agency which was started in 2005 and sold in February 2009 to WPP, the London-based global advertising and communications giant. For WPP, this is a small transaction: WPP bought 90 per cent of the business, leaving 9 per cent in H-Farm's hands and 1 per cent for H-Art's management, in a deal that valued the (already profitable) firm at 5.4 million euros. H-Care, a developer of software for customer services departments, was sold in 2008 to an Italian call-centre firm, Comdata, earning H-Farm a little more than 2 million euros. And in June 2009, 51 per cent of the travel books firm, LOG607, was sold to RCS in a deal which stands to earn H-Farm up to 2.2 million euros. These are healthy sales, but to cover its costs and become sustainably profitable H-Farm will need more of them, at higher prices.

H-Farm is an invigorating company to visit, full of young people enthusiastic about pitching their business ideas to you. Mr Rossi says that the supply of young people with ideas, capable of producing (to mix the agricultural metaphors) 'grassroots-based innovation' is not a problem. 'Creativity is in Italians' genes', he says. (Unfortunately, scientists have not identified a creativity gene and are unlikely to. But in deploying this myth, I take it that he was being metaphorical. After all, others have written of *L'Italia dei furbi*, or 'Italy of the cunning',[6] and that cunning search for advantage and protection does seem to be a tradition.) In any event, to encourage that creativity, or to blend it with confidence, H-Farm has begun holding an event called 'Storming Pizza' once every two months at home base and on tour, at which budding start-ups make their pitches to H-Farm partners and invited guests, and the 'Digital Accademia', which is an educational centre for young entrepreneurs. Mr Rossi says the idea is 'to drop the stupid paradigm of secure employment among the young. When people are in their twenties that is the best time with the best momentum to take risks and explore experiences like entrepreneurship and start-ups.'

The main problem for all ages of start-up is the difficulty in Italy of raising capital and of achieving 'exits', because there is no tradition of mergers and acquisitions, which in turn limits H-Farm's ability to raise funds for its investments. So, at a surprisingly early stage in its development, H-Farm has already become international, opening branches in Seattle, London and Mumbai, in order to gain access to capital markets and partners abroad. A good option, Mr Rossi says, could be to try to turn H-Farm into a pan-European venture business and, in two or three years' time, raise large amounts of capital through an initial public offering on the stock market. In 2012 it planned also to raise a new fund, having already attracted several new influential Italian investors in 2010–11, including Renzo Rosso, the Marzotto family (owners among other things of Hugo Boss fashions and the Ca del Bosco wine business), Banca Intesa San Paolo,

UniCredit, the RCS publishing group and, from Germany, Bertelsmann.

On the campus

H-Farm's Mr Rossi told me that he and his partners have often been asked to set up clones of themselves elsewhere in Italy: the latest enquiry came from Puglia. It is hard to see why it would make sense to clone yourself in parts of the country where it is even harder to raise capital or to sell your start-ups. Getting bigger in the Veneto, in order to be able to cover overheads more easily, is a better strategy. That doesn't mean, however, that the incubation business cannot occur elsewhere. Going by American and to a lesser extent British experience, one natural home for it is the university campus, where the commercial potential of inventions and developments made in university labs can be exploited. What, the dirty world of commerce contaminating Italy's pure halls of learning? Yes indeed: I went to two universities to see the commercial wheels spinning: the University of Ferrara and Politecnico di Torino.

Ferrara is the more surprising of the two, for it is neither a specialist technology university nor one with long-standing ties with companies. Set in the midst of the Estes' beautiful city, however, sits a university that has been shaking itself up and, just as important, starting up new companies. The shake-up has been led by the rector from 2004 until 2010, Patrizio Bianchi, who had previously founded the university's economics department in 1996, and spent a period as president of Sviluppo Italia, the state development agency. He set up a new council to encourage and organize cooperation with the city of Ferrara and with local companies. Most relevant for the present purpose, however, has been the energy he and his predecessor put into developing an incubator in the university for start-ups. Based in an old sugar mill, the 'technology pole' hosted its first spin-off company in 2000, following the new law that in 1999 made it possible for the first time for universities to commercialize their inventions. In October 2009, when I visited, it was hosting some twenty fledgling companies.

As at H-Farm, to tour Ferrara's 'technology pole' is to make a tour of youthful, though also professorial, enthusiasm. I began on the roof of one of the incubator's buildings, looking at experimental devices used to focus sunlight on to a small slice of silicon in order to boost the efficiency of solar power. I finished my tour at AmbrosiaLab smelling oils and creams, for here a group of young women are working on cosmetics and nutritional supplements, chiefly as an outsourced research lab for other companies. Founded in 2003, the firm finally had to become independent in 2010, as the university grants its spin-offs six years of incubation, during which they have free use of the campus's labs and workshops. AmbrosiaLab has a joint venture with the Baobab Fruit Company of Senegal to develop products derived from the fruit of the baobab tree, which contains powerful anti-oxidants. In between, I passed through Geotema, whose specialty is testing and measuring pollutants, and another firm developing instruments to measure and monitor radioactivity involved with nuclear medicine, chiefly in cancer treatments.

After four to six years of operation, these businesses are making annual sales of between 150,000 euros and 1 million euros. So they are small, but starting to grow. The jewel in Ferrara's crown, however, is a company called PharmEste. Founded in 2003 by two professors from Ferrara with one from the University of Firenze, PharmEste has raised an impressive 14 million euros of financing in two rounds in 2007 and 2008–11, chiefly from Zambon (an old, medium-sized pharmaceutical firm based near Vicenza), Quantica SGR (an Italian venture capital fund), Emilia Venture (linked to the Monte dei Paschi banking group of Siena) and MP Healthcare Venture Management (linked to the Mitsubishi group of companies in Japan). Its main hope, and attraction, is a treatment for chronic neuropathic pain (e.g. back pain) which began its first phase of clinical trials in 2009 using human volunteers in Switzerland. If the trials are successful, the hope is to sell the company shortly thereafter. At that point, the sale could earn the university several million euros.

The Emilia Romagna region has been more encouraging than most in pressing its universities to develop incubators in this way. As the Ferrara example shows, the incubators are growing nicely, but from small beginnings. To succeed in the spin-off game you need 10–15 years, in order to build up a large enough portfolio of companies to diversify the risks, spread the costs and provide encouragement to others. Conservative faculties, dependent on public funds and often run like feudal city-states, do not open their eyes or minds swiftly to commerce or to the new opportunities that commerce can provide. The election in 2010 of Pasquale Nappi, head of the jurisprudence faculty, as Professor Bianchi's successor as rector, signified a backlash against the recently reformist and more commercial spirit: not one that necessarily brings everything to a halt, but one that might well slow progress and change down.

To find out how a commercial spirit can be applied on a larger and more sustained scale, I visited Francesco Profumo, then rector of Politecnico di Torino, a specialist university that focuses on engineering and architecture, in particular. Immediately, seeing buildings named after the Agnelli family reminded me that commerce has long been a lot closer to this institution than to most Italian halls of academe. Like the city of Turin as a whole, moreover, the Politecnico has been remaking, reshaping and rebuilding itself over the past two decades, a process that will continue for several years more. It is particularly notable and exceptional, though, for three things.

The first is the much bigger presence of foreign students (15 per cent in 2010, up from just 2.5 per cent in 2005 when Professor Profumo began as rector) than in other Italian universities. Half the teaching is in English. The impetus to promote this internationalization began, Professor Profumo told me, when he had dinner with the head of a local industrial association who said his members were finding it hard to recruit and retain foreign workers. More than half the students are still from Piedmont and a third from the rest of Italy, but the 15 per cent from abroad and the English tuition together give courses an international flavour. Now, he says, more students are wanting tuition in English and more are wanting to spend a year of their studies abroad. This would not be notable in a university in Britain or the Netherlands, say, but it is unusual in Italy.

The second notable feature of Politecnico di Torino is how much of the university's funding now comes from sources other than the government: an impressive 70 per cent of the €300 million annual budget, a much higher proportion than at other Italian universities, and unusually high by European standards too. That 70 per cent comes from industrial companies funding research labs, from consultancy, from tuition fees (roughly, 28,000 students at 1,000 euros per head, providing about 10 per cent of the budget) and from grants for European Union projects.

The third notable feature, which is in a way a subset of that funding point but also has much larger implications, is the depth and breadth of the university's commercial activities. There are eighteen research centres established on the campus by companies, including Microsoft, Alenia, General Electric, Yahoo! and Indesit, with the biggest of them all being GM Powertrain Europe, a facility set up by General Motors. Its premises look bigger than many whole companies, and it houses 550 researchers alone. Given that Turin is Italy's 'motor city', you might think this relationship goes back decades. But actually GM's research facility dates back only to 2006, when some smart footwork by Professor Profumo and his colleagues lured GM to come and build their centre on a new site being developed next to the Politecnico, which was formerly occupied by industrial buildings. In all, the research centres employ some 2,500 people, 90 per cent of them graduates and PhDs of the Politecnico. In addition, there are forty partnership agreements between university departments and private companies, for specific research projects.

The Politecnico's incubator, I3P (which stands for Incubatore di Imprese, Innovative del Politecnico), is the country's largest and most active. Since its foundation in 1999 it has hosted 140 new companies, only 10 per cent of which have failed. It is currently hosting forty start-ups, and allows them to stay in the incubator for up to three years. Every year there are about 200 candidates presented for backing, of which 60 are chosen for 6 months of 'pre-incubation', a testing process at the end of which the budding entrepreneurs write business plans. Around 15–20 make it into full incubation.

This sounds like a lot, and to have hosted 140 compa-nies over 10 years is quite an achievement. But it has not yet yielded big, fast-growing firms. According to I3P's website, the 140 firms have produced just 600 jobs, which is not very many. Professor Profumo acknowledges that the incubator has found it hard to commercialize the ideas it has seeded. He argues that, having hit problems three or four years ago and, as a result, having brought in a venture capital firm to help out, I3P's portfolio of firms will really only mature by 2015 or so, and will only then start to earn the university substantial sums of money.

The most important effect in the shorter term, in Turin, Ferrara and at other universities that have introduced incubators, will be to spread the virus of capitalism and entrepreneurship through their conservative, often well-cushioned faculties and departments. For too long, commerce has been seen as something of an anathema to academia in Italy. Shortages of public funds should help to concentrate minds. So should the trickle of success stories, and of money being made, at innovative places such as Ferrara and Turin. And then there is another intriguing possibility: in November 2011 Mr Profumo was appointed as Minister of Education in the new government led by Mario Monti. Now he will at least have a chance to try to bring about change throughout the university system, just as the Monti government as a whole attempts the mammoth task of transforming Italy with almost no time in which to achieve it.

CHAPTER 8

Good Italy, Bad Italy

In his *Divine Comedy*, his epic poem set in fourteenth-century Florence, Dante Alighieri met his symbol of love and hope, the beautiful Beatrice, and she showed him that, despite his doubts and fears, there was indeed a Paradise, cleansed of the sins of Hell and Purgatory that had made Florence a nest of corruption, self-indulgence, internecine warfare and moral cowardice.

Few of us doubt that Italy itself remains beautiful today, yet there is little that is beautiful or paradisiacal in the slum cities around Naples where the Camorra mafia rule, where drug-dealing is a main industry and used needles make the ground crunchy underfoot, nor in centres of the Calabrian mafia, the 'Ndrangheta, such as the dingy spa-town of Lamezia Terme, nor in the now ex-prime minister's bunga-bunga parties and harems of prostitutes, nor in the selfishness and corruption for which Italian politics is now sadly famed, and with which parts of Italian business are also stained, nor indeed, at a broader and more mundane level, in the fierceness with which the myriad special interest groups in Italy defend their privileges and protections. The Bad Italy, *la Mala Italia* of the country's modern Hell and Purgatory, certainly exists and has become stronger in recent decades. Our question now must be similar to that of Dante: might there also be a Paradise, towards which Italy could be moved, one where *la Buona Italia* would be triumphant or at least regain the upper hand?

That question, indeed, is the one also facing the man who, as 2012 began, held the hopes not just of Italy but also of the whole of Europe in his hands, namely Mario Monti, prime minister of the 'technical government', budding saviour of the euro, and a man much tipped as the country's next president, if all goes well during his prime ministership. As was noted earlier, the contrast between Mr Monti and his predecessor in style, appearance and approach could not be starker. Asked who his role model was, Silvio Berlusconi would probably answer that it was himself, for no one could do the job better than him. When, in the course of an interview[1] for my forthcoming documentary film I asked Mr Monti who his role model might be, after a pause for thought he answered that it would be Luigi Einaudi.[2] That is not a name that is well known internationally, for what Mr Monti meant by this choice was that his model was thus an Italian who was a discreet, loyal, patriotic public servant, as well as being a true liberal. Mr Einaudi was, like Mr Monti, an economist, whose contribution to Italy's development came principally as its first post-war governor of the Bank of Italy

(1945–48), a job he briefly combined with that of Minister of Finance (1947–48), and then as the country's president from 1948 until 1955. In those roles, he can claim to have played a part in laying the foundation for the country's best-ever period of economic growth and social development, by stabilizing its finances, controlling post-war inflation and participating in a broad liberalization of the economy as compared with the fascist, highly state-controlled Mussolini period.

Neither Mr Monti nor the late Mr Einaudi would ever claim paradise as their goal or expectation. They would be too modest and realistic for that. And it would anyway be too ambitious a word for any modern society, rife as all our countries are with flaws and frictions: we cannot expect a modern Beatrice to take Italy there. However much Italy reforms, it is never going to be entirely cleansed of its sins. Nevertheless, to switch to the metaphor of the confessional, self-improvement and repentance are surely possible. If the Monti government and its successors can persuade Italy – that is, Italians – to admit their sins, to face up to them, and thus to rid themselves of many of the self-imposed burdens and constraints that have fostered those sins, the country could achieve a new *Risorgimento*, or revival, even a *Rinascimento*, a renaissance.

The sins of the Bad Italy, it must be said, are not unique to Italians. Plenty of developed, affluent societies are now finding it hard to grow, to create rising living standards, to shake off the effects of capitalism's latest crisis. Wall Street has been 'occupied', London has had its summer spate of riots in 2011, Greece's city air has been full of tear gas, even Russia has now seen big protests against an entrenched and undemocratic elite that swallows up far too much of the country's resources. The eurozone is weighed down by debts and by doubts, but they are not just Italian ones.

Moreover, Silvio Berlusconi is not the only example of an oligarch who has used his corporate power and wealth to gain dominance over democratic politics, and then used the power of government to enrich his businesses even more. In Britain Rupert Murdoch, the Australian media tycoon, has attained similar levels of power, albeit staying outside formal politics, and the business groups that circled around France's president from 2007, Nicolas Sarkozy, have caused frequent bouts of controversy over favours they may or may not have been given. Mr Berlusconi is, however, the only such oligarch to have become prime minister, and then whose resignation from that post (on 12 November 2011) provoked not a riot but rather a huge street party, with an orchestra in the square outside the Quirinale, the residence of Italy's president, playing the Hallelujah Chorus from Handel's *Messiah* – not to call him a Messiah but rather to celebrate his departure.

Plenty of countries have, like Italy, built up bad political habits of using taxpayers' money to bribe voters with promises of welfare, jobs, pensions and other benefits, and then when the tax revenues are insufficient (for raising taxes loses elections) borrowing more and more money to keep on fulfilling and even extending these promises. Affluence has brought rights and rising expectations but also rigid senses of entitlement, the belief that government is like a bank, into which ordinary citizens pay money but are then entitled to withdraw as much as they can from its cash machines. So public debt has become a burden, a vulnerability, hanging over most of us. We in the West have been living beyond our means.

Plenty, too, have found, like Italy, that problems of inequality, of the distribution of wealth, incomes and opportunities, were much easier to deal with in times of rapid economic growth, when there was money to spare, than in today's leaner times. That very leanness of the times makes different groups fight harder to hang on to their protections and privileges, less willing to accept change. The fight is not to gain more, as before, but to lose less and to force the bigger losses onto others. And the extremes of inequality that were overlooked or accepted in the good times as being a reward for success or good luck to which everyone might, at least in theory, aspire, rather like winning a lottery, become much more politically inflammatory when economic growth ceases and goes into reverse. A perceived lack of opportunities comes to feel like a permanent trap, not just a temporary blockage.

Italy is not different in kind from other western countries in any of these respects, nor in others, such as its organized crime, its lack of technological innovation or its demographic trends of low birth rates and an ageing population. Where it is different is in the extent of these problems, and in the particular cocktail of combined problems with which it has to deal.

In the immediate future, it is the Monti government that will be trying to deal with that cocktail, if it maintains sufficient political support, or at least tolerance, to survive. At the latest, general elections for the two houses of parliament have to be held by May 2013, so in effect the Monti government will have had barely fifteen months from inauguration to the point when parliament has to be dissolved for the election campaign. Recalling that Margaret Thatcher had a decade in which to transform Britain, fighting many entrenched interest groups and much resistance to change, fifteen months is never going to be adequate. So the real test will be whether the Monti government can start the process off, and can convince political parties and the public alike that this is not just a one-off adjustment but rather needs to be a programme for long-term change. Then, the test will be whether which-ever coalition of parties succeeds the Monti government decides to continue and extend what Mr Monti's team will have begun.

There is no real mystery about what needs to be done. The mystery is about how to do it and sustain it. Mr Monti, even in his earliest days in office, laid out a programme that was familiar to any moderately liberal critic of Italian policy and politics over the past two decades: budget cuts to start the job of repairing the public finances; reforms to the labour law to make hiring condi-tions more equal but also flexible enough to encourage investment; the removal of barriers to competition and new entry into a wide variety of markets and professions, especially in services; reform of the justice system to speed up trials, both civil and criminal; cuts to the cost of politics; investment in infrastructure of as many kinds as can be afforded; the promotion of, and where possible insistence on, meritocracy, especially in state universities; the accel-eration and intensification of the fight against tax evasion, corruption and organized crime.

The difficulty for Italy, as for the other highly indebted southern European countries, will be that the easily and quickly measurable actions available to the government are those that cut public spending and raise tax rates, and thus cause immediate pain, both to people and to economic growth, while measures that might in the end bring pleasure, such as the removal of barriers, the promotion of meritocracy or the speeding up of justice, will take many years. Moreover, the particular losers from every liberalizing or merit-encouraging action will feel pain and fight the action noisily and fiercely, while the winners from those actions will generally be too diffuse to really organize and fight in their favour.

That is a problem familiar to anyone studying interest-group politics, one that was ably summarized and explained by the late, great Mancur Olson, an American economist, as long ago as 1965 in his book *The Logic of Collective Action*. Olson then extended that analysis to become a general, pessimistic theory about how the entrenching of interest groups brings about the decline of previously dynamic countries, in his 1982 tome, *The Rise and Decline of Nations*. His point was very much the same as that made by Mario Draghi, then governor of the Bank of Italy, now president of the European Central Bank, in the speech cited in Chapter Three[3] about how and why the powerful city-states of Venice and Amsterdam went into their own declines: that interest-group privileges, once entrenched and taken for granted, are hard to remove and hinder the creative evolution that all successful societies need.

Yet in truth, as Mr Draghi himself would agree, this argument is a reason for accepting that a huge effort of political and national will is required to shift those obstacles, not for throwing up your hands and admitting defeat. Otherwise no nation would ever reform itself, and plenty have, whether one is talking of Britain and America in the 1980s, say, or eventually post-unification Germany, or, in different circumstances, Poland after the fall of communism. Clearly, as both the British and the Polish cases illustrate, a sense of crisis helps enormously, and for the time being Italy has just that. There is vanishingly little prospect that Italians will be free of their financial crisis any time soon, so large are the country's public debts and so damaged is the credibility of all euro sovereign debts: the real choice is whether they become crushed by the weight of trying to deal with these debts and descend into internecine battles, or whether that task inspires a new sense of common purpose, analogous, even, to the postwar feeling of the need to reconstruct the nation after the fall of Mussolini and the devastation of war.

If that sense of common purpose does emerge – helped by leadership from President Giorgio Napolitano, currently the country's most popular (perhaps only popular) politician thanks to his statesmanlike role in bringing in Mr Monti's technical government and in speaking out for truth rather than evasions – from both Mr Monti's government and whatever succeeds it, the test of its success will best be thought of as being the changes that occur cumulatively during at least the next five years, though probably really ten, and the results of those changes. Looking back from the vantage point of, say, 2020, the process will be able to be considered a success if substantial progress has by then been made on the following big themes, all of which have featured in this book at various junctures, and all of which feature in the Monti government's shopping list.

Public finances and the size of the state

The crisis has begun as a financial one, so that must plainly be the most fundamental theme: Mr Monti hence called his first package of budgetary measures the 'Save Italy' package. What is really needed to achieve financial salvation, however, is not short-term measures but rather a credible long-term programme to reduce the country's public debts. According to the agreement Mr Monti made with his fellow eurozone governments at a summit on 9 December 2011, Italy's debts, like those of all other eurozone members, should be reduced from their current 120 per cent of GDP to 60 per cent.

A credible long-term programme is needed both for long- and short-term reasons, since one of the biggest costs in the Italian government budget is interest on the debt. If investors become convinced that the debt is really going to be cut, and that the cutting and restraint are permanent, then they will charge less for their loans. Or vice versa. In recent years, interest payments on government debts have amounted to 4–5 per cent of GDP. So if interest rates double or treble, as they have for Greece and Ireland, the drain on GDP could soar beyond 10 per cent. Yet if they fall to British or German levels, thanks to a credible debt-reduction programme, the very task of reducing debt could become easier, as less money would be being spent on interest.

But how, and how quickly can the debt burden be reduced? It is hard to cut public debt back sharply once it has risen so high, but it is not impossible. In 1995, Belgium's public debt level was worse than Italy's at 135 per cent of GDP against Italy's 122 per cent. By 2007, Belgium's debt was down to 88 per cent of GDP, while Italy's was still 112 per cent. That is still insufficient by the standards of the eurozone's fiscal compact, and starting from now would mean that Italy would still be violating the euro's rules in 2024. So Italy needs to do even more than Belgium did.

Part of Belgium's achievement can be explained by economic growth, which helped tax revenues rise. That, certainly, will be the Italian aim too, by means of liberalization and encouraging more competition. If an average annual GDP growth rate of 2 per cent can be achieved, the task will become a great deal easier, and the programme more credible. The heavy lifting, though, will still have to be done by cuts in public spending and the overall size of the state.

Obvious places to start are privatizations of the country's remaining state-owned enterprises: Finnmeccanica, the state railways, perhaps the postal service, RAI public broadcasting, and sales of the residual 30 per cent shareholdings the state has retained in ENEL (electricity), ENI (oil and gas) and Telecom Italia. This would mostly bring in one-off income with which debt could be paid down, but in the case of RAI it would also end a constant annual drain on public funds. It might seem surprising to some readers that an author from the land of the BBC should favour privatizing Italy's state broadcasting system. But RAI is so impossibly politicized that its ability to serve a public purpose has already been destroyed, and anyway it followed Silvio Berlusconi's Mediaset channels downmarket during the 1990s and beyond. Selling it would serve a treble purpose of raising money, drawing the political sting of national television and boosting competition in the media. Naturally, for anti-trust reasons, Mediaset would have to be forbidden from buying any of it, and foreign owners would have to be welcomed.

Beyond privatization, there would be two further tests of success. One has to be the reduction in the costs of public pensions: as stated in Chapter Three, Italy's pension system, at about 15 per cent of GDP, is the costliest in Europe. A second would be a drastic restructuring of ministries and other public agencies, which are also more common and costlier than is typical in Europe, for all such public entities have been favoured tools for political patronage. Along with that restructuring must come, at least symbolically, the end of the amazing perk of official cars, or 'Auto Blu', of which, according to the *Corriere della Sera*, Italy has 72,000 – compared with just 261 in Britain – and which cost a total of 1.85 billion euros annually.[4] A third, for the same reason, would be the much-mooted elimination of the middle layer of local government, the provinces, which sit between municipal and regional governments, and whose powers overlap with both. If those changes have not been made by 2020, then it will mean that no serious effort has been made to reduce the cost of politics in Italy and that 'politics as usual' has resumed.

The electoral law

Drastic changes to the size and cost either of the state or of politics itself will not be possible without a broad consensus. The same applies to other contentious issues, such as labour laws or judicial reform. So if Italy's electoral law has not been reformed by 2020, it is likely to mean that consensus will not also have been achieved on those other matters.

After the crises of the early 1990s, discussion of the electoral law centred on the desire to avoid the situation that led to that period's corruption scandal, namely the creation of a seemingly permanent presence in government of one or two central parties, symbolized by the figure of Giulio Andreotti, the many-times Christian Democrat prime minister of the 1970s and 1980s. Following the discrediting of that system, alternation in government, with truly competitive parties or party-blocks, became the goal and laws were introduced to try to achieve that.

Yet the new system, with its extra seats given to winning majorities, and its requirement for coalitions to run behind a single, declared candidate as prime minister, has failed either to yield a durable bi-polarism or to make reforms easier to achieve. One can blame coincidental or temporary influences: the end of a sense of crisis, once the public finances had been stabilized in the mid 1990s; or the personal agenda of Silvio Berlusconi, which has deepened divisions and turned politics into a form of warfare. But a more plausible explanation is that the push towards bi-polar, majoritarian government goes against the grain of Italian society. The deep division between left and right in the country might imply the need for alternation, but the entrenched power of interest groups and the lack of national unity imply a need for a consensual system instead, one that ensures a broad representation in parliament but also requires governments to build bridges rather than blow them up. Now that there are no longer extreme parties on left and right that need to be kept out of government, as during the Cold War, a consensual system has the chance to be broader, and to accommodate changes in government rather than ossifying as it did before.

A new, consensus-seeking electoral system for the Chamber of Deputies would have three characteristics: it would be proportional, rather than a winner-takes-all system, to ensure fairness and breadth of representation; it would have direct voting for candidates, rather than a party list system as now, in order to connect politicians more closely with voters and reduce the power of party leaders; and it would have a simple threshold of 5 per cent of the votes that parties would have to cross to win seats, to avoid the extremes of fragmentation. As I like simplicity, I would propose that the system used should be the 'single transfer-able vote' method that is used in Ireland, under which voters rank the candidates according to their preferences. This achieves a proportional outcome, while smoothly redistributing the votes of parties that fail to reach 5 per cent. But other systems could also be considered. The important point is that they must be ones that discourage bi-polar politics and force consensus-seeking instead.

Labour laws

The main fruit of the more consensual form of politics that this electoral reform would bring would be a reform of the labour laws. This is the biggest single constraint on the country's entrepreneurial energy, the biggest single reason why small companies stay small, why productivity growth has been so disappointing and why corporate research and development spending is so low. It is also the biggest single reason why young people are frustrated and disillusioned, and, after budget cuts, the biggest single item on the agenda of the Monti government.

Partial reforms to labour laws, passed in 1997 and 2003, which extended the scope of fixed-term contracts and part-time working, have been widely praised for having increased employment, which they have. Similar laws were introduced during the same period in Japan, with a similar effect. In both cases, about 20–30 per cent of the workforce now consists of people on fixed contracts or working part-time. In both cases, however, the measures also produced a short-term gain but created a long-term problem.

The short-term gain was that employers were able to cut their labour costs, at a time when the traditional way to boost competitiveness – currency devaluation – had been eliminated by joining the euro. But the rigidity and ultra-security of most employment terms was left unchanged, and the burden of this adjustment in costs – that is, in wages – was borne by newcomers to employment, which essentially means young people, immigrants and women. A generation is being created which is used only to such precarious employment terms, and which employers are not bothering to train very much because they are only on short-term contracts. Moreover, this has helped to depress consumer spending and hence the domestic economy, by lowering the incomes of the young, a group that would normally be expected to be high spenders and low savers.

As a result, the labour laws continue to do what they have always done: deter companies from expanding, from hiring new workers, even in many cases from growing beyond the level of fifteen employees at which the laws begin to apply. The right to employ young people on a fixed contract or on inferior part-time terms discouraged businesses from using technology and more capital investment to increase productivity. And the average age of those with full employment protection rises, year by year.

The reform that most economists favour, the introduction of which should be the test of success when looking back from 2020, is one that replaces the current dual labour market with widely differing contractual rights with a single set of contractual rights for all workers, full or part-time, with these rights increasing by stages. It would be important with such a reform to avoid creating an incentive for employers to dismiss workers when they approached each next stage. The way to do that has to involve also making it easier for employers to dismiss workers even when they have been at the company for many years, requiring adequate compensation for such dismissal and creating a more generous social safety net, or unemployment insurance, to support the jobless – one that covers all workers, rather than the patchwork of safety nets that exists now. The extreme gap between the rights for permanent workers and fixed contract workers needs to be eliminated, but permanent contracts must also be made more flexible.

Giving the same rights to all workers would bring Italy in line with Britain; creating a blend of flexibility and security would bring it in line with Denmark, the Netherlands and much of northern Europe. Then, if a further reform could be added to make it easier for companies to negotiate contracts locally rather than adopting national agreements, as now, this would bring Italy into line with Germany.

This is all, of course, hugely controversial. It could be achieved only through a broad consensus. To achieve that, and to make a single contract work in a flexible way, the crucial element will be the introduction of a comprehensive unemployment insurance system, a social safety net, as that will make workers more willing to take the risk of changing jobs. In the spring of 2012 the Monti government was proposing just this, but facing big trade-union resistance. The introduction of such a system is a big test for reformist success, for it costs money. If by 2020 this has been achieved, while the programme to cut public debt down well below 100 per cent of GDP has been carried out, then this period of reform will have achieved a remarkable amount.

Women

Broadly, the biggest beneficiaries of such a labour law reform would be the young, who currently suffer most from the dual labour market. A second broad group of beneficiaries, however, would be women. For not only are many women also on short-term, precarious contracts if they are in work at all, but also those contracts deprive them of maternity rights, which gives Italian women a starker choice between work and family than exists in other western European countries.

It would not be an exaggeration to say that those labour conditions, combined with the country's domination by old men and the image given to women by Silvio Berlusconi's television channels, have made Italy the worst place in Europe in which to be a woman: the opportunities that could have allowed better-educated new generations to enjoy more freedom have become blocked, the money to provide public child-care facilities for working mothers is non-existent, and the exploitation of women as objects for decoration and sex has become harder and harder for women to dodge. The problem does not just lie in television. Only in 2011, on the front page of the country's most respectable daily newspaper, the *Corriere della Sera*, a former editor-in-chief of that paper, Piero Ostellino, was allowed to write a column in which he said that women were 'sitting on their fortunes', and that using their bodies to get money or jobs did not make them prostitutes:[5] it was just an expression of liberty and, presumably, of the fact that all power lay in the hands of men. If in Britain *The Times*, or in America the *New York Times* were to publish such a commentary there would be a huge outcry. In Italy, to many, these views just seemed normal.

For this has long been a male-dominated society, one in which within living memory women in some parts of the country were made to wear veils and forbidden to leave the family house unescorted, and in which rape was not made a proper felony until 1996. In the past 20–30 years, that male domination has come to be expressed in a new, exploitative way, the way of showgirls, prostitutes and former topless models becoming Minister for Equal Opportunities, while in the rest of western Europe the lot of women has steadily improved. Suddenly, however, as 2011 came to a close, there was a glimmer of change: the new Minister for Equal Opportunities (but a responsibility now merged with that of Labour and Welfare), a female university professor called Elsa Fornero, walked out of a meeting with an association of young Italians because the group's steering committee consisted entirely of men. They clearly, she implied, did not in fact represent young Italians.

If reforms and new attitudes do take hold, as undoubtedly people like Mrs Fornero would like them to, then they are likely to have to include a spate of affirmative action programmes to help women advance in many fields. Liberals such as your present author do not like the use of 'pink quotas', nor quotas of any kind, for they offend against ambitions for meritocracy and risk introducing a new distortion to supplement all the old ones. But their broad application would at least be a sign of seriousness, as opposed to tokenism. Ideally, all such pink quotas would have attached an expiry date, so that this affirmative action programme can fade away.

Justice

Labour laws are top of the entrepreneurs' list of complaints, the list of factors that obstruct their progress and their expansion. Second on that list is justice, the interminably slow, costly and often arbitrary nature especially of civil justice but also of the criminal system. This is also one of the main obstacles cited by foreign companies as a reason why they have not chosen to invest in Italy. Why does Britain have a bigger car industry than Italy, despite not having had a successful large British car manufacturer of its own for half a century? The reason is that Japanese, French, German, Indian, Chinese and American car firms find Italy's labour laws too onerous, its justice system too slow and dangerous, its visa rules and procedures for foreigners incredibly unwelcoming.

As with the labour laws, there needs to be a broad consensus if the justice system is to be reformed. Any reform needs to preserve the principle of the independence of the judiciary from political interference, hard though that principle has been to enforce and protect. It ought also to separate properly the role and status of judges from those of prosecutors, for the closeness between the two has helped to undermine public trust in the judiciary at all levels, with the notable and admirable exception of the Constitutional Court. Most of all, it needs to speed up judicial procedures without simply encouraging miscarriages of justice or the elimination of valid cases by the manipulation of the statute of limitations.

Curing these ills will require resources, structural changes and legal changes. Resources are required even for the simple task of cataloguing and computerizing all the country's judicial cases, so that they can be monitored and properly organized, and so that judicial communications with lawyers, witnesses and defendants can also be computerized. Then there are the resources needed to increase the number of prosecutors and to give them the chance to do their jobs.

Structural changes are needed to separate prosecutors formally from judges, in their training, recruitment and promotion, and to remove and replace the open prosecutorial power to initiate any investigation they please, with a system to prioritize and justify investigations. This would reduce wasteful and needlessly provocative activity by prosecutors. Such a system would need a body to run it – the equivalent of the Crown Prosecution Service in Britain or Sweden's Office of Public Prosecutions – which would need its own independence preserved, perhaps by making appointments to it in a manner analogous to those on the Constitutional Court, with seats elected by judges, by prosecutors and by, say, a regional assembly, if these bodies were to be regional.

New laws would be required to alter that prosecutorial power but also to strengthen the role and responsibility of judges in managing the conduct and speed of cases. Judge Barbuto in Turin, and his equivalents in Bolzano and Trento, have shown that this can be done without new laws. But with them, it would be easier to make the cures national rather than simply local.

Reforms such as these also require a kind of grand bargain, one that has been unattainable during the periods of fierce conflict between political parties and the judiciary, especially during the Berlusconi governments. The post-Berlusconi era that began with his fall from office at the end of 2011, ought, however, to provide an opportunity for just such a bargain. Looking back from 2020, it will be the presence or absence of such a grand bargain that will determine whether justice is truly reformed.

Competition

One of the appealing features of labour reform in these straitened times is that it does not cost the Treasury very much. Nor would the other big area of economic reform, competition. In fact, the two sorts of reform would reinforce one another, too. A country that succeeds in deregulating and liberalizing markets for goods and services at the same time as reforming its labour laws stands a better chance of encouraging the creation of new jobs, which makes the labour reform more palatable; while a less rigid labour market will make the exploitation of new competitive opportunities easier for companies to contemplate.[6]

The walled gardens that many Italian entrepreneurs have created are the result of the plethora of regulations and state interference, both at national and regional level, that restrict competition in Italy. The domestic competition authority, the Autorità Garante della Concorrenza e del Mercato (AGCM, the Competition and Market Guarantee Authority) knows already most of what needs to be done. By international standards Italy has a very modern competition law, thanks to it being adopted only in 1990, and so it also has a very modern anti-trust agency, but the agency is nevertheless unable to create a genuinely competitive market. Under the power granted to it to propose a new law on competition every year, it makes regular recommendations for liberalization. The AGCM, however, lacks resources – it has just 270 employees, which is tiny when you have the task of investigating infractions of anti-trust law throughout the country – but also lacks power. Its recommendations are often ignored, and its resources and strength have been depleted by requiring it to take on the job of policing conflicts of interest (rather pointlessly, given the identity of the prime minister in 2008–11) in addition to competition.

As its then chairman, Antonio Catricalà, explained to me in 2010, the AGCM would like the power to challenge regional laws in front of the Constitutional Court, for it is from those regional laws that many restrictions on competition arise. Moreover, the AGCM is not a regulatory agency, so although it can impose fines for infractions, it cannot then force companies or local governments to change how they operate, except for limited periods of time. The Bersani reforms of 2006–08 led to 3,000 new pharmacies being opened, and chipped away at restrictive practices among taxi drivers, notaries and some other professional services, and the Berlusconi government has been quite successful in simplifying administrative procedures. In November 2011, Mr Catricala was made the top under-secretary in the Monti government, in effect the prime minister's right-hand man, and a drive for liberalization began.

Similar effects, generating new jobs especially for the young, could be obtained if, for example, restrictions on petrol stations selling other products were removed, or limits on the number of opticians in Sicily were abolished, or if markets for services such as insurance, lawyers and, yes, journalists were opened up. Electricity, gas, telecommunications, water and other utilities, both national and local, are other vital areas for liberalization, identified regularly by the AGCM. So, I would add, should be the markets for television and for advertising, given that one company, Mediaset, controls 90 per cent of commercial television, and its sister company, Publitalia, about 40 per cent of advertising sales – a level of concentration which would spark anti-trust enquiries in most developed countries, and certainly in America.

Competition is often considered a taboo word in Italy. Yet a drive against restrictions on competition would in reality be a national effort to unleash entrepreneurship, to allow the thousand flowers of Italian initiative and enterprise to bloom, to use the pressure of international and domestic competition as the means to prevent capitalists, politicians or anyone else from accumulating so much power that it endangers society and democracy. If that hasn't happened by 2020, then there is little chance that Italy's economy will really become dynamic again.

Human capital and meritocracy

The greatest asset of Italy, it is often said, is the Italians themselves, with their spirit of initiative, of inventiveness, of building relationships with one another. That asset, however, doesn't just develop on its own. Training, education and technology all build it and provide it with opportunities to flourish. Most of all, however, what has been lacking has been a spirit and practice of meritocracy: ability and top-class performance have neither been valued nor rewarded, especially in the universities.

Universities are one of Italy's greater tragedies: a proud history, many fine individuals, but a mediocre collective outcome. The lack of foreign students and foreign faculty, in a country that is otherwise one of the most attractive in the world to study and live in, is a symptom of this mediocrity. A study[7] by Vision, a think-tank in Rome attached to a small consultancy, Vision and Value, found in 2010 that Italy is the only OECD country in which the number of domestic students leaving to study abroad is greater than the number of incoming foreign students. It also found that among the foreign students there are more Albanians than those coming from France, Germany, Britain, America, Brazil, China and India put together. This is an enormous lost opportunity – for fees, but also for the exchange of ideas and the development of Italians' own human capital.

In times of austerity, universities are not going to be improved by new injections of public money. So any determined reformer must seek to improve them by bringing in private capital and giving them a strong incentive to introduce meritocracy and to seek to produce world-class research. Above all, such a reform must exploit the opportunity for renewal provided by the imminent compulsory retirement of (in many universities) 30 per cent of the professors. The same Vision study showed that in 1990 the average age of professors in Italian universities was the lowest among the G8 rich nations; by 2008 it was the oldest.

Most of all, the main test of a reform's seriousness will be whether it alters university governance, making public universities formally independent of the state and with each governed by a board of directors which would appoint the rector, taking that power away from the faculty. This structure is the one used by Bocconi, of which Mr Monti was president until 2011. In Japan, state universities were given this formal independence in 2004, as well as an advance warning that their public grant would in future be reduced by a small percentage every year. This has obliged them to begin raising private funds and to build closer relationships with private companies, as well as to seek foreign students to gain more income from tuition fees. It has also put pressure on their presidents to promote efficiency, to promote young researchers and teachers, and, if students are to be attracted, to demonstrate merit.

The same needs to be done in Italy, with public money for university research departments being distributed solely according to their research quality and performance (currently less than 10 per cent is handed out in this way). The aim would be that as a result small universities would then merge or else collaborate with one another to eliminate wasteful duplication and raise standards, that the proportion of foreign students would rise, that rectors would be appointed with a strong incentive to promote merit and performance rather than protecting the professors, and that there would be an influx of private capital into the university system.

Such an investment in human capital, or rather in its formation, would not pay off immediately, but new generations would quickly benefit. Another focus for investment could bring faster, broader rewards, by developing faster, more widely accessible broadband internet connections throughout the country. This is being held back by the huge debt burden weighing down Telecom Italia, along with restrictions on the ability of competitors to step in where Telecom Italia cannot. The overweening power of Mediaset in commercial television is another obstacle, because the likeliest future source of competition against Mediaset's near monopoly is video transmitted and watched over the internet – which is possible only with superfast broadband connections. The result is that only 18 per cent of Italians have access to fast, fixed-line broadband, well below the level in other developed countries.

So will it happen?

Eppur si muove,[8] as Galileo said. Italy can move, if Italians want it to. It can move, if constraints are removed and if positive ideas and energies are allowed to inspire and influence one another. A liberal agenda, which reformed the justice system to make laws much more enforceable and respected, as well as removing the myriad barriers to initiative and enterprise, would enable that movement to occur.

This does not, of course, mean that it inevitably will. The fall of Silvio Berlusconi and the sovereign debt crisis have created a new opportunity for this to happen. The nation's president, Giorgio Napolitano, has said that this is a moment when Italy needs to, and must, both tell the truth to itself and face up to the truth about what needs to be done. In 2011, he presided over the country's year of celebrations of its 150th anniversary as a unified nation, a process that revealed Italians' pride in their country, underlined their common national roots and heritage, but also exposed some of the limits to that unity. Patriotism, a sense of national identity, were shown to be present, but in a somewhat lukewarm form compared with the corresponding feelings in France, say, or Germany, both of which manage to combine strong regional identities with strong national ones, even with some sense of a common purpose.

It is that sense of a common national purpose that Italy lacks, but now needs to find, or at least to rebuild. The effort to do so, in the wake of the financial crisis of 2011, and the moral and democratic crises of the Berlusconi years, will require an enormous amount of truth-telling, a great deal of moral courage. For the desire to evade or prevent change and reform, to ensure that sacrifices are made by others rather than by oneself, naturally remains strong. So, sadly, does the power of organized crime, and the instincts and channels of the selfish political and corporate power that makes up *la Mala Italia*. The future of Italy, of the hope for *la Buona Italia*, remains in the balance.

Notes

Chapter 1: Italy's second chance

1. Described especially aptly in *The Liberty of Servants: Berlusconi's Italy*, by Maurizio Viroli (Princeton University Press, 2011).
2. London correspondent of *l'Espresso* magazine, and formerly correspondent for La7 television, she is now the director of a documentary film on Italy, focusing on this divide, for which your present author is the narrator.
3. Bettino Craxi (1934–2000), was leader of the Socialist Party from 1976 to 1993, prime minister from 1983 to 1987, and, together with Giulio Andreotti and Arnaldo Forlani of the Christian Democrats, was the lynchpin of Italian politics during the 1980s. He also became a close ally of Silvio Berlusconi, then just a rising property and media magnate, granting him the national commercial TV licences he needed to build what is now a virtual monopoly. In 1994, after the Tangentopoli scandal broke and magistrates led by Antonio di Pietro opened more and more investigations, Craxi fled the country to live in exile in Tunisia. He was sentenced *in absentia* to twenty-seven years in jail.
4. 'US Crown Slips', *Financial Times*, 21 June 2010.
5. See *The Economist*, 26 April 2001.
6. The first of those libel suits, brought in 2001, was won by *The Economist* in 2008, when the Milan court rejected Mr Berlusconi's claim and charged him the costs of the case. He has appealed against the judgment. The second case, brought in 2003, was also subsequently won by *The Economist* in 2010, but Mr Berlusconi chose not to appeal.
7. Under Italian law, Silvio Berlusconi is not allowed to own any daily newspapers directly because he also owns television channels. So he controls *il*

Giornale through his brother and *il Foglio* through the nominal ownership of his ex-wife, Veronica Lario.

Chapter 2: *L'inferno politico*

1. The title of Federico Fellini's 1960 film, starring Anita Ekberg and Marcello Mastroianni, the dim image of whose scene in the Trevi fountains in Rome attracts thousands of tourists there every day.
2. Although the age of consent in Italy is 14, and prostitution is legal, it is illegal to pay anyone for sex who is below the age of 18.
3. She is of Moroccan birth but her parents live in Sicily; and her chosen alias is the more memorable 'Ruby Rubacuori', or Ruby the Heartstealer.
4. Which, it should be noted, means only the 25–30 per cent of electors who have voted for his parties. He has won elections through multi-party coalitions that together nominated him as their candidate to be prime minister.
5. See *I senza Dio: l'inchiesta sul Vaticano* (The Godless: The Inquiry into the Vatican), by Stefano Livadiotti (Bompiani/RCS Libri, 2011).
6. Leader and founder of Italia dei Valori, or Italy of Values, a party generally described as left-wing, although it is actually hard to pin down on a left–right divide.
7. The PCI won an extraordinary 36 per cent of the seats in the Chamber of Deputies in 1976, its best result, while its worst result was a still impressive 23.5 per cent of seats in 1958. In 1992, following the party's collapse and dissolution, the two parts formed from its pieces, the PDS or Democratic Party of the Left, and the RC, or Refounded Communists, won 17 per cent of seats and 5.6 per cent respectively.
8. Short for 'Propaganda Due', i.e. Propaganda Two. The network was discovered during an investigation into the collapse of a bank connected to the Vatican, Banco Ambrosiano, which hit the British headlines when its president, Roberto Calvi, was found hanging from Blackfriars Bridge in London in 1982.
9. In his book *Berlusconi's Shadow* (Allen Lane, 2004), David Lane quotes a British judge, Lord Justice Brown, who in 1996 had to rule on a dispute concerning whether some confidential documents linked to Mr Berlusconi should be transferred to magistrates in Italy. In response to Mr Berlusconi's insistence that the magistrates were persecuting him for political reasons, Lord Justice Brown said in his judgment:

> It is a misuse of language to describe the magistrates' campaign as being for political ends, or their approach to Mr Berlusconi as one of political persecution. On the contrary, all that I have read in this case suggests rather that the magistracy are demonstrating both their proper independence from the executive and an even-handedness in dealing equally with the politicians of all political parties.

10. Marcello Dell'Utri was convicted in the court of first instance in December 2004 of conspiracy with the mafia, and sentenced to nine years in jail. His

appeal began in 2006 and the original verdict was upheld in 2010, with the sentence reduced to seven years. He has now launched the third and final level of appeal, to the Court of Cassation, remains a senator, and has not yet served any either of this sentence or of a 1999 jail sentence (confirmed at the Court of Cassation) for tax fraud and false accounting.

11. His 'Olive Tree' coalition lost by 400,000 votes.

12. 'The Controversial Legacy of "Mani Pulite": A Critical Analysis of Italian Corruption and Anti-Corruption Policies', *Bulletin of Italian Politics* 1(2), 2009, pp. 233–64.

13. 'La misura dell'economia sommersa secondo le statistiche ufficiali, anni 2000–2008', ISTAT, 13 July 2010.

14. Sergio Rizzo and Gian Antonio Stella (Rizzoli, 2007).

15. Normally, a book is considered a non-fiction ('*saggistica*', in Italian) bestseller if it reaches 50,000 sales.

16. This has since been changed to five years.

17. *Il costo della democrazia* (The Cost of Democracy) (Mondadori, 2005). Mr Salvi was a senator himself at the time of publication, for the Democrats of the Left party.

18. Published on 6 August 2009.

19. It is true that Italy's first republic began when a referendum in 1946 voted to abolish the monarchy and then a Constituent Assembly wrote the new Italian Constitution. As David Gilmour points out in *The Pursuit of Italy* (Allen Lane, 2011), the paradox of this was that the unification movement in and after 1861 had been essentially liberal, nationalist and anti-clerical, but after the first republican Constitution the country's main parties followed the anti-nationalist ideologies of communism and Christian democracy. But where would Italy be without paradoxes?

20. See *Between Commodification and Lifestyle Politics: Is Silvio Berlusconi a New Model of Politics for the Twenty-First Century?*, by Paolo Mancini (Reuters Institute for the Study of Journalism (RISJ), 2011).

21. Mancini, *op. cit.*

22. Mancini, *op. cit.*

23. Public subsidies to the media, excluding RAI, totalled 177 million euros in 2009, in addition to which discounted mail tariffs for newspapers, magazines, books and non-profits cost a further 240 million euros (see: http://www.governo.it/DIE/dossier/contributi_editoria_2008/stampa. html).

Panorama magazine, 14 April 2010, 'Caro-Posta per I Giornali', by Stefano Caviglia.

24. For which I write regular columns as a contracted freelancer.

25. Author of *Gomorra* (2006), about the Neapolitan mafia, the Camorra.

26. Published by Rizzoli in 2010. Published in English in 2011 as *Mamma Mia! Berlusconi Explained for Posterity and Friends Abroad* (Rizzoli ex Libris).

27. Umberto Bossi, leader of the Northern League, was found guilty in a 1995 trial of receiving a 200 million lire bribe, and was given an eight-month suspended sentence, which was upheld on appeal.

28. *OECD Factbook 2010* (OECD, 2011), p. 23.

29. See: http://www.doingbusiness.org/reports/global-reports/doing-business-2011/

30. If the name is faintly familiar to anyone following Italian politics during 2011 that is because Pisapia's son, Giuliano Pisapia, won a shock victory to become mayor of Milan in that year, a development widely seen as signalling the end of the Berlusconi era. During the election campaign none other than Silvio Berlusconi himself accused the young Pisapia, who is also a lawyer, of having been a terrorist during the 1970s.

Chapter 3: *Il purgatorio economico*

1. Angus Maddison, *Monitoring the World Economy 1820–1992* (OECD, 1995), cited in Andrea Boltho, Alessandro Vercelli and Hiroshi Yoshikawa (eds), *Comparing Economic Systems: Italy and Japan* (Palgrave, 2001).

2. 'Italy and the World Economy 1861–2011', by Gianni Toniolo: presentation of research for Bank of Italy conference, Rome, 12 October 2011.

3. Marcello de Cecco and Francesco Giavazzi, 'Inflation and Stabilisation in Italy, 1946–51', in Rudiger Dornbusch, Wilhelm Noelling and Richard Layard (eds), *Postwar Economic Reconstruction and Lessons for the East Today* (MIT Press, 1993).

4. Massimo di Matteo and Hiroshi Yoshikawa, 'Economic Growth: The Role of Demand', in Boltho et al., *Comparing Economic Systems, op. cit.*

5. Vera Zamagni, *The Economic History of Italy 1860–1990* (Clarendon Press, 1993).

6. 'Italy, Germany, Japan: From Economic Miracles to Virtual Stagnation', by Andrea Boltho, Economic History Working Paper no. 14 (Bank of Italy, October 2011).

7. Boltho, 'Italy, Germany, Japan', *op. cit.*

8. Boltho, 'Italy, Germany, Japan', *op. cit.*

9. Special report on Italy, 'Oh for a New Risorgimento', by John Prideaux (11 June 2001).

10. Zamagni, *op. cit.*, p. 382.

11. Opening speech, Bank of Italy conference, 'Italy and the World Economy, 1861–2011' (12 October 2011; author's translation).

12. This phrase is a relatively ancient one in economics, having been coined by Alfred Marshall, an English scholar, in his *Principles of Economics* in 1890.

13. Boltho, 'Italy, Germany, Japan', *op. cit.*

14. Boltho, 'Italy, Germany, Japan', *op. cit.*

15. *The Economist*, special report on Germany: 'Older and Wiser', by Brooke Unger (13 March 2010).

16. *OECD Economic Survey of Italy, 2007*, Policy Brief, June: Table 1.6, p. 32.

17. *OECD Economic Survey of Italy, 2007, op. cit.*, p. 32.

18. Even on the measure used by the national statistics institute, ISTAT, which leaves out the pension adjustment, the propensity to save has fallen steadily, to 11.5 per cent in 2011. It is worth noting also that the president of ISTAT, Enrico Giovannini, was previously head of the statistics division of the OECD which produced those adjusted (and gloomier) figures

19. Zamagni, op. cit., p. 346.
20. Carmen M. Reinhart and Kenneth S. Rogoff, *This Time is Different: Eight Centuries of Financial Folly* (Princeton University Press, 2009).
21. Zamagni, op. cit., Table 12.1, p. 345.
22. Vito Tanzi, *Government versus Markets: The Changing Economic Role of the State* (Cambridge University Press, 2011), Table 4.4, p. 103.
23. *OECD Economic Survey of Italy 2011* (OECD Publishing, 2011).
24. *OECD Factbook 2010, op. cit.*, p. 57. 'Value added' is used as a measure simply because GDP also includes value added tax and some other product taxes, so provides a misleading denominator for such ratios.
25. 'Oh for a New Risorgimento', *op. cit.*, 11 June 2001, p. 10.
26. *OECD Economic Survey of Italy, 2007, op. cit.*, p. 60.
27. The Governor's Concluding Remarks: Ordinary Meeting of Shareholders, Bank of Italy, 31 May 2011.

Chapter 4: Inspirations from Turin

1. Although 1861 is remembered as the date when Italy was unified, it is important to note that what we now know as Italy was not completely united in that year: the very large 'Papal states' that had been ruled from Rome by the Pope and grouped together Lazio, Umbria, the Marche and Emilia Romagna were not fully incorporated into Italy until 1870. Nor did the then Venetian republic (today's Veneto, plus Friuli–Venezia Giulia) shake off Austrian rule and join until 1866.
2. Strictly, Italy's first railway was in the Kingdom of Naples. But it was Piedmont's that was exploited to a fuller commercial extent.
3. *'Anni di piombo'* in Italian, referring to the assassinations by bullet and bomb carried out by such terrorist groups as Lotta Continua ('continuous struggle') and Brigado Rosso ('Red Brigades'). Germany was the only European country in which anything equivalent occurred, with its Baader Meinhof Gang of assassins and kidnappers.
4. *Torino City Report*, by Astrid Winkler (CASE, 2007).
5. When I was editor-in-chief of *The Economist*, I published two cover stories advocating the legalization of gay marriage, on human rights grounds, on 6 January 1996 ('Let Them Wed') and on 26 February 2004 ('The Case for Gay Marriage').
6. There is now one big branch of EATALY in New York and seven shops in Tokyo. In New York in 2010 when EATALY opened there, it was for quite some time one of the city's most-visited restaurants.
7. Fiat's headquarters offices are still in the Lingotto buildings, but everything else has gone, bar the rooftop test-track, on which is now perched an art gallery.
8. The museum was founded in 1824, when the then Savoy king, Carlo Felice, bought a collection of more than 5,000 objects that had been gathered by an Italian amateur archaeologist, Bernardino Drovetti.
9. The Fondazione Museo delle Antichita' Egizie di Torino.
10. Collegio degli Avvocati.

11. See: *UEFA Club Licensing and Financial Fair Play Regulations 2010* (http://
www.uefa.com/MultimediaFiles/Download/uefaorg/Clublicensing/01/
50/09/12/1500912_DOWNLOAD.pdf)

Chapter 5: Hope in the South

1. The *Spedizione dei Mille* or Expedition of the Thousand was Garibaldi's
second, but this time successful, attempt to push the Spanish Bourbon
occupiers out of Sicily and southern Italy. Against overwhelming, but
poorly prepared and motivated opponents, he succeeded surprisingly
quickly and easily in defeating the incumbent forces and seizing Palermo,
where he became, in effect, dictator, before later marching on Naples, the
Bourbon capital. It was this initiative which made unification of most of
Italy possible the following year.

2. 'Se un commerciante aderisce ad Addiopizzo o a un'associazione anti-
racket non ci andiamo, non gli chediamo niente' ('If a shopkeeper joins
Addiopizzo or an anti-racket association, we don't go there, we don't ask
anything of them'), *Giornale di Sicilia*, 30 April 2010.

3. Published by Mondadori in 2006 under the title *Gomorra*, in English translation as *Gomorrah* (Farrar Straus and Giroux, 2007), and as a film directed
by Matteo Garrone in 2008.

4 You can find it, and offer your support, at www.ammazzatecitutti.org

5 See: http://video.ilsole24ore.com/SoleOnLine5/Video/Notizie/Italia/
2010/intervista-Santoro-Libero-Grassi-1991.php

6. See: http://www.bancaditalia.it/pubblicazioni/seminari_convegni/mezzo-
giorno_4/4_volume_mezzogiorno_2010.pdf. A much shorter summary of
the findings of this excellent set of studies by the Bank of Italy can be found
in *Critica della ragione meridionale: il Sud e le politiche pubbliche*, by Luigi
Cannari, Marco Magnani and Guido Pellegrini (Editori Laterza, 2010).

7. Domenico La Cavera died later that year, in 2010.

8. On 9 December 1957 (http://www.time.com/time/magazine/article/
0,9171,810167,00.html).

9. Annual reports by SVIMEZ (Sviluppo Mezzogiorno, or Southern
Development Agency), 2010 and 2011. The South's GDP shrank in 2009
by 4.6 per cent, the Centre–North's by 5.4 per cent. In 2010, however, the
Centre–North rebounded more strongly, by 1.7 per cent, against the
South's 0.2 per cent.

10. They are at Mirafiori, Cassino, Melfi, Termini Imerese and Pomigliano
d'Arco. The Termini Imerese plant, in Sicily, closed at the end of 2011.

Chapter 6: Enterprise obstructed

1. See, for example, *The Economist* survey on capitalism and democracy,
'Radical Birthday Thoughts', 28 June 2003, by your present author, or
indeed an *Economist* survey much earlier by my predecessor, Rupert
Pennant-Rea, 'Punters or Proprietors?', 5 May 1990.

2. Peter Drucker, 1909–2005, was born and educated in Austria but became a naturalized American in 1943, and thereafter taught and wrote first at New York University and then at Claremont College in southern California.

3. The Amato Law of 1990 transformed the banking industry by replacing mutual ownership with stock-exchange listed shares and converting the original banking entities into foundations. In a vast exception to the general rule that mergers and acquisitions are alien to Italy, there have been over 300 bank combinations since 1990. Indeed, the Amato Law is one of the rare triumphs of structural economic reform during the past two decades, and it shifted the balance dramatically between the Bad Italy and the Good Italy, for before 1990 banks were essentially political tools, instruments of manipulation and control.

4. Pennant-Rea, *op. cit.*, 5 May 1990.

5. Bank of Italy, 'The Euro and Firm Restructuring', Discussion Paper no. 716, June 2009.

6. Bank of Italy, 'Employment, Innovation and Productivity: Evidence from Italian Microdata', Discussion Paper no. 622, April 2007.

7. Centro di Ricerca Interdipartimentale di Economia delle Istituzioni, Roma Tre, Working Paper no. 3, 2007 (http:/host.uniroma3.it/centri/crei/pubblicazioni.html).

8. Wikipedia reports that Goering did not in fact say this, though it is nice to think that he did. The line was apparently spoken in a pro-Nazi play, *Schlageter*, written by Hanns Johst, that was first performed in 1933.

9. The Governor's Concluding Remarks, Ordinary Meeting of Shareholders, 29 May 2009.

10. *The Shock of the New* (revised and updated edition published by Thames and Hudson, 1991).

11. *OECD Factbook 2010, op. cit.*, p. 151.

12. See: http://www.timeshighereducation.co.uk/world-university-rankings/

13. See: http://www.cwts.nl/ranking/LeidenRankingWebSite.html

14. TED stands for 'technology, entertainment, design' and is a non-profit devoted to 'ideas worth spreading', which it does through annual conferences in California and abroad.

15. *OECD Factbook 2010, op. cit.*, p. 155.

16. *OECD Factbook 2010, op. cit.*, p. 159.

17. *Italy in the Creative Age*, Creativity Group Europe (September 2005).

18. According to Irene Tinagli, in her 2008 book *Talento da svendere*, or 'Talents for Sale'. She took part in the research conducted by Creativity Group Europe.

19. Tinagli, *Talento da svendere, op. cit.*, p. 52.

20. *OECD Factbook 2010, op. cit.*, p. 182.

21. *OECD Factbook 2010, op. cit.*, p. 163.

Chapter 7: Potential displayed

1. *New Yorker*, 29 March 2010.

2. 'L'abate si mostri insieme severo, dolce, esigentissimo maestro, tenerissimo padre.'
3. *The Rational Optimist: How Prosperity Evolves*, by Matt Ridley (Fourth Estate, 2010).
4. Adriano Olivetti, 1901–60, was the son of the founder of the Olivetti business, but he was the one who really established the firm as a maker of measurement devices (like Loccioni), typewriters, calculators and computers, and was known as a paternalist, even utopian, employer.
5. London Business School CS-10-018.
6. Title of a book by Renato Mannheimer and Paolo Natale (Gruppo 24 Ore, 2009).

Chapter 8: Good Italy, Bad Italy

1. In December 2011.
2. Luigi Einaudi, 1874–1961. In addition to the formal roles listed in the text, before the fascist period Mr Einaudi was also a noted journalist and liberal critic, principally for the *Corriere della Sera* but also for *The Economist*. During the fascist period Mr Einaudi ceased working as a journalist in Italy, but continued to contribute anonymously to *The Economist*: see *The Pursuit of Reason: The Economist 1843–1993*, by Ruth Dudley-Edwards, pp. 508–11 (Hamish Hamilton, 1993).
3. See Chapter Three, this volume, p. 81. Opening speech, Bank of Italy conference 'Italy and the World Economy, 1861–2011', 12 October 2011.
4. See: http://bigben.corriere.it/2011/11/la_vergogna_delle_auto_blublu.html
5. 'Una donna che sia consapevole di essere seduta sulla propria fortuna e ne faccia, diciamo così, partecipe chi può concretarla non è automaticamente una prostituta' ('A woman who is aware that she is sitting on her fortune, and uses it, as we say, is not automatically a prostitute'), *Corriere della Sera*, 17 January 2011.
6. That beneficial interplay between labour and product-market reform was the main conclusion of an IMF Working Paper, WP/09/47, 'The Italian Labor Market: Recent Trends, Institutions and Reform Options', by Martin Schindler (March 2009).
7. See: www.visionwebsite.eu
8. 'And yet it does move.'

Further reading

The most helpful general English-language histories are Christopher Duggan's *The Force of Destiny: A History of Italy since 1796* (Allen Lane, 2007) and David Gilmour's *The Pursuit of Italy* (Allen Lane, 2011). Luigi Barzini's *The Italians* (Penguin, originally published in 1964) still provides an incomparable analysis of the interplay between Italianness and history. Paul Ginsborg's two-volume postwar history, *A History of Contemporary Italy, 1943–1988* (Allen Lane, 1990) and *Italy and Its Discontents* (Allen Lane, 2001) provide a magnificently detailed study of political, social and economic developments. The annual studies all called 'Italy Today' by the Censis think-tank and published in English a year later by FrancoAngeli, provide a great deal of social data.

For economic history, the best if now outdated is Vera Zamagni's *The Economic History of Italy, 1860–1990* (Clarendon, 1993). Helpful for the context is *Economic*

Growth in Europe since 1945, edited by Nicholas Crafts and Gianni Toniolo (Cambridge, 1996) For a fantastic and fascinating set of papers on numerous aspects of Italy's economic history in its first 150 years as a nation, from 1861 to 2011, go to the Bank of Italy's website at www. bancaditalia.it/studiricerche/convegni/atti/storico-internazionale. Some are quite academic in nature, but most are highly accessible for the general reader, including in particular the overview paper by Gianni Toniolo.

On politics, a thorough and balanced textbook is *Italian Politics* by Martin J. Bull and James L. Newell (Polity Press, 2005). *Machiavelli's Children: Leaders and their Legacies in Italy and Japan* by Richard J. Samuels (Cornell, 2003) also provides a helpful comparative context. There is a large literature on Silvio Berlusconi, of which the pick of the crop are Alexander Stille's *The Sack of Rome* (Penguin, 2007) and Paul Ginsborg's *Silvio Berlusconi: Television, Power and Patrimony* (Verso, 2004).

There is also a large literature on organized crime, among which I would particularly recommend Roberto Saviano's novelistic and compelling *Gomorrah* (Macmillan, 2007), David Lane's *Into the Heart of the Italian Mafia: A Journey through the Italian South* (Profile, 2009) and Federico Varese's *Mafias on the Move: How Organised Crime Conquers New Territories* (Princeton, 2011).

Index

Bold page numbers indicate figures.

absenteeism 182
abuses 67
ad personam laws 4, 38
Addiopizzo 140–3
ageing population 80
aid, and development 165
Alessandri, Nerio 223–6
Alighieri, Dante 15, 77–8, 106, 254
Alitalia 241–2
Alliance for Italy 42
Amato, Giuliano 185–6
ambivalence, towards state 25,
    94–5
AmbrosiaLab 248
Ammazzateci Tutti 146–8
Andreotti, Giulio 52, 68
Anemone, Diego 44
anni di piombo 93
anti-mafia campaigning 139–45,
    146–7
    collective action 148–9
    lack of institutional support 154–5
    role of judiciary 150–3
anti-trust law 102

Antica Focacceria San Francesco
    144–5
art 26–7
assassinations 88–9
Auto Blu 48–9
Autogrill 237–42
Autoritá Garante della Concorrenza
    e del Mercato (Authority for
    Guarantee of Competition and
    of the Market) 102, 274–5

balance 24
Balsamo, Judge Antonio 152–3
Bank of Italy, surveys of industry
    189–90
banking 184–6, 199
Barbuto, Judge Mario 132, 133–4
Bari 157
Bavaglio Law 153
Belgium 98, 263
bell-towerism 14
Benetton 240
Berlusconi governments 3, 4–5, 135,
    152–3

Berlusconi, Silvio 3–4
  anti-communism 39
  approach to politics 31–2
  attitude to business 196–7
  as business innovator 38–9
  business interests and public
    role 58
  claims of economic strength 7
  continued presence 30–1
  image 35
  innovation 60–1
  judicial history 37–8
  legacy 30
  lifestyle 29
  media power 5
  as political genius 32–3
  political survival 52–61
  relationship with Catholic
    Church 32–4
  scandals 20–1
  use of power 52
Berlusconismo 31
Bersani, Pier Luigi 102–3
Bersani reforms 275
Bertolaso, Guido 44, 48
Bianchi, Patrizio 247–8
Big Society 20
black economy 87
borrowing costs 9–10
Borsellino, Piero 39
Borsellino, Rita 154, 155
Bribesville see Tangentopoli
broadband 278
budget deficit 78
budget surplus 97
bunga-bunga 30, 31
business
  attitude to mafia 162
  failure to grow 187
  incubation and investment 243–4
  political control of 199
  and political status 197–8
  risk avoidance 195–6
  self-image 201–2

Calabresi, Mario 56
Cameron, David 20

Camorra 180
campanilismo 14
capital, raising 246–7
capitalism 184–5, 186–7
  see also global capitalism
car industry 241
  see also Fiat
cashmere 212–17
Cassa Integrazione Guadagni 99
Casta, La 49
Castellani, Valentino 114, 115–16,
    117
Catholic Church 4, 32–4
Catricalà, Antonio 275
Cavera, Domenico (Mimi) La 167–9
Cavour, Count Camillo Benso di
    105–6, 108–11
Centopassi 143
change
  long-term 259
  motivation for 261
  need for acceptance 106
  political 51–2
  resistance to 18
Chiamparino, Sergio 115, 116,
    117, 138
Christian Democrats (DC) 37
Ciampi, Carlo Azeglio 2
cinema 122, 230–1
civil justice 132–3
Clean Hands 35–6
coalition governments 36–7, 40–1
Cold War, political legacy 36–7
collective action, anti-mafia
    campaigning 148–9
collective bargaining 84–7
common purpose 261, 279–80
Communist Party (PCI) 36–7
compensation, for slow justice 133
competition 99–103, 273–6
competitiveness 190–1
complacency 5–6, 10
complicity 4
Confindustria 85, 99
Confindustria Sicilia 144, 162–3
conflict, between political
    institutions 66–7

conflict of interest 58–9
consent, and criminal power 153–4
Constitution 70
Consumo Critico 141, 142
context, international 256–8
Conticello brothers 144–5
continuity and change, in politics 40
contracts 69, 88
contradictions 25
Contratti Collettivi Nazionali di Lavoro
   (National Collective Labour
   Contracts) 85
corporate social responsibility 237
Corriere della Sera, il 55
corruption 257–8
   assessing extent of 44–8
   attempts to expose 67
   effects on business 199
   Mani Pulite campaign 36
   perceptions of 46
   research into 45–7
   tacit rules of 47–8
Corte dei Conti (Court of
   Accounts) 133
Cosa Nostra see mafia
così fan tutte 17–18
Craxi, Bettino 17, 36, 37, 52
creativity 206–7, 245–6
Criminal Code 70
criminal proceedings, slow pace 69
crises
   comparison 2
   as motivation for change 261
   research into 92–3
crisis, 1992–4
   devaluation 87–8
   economic reforms 17
   effects on government
      spending 96
   failure to learn from 3–4
   government debt 92
   as learning opportunity 2
Cucinelli, Brunello 212–17
cultural heritage 130–1

D'Addario, Patrizia 50–1
debt burdens 6–7

debt crisis, inevitability of 10
debt restructuring 9
debts 8, 78, 91–9
default 9
defeatism 12–13
Dell'Utri, Marcello 39
Democratic Party (PD) 41–2, 43
demographic change 80
Detroit 113
devaluation, lira 87–8
development, and aid 165
Digital Accademia 246
dismissal 82, 88
diversity, of success 23
Divina Commedia, La 15, 77–8,
   106, 254
Divine Comedy 15, 77–8, 106, 254
divisions 14–15
Donadon, Riccardo 244
Draghi, Mario 81–2, 104–6, 166–7,
   200, 260
Drucker, Peter 185
dynamism, loss of 28

EATALY 118
economic growth
   1950s and '60s 74–5
   1970–90 75
   lack of 7, 73–4
   long term 77
   post-war 75–7
   reasons for slowdown
      see economic slowdown
   slowdown 77–80
   underperformance 78
economic models 6
economic reality 7
economic reforms 17
economic situation, denial 5
economic slowdown
   additional factors 103–6
   competition 99–103
   labour 82–91
   public finances 91–9
economic status 72–3
Economist, The on Berlusconi 20–1
economy, parasitical 164–5

education, tertiary level 207
  see also universities
Egyptian Museum, Turin 127–31
Einaudi, Luigi 255–6
elections
  forthcoming 258–9
  mayoral 115, 155–6
electoral reform 17, 40, 264–6
Elkann, John 56
emerging economy 74
Emiliano, Michele 156, 157
employers' associations 85
employment statistics 87
entertainment industry 230–1
entitlement, sense of 257–8
entrepreneurship 177, 186–7,
  209–10
environmental controls 25
Euro 3, 5, 9, 78–9, 91–2
European single currency 5
Eurozone 8–9
executive, conflict with judiciary 67

Falcone, Giovanni 39
families, importance 26
favours 4
fellow-feeling 19–20
Ferrara, Giuliano 57–8
Ferrero 234–7
Ferrero, Michele 235
feudalism 28
Fiat 56, 86, 112, 113–14, 181–2,
  196, 241
Fini, Gianfranco 41, 57
firm size 84, 192–5
fiscal federalism 64, 164–6
Foglio, Il 57–8
football 135–8
Fortugno, Francesco 147
Forza Italia 31
  see also Popolo della Libertà
France 94–5, 100
'From Concept to Car' 119
Future and Liberty (FeL) 41

Gabanelli, Milena 57
Garibaldi, Giuseppe 109

gender equality 124–5
GEOX 191, 217
Germany 84, 87, 100, 188–9, 201
Giornale, il 57
global capitalism
  Autogrill 237–42
  Benetton 240
  Brunello Cucinelli 212–17
  Ferrero 234–7
  Loccioni Group 218–22
  Luxottica 231–4
  Rainbow 227–31
  as source of optimism 211–12
  Technogym 222–7
  see also capitalism
global economic crisis
  response to 5–6
  shock of 1–2
global trade, liberalization 101
globalization, three hub
  model 226
government debt 2, 7, 91–9, **94**,
  257–8, 262–3
government spending 95–6
government, technocratic 2–3
Gramsci, Antonio 211
Grassi, Libero 140, 153–4
Grassi, Pina 142
Great Britain 100
Greece 9–10, 73
gross domestic product (GDP) 2, 7
  eurozone 9–10
  growth **79**
  North–South divide 169–70
Guerra, Andrea 233

H-Farm 242–7
hindsight, applied to economy 10
history 26–7
'Hoover' factor 60
Hosoe, Isao 218–19
household savings 74, 90–1
human capital 209, 276–8
'human' factor 60

illegal economy, size of 47
immigration 64–5, 117

Impastato, Giovanni 155
Impastato, Peppino 143
incubation, of business ideas
243–4
independent politicians 155–6
industrial action 182
industrial conflict 83
industrial districts 83–4
industry 76, 99–100
links to universities 220–1, 242
poor growth 188–9
reluctance to modernize 189
restructuring 189
surveys of 189–90
and universities 247–53
inequality 90, 258
inflation 78, 83
informal economy 87
information and communication
technology (ICT), investment
206, 209
infrastructure 76–7, 200, 230
innovation 189–90
Berlusconi 60–1
and entrepreneurship 209–10
H-Farm 242–7
need for 38
resistance to 202–3
science and technology 187
and universities 247–53
Interaction Design Institute 121–2
interest groups 260
interest rates 78–9, 262
internet, availability 278
investment 243–4, 246–7
Ireland 72–3, 165
isolation 230
ISTAT 47
Italian Social Movement (MSI) 37
Iuculano, Carmela 151

Japan 23–4, 74–5, 76
joint ventures 248
judiciary, conflict with executive 67
justice 59–60
anti-mafia campaigning 150–3
need for reform 67–9

reform efforts 69–71
reform needed 271–3
Turin 131–5
Juventus 135–8

Kennedy, John F. 15
knowledge economy 185
knowledge worker 185

labour, and economic slowdown
82–91
labour costs, increases 88
labour laws 82, 88–9, 180, 190, 200,
266–9
labour market, two tier 89–90
labour participation 87
labour practices 180–3
Lario, Veronica 50
laws, ad personam 4
leadership 234
Lega Nord per l'Indipendenza di
Padania see Northern League
for Padanian Independence
LegalItalia 148–9
Libera Terra 143
liberalism, possible acceptance
of 11
liberalization, global trade 101
Libero Futuro 142
Lingotto factory 118
lira, devaluation 87–8
lobbying 59, 101
Lobello, Ivan Hoe 162, 163, 164
local loyalties 14
Loccioni, Enrico 219
Loccioni Group 218–22
logistics 200–1
Lombard League 64
long-term change 259
loyalties, local 14
Luca, Vincenzo De 156–7
Luxottica 193–4, 231–4

Maastricht Treaty 8
mafia
political associations 39
reports to police 142

mafia (*cont.*)
  young people's opposition
    139–45, 146–8
  see also organized crime
Mahroug, Karima El 33
Maio, Giuseppe di 142–3
Mani Pulite 35–6, 48
manufacturing 99–100
Marchionne, Sergio 86
mayoral elections 155–6
mayors, direct elections 115
media
  Berlusconi's use of 53–4
  concentration of power 4
  failure of legislation 58–9
  investigative role 54–5
  lack of independence 55–7
  ownership and control 55–7
  political power 257
  politicized 55
  role in democratic crisis 4
Mediaset 196–7, 230–1, 278
mergers and acquisitions 246
  Autogrill 238–9, 240
  Luxottica 232–3
meritocracy 100–1, 104, 276–8
migration 104
Milan, organized crime 145–6
minimi tabellari 86
minimum wages 86
monopolies 197
Monti government, need for support 5
Monti, Mario 3, 30, 115, 255–6,
    258–9
moral arbitration, lack of 4
moral divisions 15
Morellato 191
municipal government 115
Murdoch, Rupert 257

Naples 177–8
Napolitano, Giorgio 261, 279
National Alliance (AN) 41
National Association of
    Magistrates 70
'Ndrangheta 146, 147
Newcastle 118–19

newspapers 55–7
Nobel prizes 205–6
North–South divide 13–14, 103,
    104, 166, 169–70
Northern League for Padanian
    Independence 51–2, 61–6
Northern separatism 61–6
Nutella 235

official cars 48–9
oligarchs 257
Olivetti, Adriano 221
Olson, Mancur 260
optimism 13, 18–19
ordine 101
organized crime 145–6
  Addiopizzo 140–3
  Ammazzateci Tutti 146–8
  and consent 153–4
  effects on industry 180, 181, 199
  see also mafia
outsourcing 190–1

Padania 62
Palma, Giovanni Di 236
parasitical economy 164–5
Pascale Langer, Luigi 178–9
Pascale Langer, Paolo 177,
    178–9, 180
patents 206
patronage 4, 48, 49
Pecora, Aldo 145, 147, 148
pensions 95, 96–7, 264
pessimism 12–13, 171
Petrini, Carlo 123, 124, 125, 126, 127
PharmEste 249
philanthropy 215, 237
philosophical divisions 15
Piedmont, role in unification 110–11
Pietro, Antonio Di 35–6
PIGS 72–3
PIIGS 73
Pinto Law 133
Pisapia Committee 70
pizzo 140–5
Planeta, Diego 171–6
People of Liberty (PdL) 41

policies, implementation 166–7, 260
Politecnico di Torino 250–3
political change 51–2
political control, of business 199
political institutions, conflict 66–7
political parties 41–3
political sins 34–5, 43
political status, and business 197–8
political tradition 37–8
political will, importance of 261
politicians
    failure to govern 17
    incomes 49
politics
    and banking 199
    continuity and change in 40
    cost of 49–50
    nature of 59
    as source of income 49
pollution 157–62
Poltrona Frau Group 191–2
Popolo della Libertà 33
    see also Forza Italia
populism 53–4, 60
precari 89–90
privatization 78, 96, 263–4
    see also state ownership
product market regulation (PMR)
    101–2
productivity 181–2, 188
Profumo, Francesco 250–3
'Propaganda Due' 32
proprietors 186–7
prosperity gap 103, 104
protection money 140–5
protests 256–7
public debt see government debt
public finances 91–9, 262–3
public money, for political
    patronage 49
public sector employment,
    politicization 95
public spending 166–7
Puglia 157–62

railways 122
Rainbow 227–31

reform
    likelihood of 279–80
    resistance to 260–1
regional differences 13–14
regional divisions 62
Reinhart, Carmen 92–3
RENA (Rete per l'Eccellenza
    Nazionale) 22
rent-seeking 195–7
Renzi, Matteo 43
Repubblica, la 55
research and development (R&D)
    104, 203, 208
research professionals 208
restructuring, of state institutions 264
Rogoff, Kenneth 92–3
Romania 190–1
Rossi, Maurizio 242–3
Rutelli, Francesco 42

Salerno 156–7
Salone del Gusto 126
Salvi, Cesare 49
Sava, Lia 150–1
Save Italy 262–3
Saviano, Roberto 146
savings and earnings 89
Scajola, Claudio 44–5, 47–8
scala mobile 82–3
scandals 44
self-congratulation 6
self-interest 15–16, 19
selfishness 15–16
semi-private management 129–30
service industries 100, 120–1
    Autogrill 237–42
Settesoli wine cooperative 172
Sicily
    anti-mafia campaigning 139–45
    development opportunities 176–7
    economy 163–4
    future expectations 171–2
    independent politicians 155–6
    role of politicians 176–7
    wine 172–6
Sinistra, Ecologia, Libertà 161–2
sins, political 34–5, 43

Slow Food 118, 123–7
small and medium enterprises
    82–4, 187
Smith, Adam 19
soccer 135–8
social pacts 85–6
sovereign debt 92–3
Spaventa, Alessandro 190
Stampa, La 55–6
state 94, 95
state control, ambivalence
    towards 25
state ownership 102, 262–3
    see also privatization
status quo, maintaining 39
Statuto dei lavoratori (Workers'
    Statute) 82, 88, 93
Storming Pizza 246
Straffi, Iginio 228–30
success, diversity of 23
Superior Council of the Judiciary
    (CSM) 70
Sweden 94–5

Tangentopoli 16, 35–6
Tarantini, Giampaolo 50
tax evasion 95
taxation 34, 95, 97, 199
technocratic, government 2
Technogym 222–7
Tecnam 177–80
television 4, 51–2, 53–4
tertiary level education 207
    see also universities
Terzi, Vittorio 192–3
Theory of Moral Sentiments, The
    (Smith) 20
TINA (there is no alternative)
    factor 61
Tod's Group 194
Tomb of Kha 128
Tommy & Oscar 228–31
Tondato da Ruos, Gianmario 238–9
'Torino Internazionale' 117
tourism 26–7, 121
trade liberalization 75
trades unions 85, 129–30, 181–2

tradition, political 37–8
Transparency International 46
Tremonti, Giulio 57
trials 68–9
Turin
    1970s 111–12
    as capital 109
    dependence on Fiat 113–14
    Egyptian Museum 127–31
    football 135–8
    global economic crisis 112–13
    infrastructure 116, 117
    internal and external connections
        116–17
    judiciary 131–5
    'New Urban Masterplan' 116
    Politecnico di Torino 250–3
    regeneration 111, 114, 116, 118
    service industries 121
    Slow Food 123–7
    strategic planning 117
two-party system 40–1

UEFA, 'financial fair play' 136
unemployment 87
unification 62, 108–9
unionization 85
universities 103, 104
    Ferrara 247–50
    and innovation 247–53
    links to industry 220–1, 242
    Politecnico di Torino 250–3
    reform needed 276–8
    status and quality 203–5, 242
    Turin 120
university education 207
University of Ferrara 247–50
University of the Gastronomic
    Sciences 126–7
urbanization 75–6
utilities, prices 200

Vannucci, Alberto 45–6, 47
Vassilika, Eleni 127–31
'Vecchia Signora', La 135–8
Vecchio, Leonardo Del 232, 234
Vendola, Nichi 157–62, 164

venture capital 242–7
vertical integration 232
Villone, Massimo 49
viticulture 172–6
Vittorio Emmanuele 109
voters, attitude to Berlusconi 32–3

wages 82–3, 86
Wealth of Nations (Smith) 19
welfare state 93
Wen Jiabao 20

wine 172–6
Winx 227–31
wiretaps 45, 153
women 269–71
Workers' Statute 82, 88, 93

young people 21–2, 139–45,
146–8, 210

Zamagni, Vera 81, 91, 93
'Zelig' factor 60–1